T0328757

Professions

Professions and professionalism have played an integral part in business and society. In this book, Mike Saks provides a thorough overview of this field through an analysis of a range of professions, including, amongst others, accountants, doctors and lawyers.

The book offers a critical analysis of such privileged occupational groups in modern societies. Anticipating a positive if changing role for such groups in the years ahead, the book outlines conflicting theoretical perspectives on professions and discusses current developments in an accessible, multi-disciplinary style. The book documents their evolution and contemporary transformation from medieval guilds to fully-fledged professions and international professional service firms, while pointing a path towards their future in the world of work and beyond.

With insights into the recent challenges provided by clients, citizens, the state and corporations in neo-liberal societies, *Professions* provides a concise overview that will be essential reading for students, academics and others interested in the operation of these key occupational groups in business and society.

Mike Saks is Emeritus Professor at the University of Suffolk, UK, and Visiting Professor at the University of Lincoln, Royal Veterinary College, University of London, University of Westminster, UK, and University of Toronto, Canada.

Key Ideas in Business and Management

Edited by Stewart Clegg

Understanding how business affects and is affected by the wider world is a challenge made more difficult by the disaggregation between various disciplines, from operations research to corporate governance. This series features concise books that break out from disciplinary silos to facilitate understanding by analysing key ideas that shape and influence business, organizations and management.

Each book focuses on a key idea, locating it in relation to other fields, facilitating deeper understanding of its applications and meanings, and providing critical discussion of the contribution of relevant authors and thinkers. The books provide students and scholars with thought-provoking insights that aid the study and research of business and management.

Titles in this series include:

Global Oligopoly
A Key Idea for Business and Society
Chris Carr

Luck
A Key Idea for Business and Society
Chengwei Liu

Feminism
A Key Idea for Business and Society
Celia V. Harquail

Hierarchy
A Key Idea for Business and Society
John Child

Professions
A Key Idea for Business and Society
Mike Saks

For more information about this series, please visit: www.routledge.com/Key-Ideas-in-Business-and-Management/book-series/KEYBUS

Professions

A Key Idea for Business and Society

Mike Saks

Routledge
Taylor & Francis Group

LONDON AND NEW YORK

First published 2021
by Routledge
2 Park Square, Milton Park, Abingdon, Oxon OX14 4RN

and by Routledge
52 Vanderbilt Avenue, New York, NY 10017

Routledge is an imprint of the Taylor & Francis Group, an informa business

British Library Cataloguing-in-Publication Data
A catalogue record for this book is available from the British Library

Library of Congress Cataloging-in-Publication Data
Names: Saks, Mike, author.
Title: Professions : a key idea for business and society / Mike Saks.
Description: Milton Park, Abingdon, Oxon ; New York, NY : Routledge, 2021. | Includes bibliographical references and index.
Identifiers: LCCN 2020045300 (print) | LCCN 2020045301 (ebook)
Subjects: LCSH: Professions. | Professions–Sociological aspects.
Classification: LCC HD8038.A1 S25 2021 (print) | LCC HD8038. A1 (ebook) | DDC 331.7/1–dc23
LC record available at https://lccn.loc.gov/2020045300
LC ebook record available at https://lccn.loc.gov/2020045301

ISBN: 978-1-138-61043-9 (hbk)
ISBN: 978-1-138-61041-5 (pbk)
ISBN: 978-0-429-46580-2 (ebk)

Typeset in Times New Roman
by Taylor & Francis Books

Contents

Illustrations

Boxes

Tables

Acknowledgements

This book is on a topic – the professions – for which I have held a passion throughout my academic career, going back some four or five decades. This is reflected in my many books and other publications, as well as papers, and addresses both professions in general and professions operating in specific contexts. It is also mirrored in the practical policy agenda surrounding professional groups in which I have long played a part in the wider society – locally, regionally, nationally and internationally. I am driven by the ongoing importance of such groups in the modern world in business and beyond and my desire to ensure that they consistently operate to public benefit.

In this context, I thank all the universities in which I have been, and am currently, involved for the stimulus that they have provided to me on this topic. I am also extremely grateful to the multitude of authors on this subject who have inspired my thoughts on this fascinating cluster of occupations – and to all those, academics, policy makers and professionals alike, who have refined my views on this area through debate. I must also thank Terry Clague, Senior Publisher at Routledge, who encouraged me to contribute to this Key Ideas series. It has proved a most appropriate vehicle to bring together many aspects of my work in an extremely helpful way to readers interested in this subject.

Aside from these most important wider acknowledgements, I must finally thank my partner, Julie Search-Whittaker, for her patience in coping with my intensive writing of this book over a short period. This has been essential in enabling me to capture and bring together my thinking on professions in what is hopefully an exhilarating manner. Without her support, during challenging times both personally and globally, the production of this book in an accessible fashion would not have been possible. I trust that the contents of the volume not only give a clearer understanding of professions, but also contribute to making the world with which they interface a better place.

1 Introduction

The context to the analysis of professions

Introduction

In this Key Ideas book on professions, the general concept of a profession will be analysed in modern neo-liberal societies. This will involve distinguishing professionals as individuals from collective professional associations. It will also allow the nature and activities of professions to be considered in an international context – not least in areas such as accountancy, law and medicine, amongst many others including relatively new and emerging professional groups. The book will also cover in an interrelated manner the major changes that have occurred in recent years with the development of national and international professional service firms. The structure and argument put forward in each of the ensuing chapters of the book will be overviewed in Chapter 1 to underline the coherence and flow of the volume. To set a context, lay and academic views on the difference of professions from non-professions will then be highlighted, along with the relationship between specific professions in terms of features such as hierarchy and jurisdiction.

The field of business and management in Britain and the United States on which this book is in large part centred is made up of several sub-disciplines based on subjects such as sociology, social policy, economics, politics and social psychology. Although this field is frequently depicted as a well-charted area, contributors typically use different theoretical approaches, generating diverse maps of what is essentially the same terrain. This is certainly true of the subject of professions about which, as will be seen, there are multiple interpretations from varying socio-political perspectives. As such, the book goes beyond the typically rather superficial accounts of professions given in textbooks in business and management covering areas like human resource management, organisational behaviour and work organisation. In so doing, it importantly enables the reader to grasp key concepts and debates about professions more holistically – in the context of a much wider discussion about such occupational groups.

In this manner, the book mirrors the philosophy of the series of which it is part. More specifically, it offers new ways of understanding professions primarily, but not exclusively, from a business and management perspective. As such, it provides an authoritative and original narrative on professional groups, locating this subject matter within differing schools of thought, giving insights into its applications and meanings, and critically discussing the contributions of a wide variety of top authors in this field. Drawing extensively on the latest published research on professions, it aspires within the series template to be a clearly written, accessible and pacey volume – delivering a thought-provoking, stimulating path into the subject for its range of potential readers, from undergraduates, postgraduates and academics to executive leaders, professionals themselves, policy makers and, of course, the educated lay person.

The contents of the book

As will be apparent from this introductory Chapter 1, while the nature of professions is debated, they are traditionally seen as an integral aspect of modern neo-liberal societies – as repositories of exceptional expertise, the mainstays of democracy and the guardians of ethical behaviour. This book continues in Chapter 2 by noting the growth in their significance by the second half of the twentieth century and charting their chronological development from more localised guilds to fully-fledged and legally underwritten professional bodies within specific nation states. While this history is focused on their classic Anglo-American socio-economic and political origins, it also considers the similarities and differences in the process of professionalisation with other countries, from continental Europe to societies with a socialist heritage like China and Russia. This highlights that professionalisation is by no means an inevitable and unilinear development in modern societies, bringing about long-term occupational convergence.

Differing theoretical interpretations of professions and professionalisation are then considered in Chapter 3. This begins with the more positively disposed trait and functionalist theories from the 1950s and early 1960s. It then outlines the work of their initial free market economist and social psychologically oriented symbolic interactionist critics – the latter of whom provide a platform for contemporary discourse analysis, which views professionalism purely as a politically deployed occupational ideology. The chapter goes on to outline the more recent macro structural theories of professions of Marxism and Foucauldianism, which also in different ways paint a less entrancing view of professions. This analysis of competing theories of professions culminates in an outline of the neo-Weberian perspective linked to exclusionary social closure in the market and the loosely interwoven Bourdieusian and neo-institutionalist approaches. The neo-Weberian perspective is particularly favoured here and frames most of the remainder of the volume.

In parallel with these theoretical shifts, the self-regulatory powers of legally enshrined professions increasingly came under attack in the wake of the counter culture from the 1960s and 1970s. It derived from both clients and citizens and the state in modern neo-liberal societies, alongside the threat of growing corporatisation. Chapter 4 considers the effects of these challenges on the autonomy and privileges of professional occupations. Although some argue that this has led to the increasing emaciation of ever more bureaucratised and externally controlled professions, others believe that the position is a good deal more complex because of hybridisation and other factors. This leads to a discussion of the extent to which professions have been able to resist the challenges to their independence and to self-interestedly protect their typically high income, status and power. This is considered mainly in terms of the deprofessionalisation thesis, which is widely debated by neo-Weberian and other contributors.

Key issues for professions in business and management are discussed in Chapter 5. These follow the question of to what extent professions have become the creatures of organisations in the private and public sector in responding to competing institutional logics. It is argued that the modern world is increasingly becoming transnational in scope, rather than simply being contained within country-specific boundaries. The chapter also considers the implications of the rise of international professional service firms in an ever more global and entrepreneurial context. The extent to which managers can be seen as professions in national settings is then explored, alongside an analysis of more established and newer and emerging business-linked professions, again primarily from a neo-Weberian perspective. The benefits or otherwise of interprofessional collaboration in a business environment are then assessed. In all this, as in the rest of the volume, it is argued that the impact of diversity in terms of gender and ethnicity on professions in the marketplace cannot be ignored.

This leads on to a consideration of the future of professions in the concluding Chapter 6. Some academics argue that the focus in modern neo-liberal societies should now be on knowledge and expertise rather than professions themselves, while others believe that professions should be disestablished. Alternatively, the future may best involve changes in particular professions and/or professions as a whole taking on such roles as risk managers or trusted interpreters of information. Here the part played by professions has been developing as a result of, amongst other things, the growing importance of technological changes – including the increasing introduction of artificial intelligence. This raises the question of whether professions can take on a more positive role in society in the future. In shedding some of their undesirable characteristics, it is argued that care should be taken not to jettison their potential future role in responsible leadership. Whatever their shortcomings, Britain and the United States and the broader contemporary neo-liberal world would be a poorer place without professional groups.

In sum, the core message of this book lies in providing a range of fascinating and topical insights into the past, present and future role of professions in business and management and modern society in general in a challenging and rapidly shifting socio-political context – not least in a world currently riven by the coronavirus pandemic, of which more in the book's conclusion. The main aims of this volume can be listed as follows:

- To increase our understanding of professions in modern societies
- To outline the history of professions and professionalisation
- To consider different theoretical interpretations of professions
- To examine the impact of the recent more critical political climate for professions
- To discuss selected business and management issues related to professions
- To consider whether and in what form professions have a future.

In covering these themes, it should be noted that, from a stylistic perspective, the pedagogic features the book adopts to enhance readability on its professional themes include:

- Accessible content based on an engaging reading style
- The inclusion of boxed entries and tables
- The bulleting of points where appropriate
- The use of metaphors where relevant to highlight pivotal points
- A guide to key further reading in addition to the general bibliography.

Readership, publications on professions and authorship

The readership for the book is potentially extensive – especially in developed English-speaking countries like Britain, the United States,

Australia and Canada, as well as continental Europe. Consideration of the historical and contemporary position of professions is very relevant to a wide range of academic business and management programmes, as well as a broad span of social science and professional courses. Its relevance extends beyond such strongly business-related areas as accounting and law to include the established fields of medicine and health and newly evolving professional areas like executive search and project management. In addition, it intersects with more general subjects such as corporate governance, responsible leadership and business ethics. In this respect, there are very few publications that generically cover such work on professions – not least in monograph form.

To be sure, as will be seen, in addition to broader Anglo-American journals like *Work, Employment and Society* and *Work and Occupations*, there are high-quality targeted journals that publish articles on professions and specific professional groups. Central amongst these are the online open-access journal *Professions and Professionalism* and Oxford University Press's *Journal of Professions and Organization*. In the former, as the author of this text, I have published a number of papers, while in the latter I have been a serial contributor and referee for new submissions as a longstanding member of the editorial board. Here I have regularly served annually on the prize-awarding body selecting the best article, the presentation of which is made at the annual conference on professional service firms at the Saïd Business School at the University of Oxford.

There are also several helpful edited and other books giving coverage of the professions field – albeit in restricted terms in relation to the year of publication and the particular professional groups or geographical locations covered. They include those by Dingwall and Lewis (1983) focusing on law and medicine in Britain, and Svensson and Evetts (2010) primarily centred on Scandinavia in a wider European context. However, despite these collections, more comprehensive international books on professions are rarely produced as monographs. The most memorable sole-authored volumes in this mould are *The Sociology of the Professions* by Macdonald (1995), which is now rather dated, and the recently reproduced and revived early 1970s book by Johnson on *Professions and Power* (2016), for which I and John Flood contributed a new Preface.

As will be seen in this volume, there are a range of excellent monographs on various aspects of specific professions in a range of different modern societies – including on the elite occupations of medicine and law (see, for instance, Berlant, 1975; Burrage, 2006) – and professions more generally in England from the viewpoint of a social historian

(Perkin, 1989). These cover areas spanning from their historical development in the very different Anglo-American socio-political milieu to their contemporary regulatory positioning in the countries concerned. In addition, there are also larger compendiums for academic researchers – as illustrated most recently by *The Routledge Companion to the Professions and Professionalism* co-edited by Mike Dent and colleagues (2016), for which I was an invited contributor. But such a collection is the exception rather than the rule and does not provide the coherence of a monograph such as this across the wider landscape of professional groups in the modern world, especially focused on neo-liberal societies.

This gives some indication of where this book is positioned in the existing literature on professions. I have found professions both a fascinating and exciting area to research. As a full academic professor for some thirty years, I have written extensively on this and related subjects like regulation and research, particularly in the health field. This has resulted in over one hundred journal articles and book chapters, alongside the many papers and keynote addresses I have given on these themes at international conferences. I have also enjoyed writing more than twenty edited and single-author volumes on cognate subjects with top publishers from Oxford University Press and Sage to Bristol University's Policy Press and Routledge – with the latter of which I have now published more than half-a-dozen books over a twenty-five-year period.

The texts with Routledge reach back to such pioneering sole and co-edited works with other authors as *Professions and the Public Interest* (1995) and *Health Professions and the State in Europe* (1995). These were followed by books with other publishers on *Professional Identity and Order in Comparative Perspective* (1998), *Professional Identities in Transition* (1999), *Regulating the Health Professions* (2002) and *Rethinking Professional Governance* (2008). Most recently I have written, amongst others, *The Professions, State and the Market* (2015), *Professions and Metaphors* (2016), *Professions and Professional Service Firms* (2018), *Professional Health Regulation in the Public Interest* (2018) and *Support Workers and the Health Professions in International Perspective* (2020). The latter two books are part of a series for which I am co-editor with Policy Press specifically on health professions in modern societies.

As such, my work spans the various social sciences covered by this volume – from politics and social policy to my base discipline of sociology which I studied at a number of British universities, culminating in my doctorate on the professions at the London School of Economics, where I once taught. My early career as a Lecturer/Senior Lecturer at De Montfort University (DMU) was helpfully spent teaching in a Law School and a Business School, alongside regular inputs on a range of other professionally accredited courses from estate management to public administration. This was in addition to later becoming Head of School and then Dean of Faculty of Health and Community Studies at DMU. This experience was expanded in my roles as Pro Vice Chancellor and Deputy Vice Chancellor at the University of Lincoln and Provost at University Campus Suffolk, where I had academic oversight over a range of professionally related disciplines.

The value of this interdisciplinary experience in professional and associated fields in writing this book has been increased by my recent roles as Research Professor and Emeritus Professor at the University of Suffolk – which runs many courses providing the higher education qualifications necessary for entry into the mainstream professions. It has also been accentuated by my present posts as Visiting Professor at the University of Lincoln, the Royal Veterinary College, University of London, and the University of Westminster in Britain and the University of Toronto in Canada. These followed my service on the Executive of De Montfort University, the University of Lincoln, the University of East Anglia and the University of Essex and my Chief Executive role at University Campus Suffolk – as well as my ongoing Board membership at Rose Bruford College of Theatre and Performance in London.

Aside from the wide-ranging insights I can therefore provide on the educational foundation of the professions and higher education itself as an academic profession, I have a strong enterprise profile as befits the author of a book focused on business and management. As indicated above, I have successfully been involved in running universities in Britain with multi-million-pound turnovers receiving *Times Higher Education* awards for Widening Participation University of the Year and Outstanding Leadership and Management Team of the Year. I have also held numerous Company Directorships and am a Fellow of the Institute of Directors and the Institute of Knowledge Exchange. In the latter role, I am a member of the Innovation Council, which includes many Chief Executives of major multinational companies. In addition, I have been a Chair/member of many National Health Service and other health committees including national charities and have advised the United Kingdom Departments of Health and professional bodies like the General Social Care Council and the General Medical Council.

To add to my motivation in writing this book, which covers a range of modern societies, I have engaged in funded international research projects on professions in countries as diverse as Canada and Russia. I have also been President of the International Sociological Association (ISA) Research Committee on Professional Groups – and am the current Vice President of the ISA Research Committee on Health with members drawn from some forty different countries. I am also a member of the Editorial/Advisory Board of various international journals and have advised governments on regulatory policy in several countries. Most recently, I became honorary Senior Advisor to the United Nations on public sector leadership and co-founder of the United Nations-sponsored Institute for Responsible Leadership, both of which centrally link to professional governance.

Debates about the concept of a profession

Having established my own knowledge base for producing this volume on professions which brings together several important threads of my previous work, what exactly is meant by the general concept of a profession in the modern neo-liberal world? As the much-revered American sociologist Eliot Freidson (1986) notes in one of his highly influential trademark books, in everyday usage there are a range of interpretations. Professionals are sometimes seen in a more refined manner as those in highly skilled or specialised jobs or at a more basic level as anyone who undertakes work from which they earn an income or a livelihood (Millerson, 1964). The latter notion hinges on the traditional distinction between professionals and amateurs which was extant through most of the twentieth century. This is manifested historically in sport when the participation of paid professionals was seriously questioned in events such as the Olympic Games, even to the point where medals were withdrawn on the discovery of minor payments in previous sporting roles (Goldblatt, 2018).

In this dialogue, professions were regarded as subverting the noble goals of society which were enshrined in the activities of the amateur. As such, as Crook (2008) observes, at the turn of the twentieth century eminent practitioners in fields from architecture to botany, often operating in an amateur capacity, joined in vociferous condemnation of paid business and academic personnel who were seen to be encroaching on their territory. Associated controversy also raged over whether groups like teachers were born not made through diploma mills in relation to the need for formalised academic qualification for their roles. In the aftermath of the Second World War, though, this position had started to be reversed with the term 'professional' referring to any job, paid or unpaid, carried out proficiently and with integrity. This mirrored the new-found reverence given to the educational credentials achieved and codes of conduct adopted by the ever-expanding numbers of professional associations on both sides of the Atlantic at this time (Saks, 1995).

On the other side of the coin, 'amateurism' itself became a pejorative concept, in the wake of the growing credence given to the altruistic service ideal. As Brundage (2008:3) notes, "The prestige attached to professions, like the word 'profession' itself, has religious roots connected with making a solemn promise or undertaking." This takes us back full circle to medieval times when theologians talked of making a 'profession of faith', with monks and nuns taking solemn religious vows as 'professed members' of their communities. Here there are direct parallels in the modern world with, for example, the contemporary Code of Professional Responsibility of lawyers in the United States (Marks, Leswing and Fortinsky, 1972) and the more historic Hippocratic Oath sworn by British, American and many other doctors worldwide to the healing gods to testify to their professional adherence to specific ethical standards in their rites of passage (Miles, 2005).

In Britain this shift symbolised the transition from 'status professionalism' where groups such as physicians, clergy and members of the Bar derived their high standing from being wealthy gentlemen with a leisured and honoured lifestyle, to 'occupational professionalism' where professional roles needed to be justified by the cultivation of an explicit ideology of public responsibility (Elliott, 1972). As previously noted, another aspect of this, with the decline of the landed gentry and the new demand for services from the industrial middle class, was also to develop training schools to demonstrate the vocational relevance of professions (Saks, 1995). Whether skilled or unskilled, the extensive myriad of paid occupational roles that exist in the current world are now therefore in a different kind of relationship with amateur engagement. This is because the involvement of unwaged lay persons potentially threatens the notion of more esteemed paid work – even if volunteers now increasingly supplement, under their control, the activities of typically more qualified and financially rewarded staff (Ganesh and McAllum, 2012).

Paid work is a very broad-brush concept and here we may also need to distinguish professionalism from trade unionism. As Watson (2017) notes, trade unions can be seen as solidaristic and defensive occupational associations that negotiate working conditions and rewards with employers mainly linked to working-class values and interests – in contrast to traditionally middle-class notions of professionalism. To complicate matters, though, trade unions include skilled, as well as unskilled, personnel. If we contain paid work roles simply to more skilled workers, we end up with a much larger number of groups from car mechanics and undertakers to newer occupations like information technology analysts and financial consultants. But not all of these skilled workers are actually professions in the classic mould like law and medicine in modern neo-liberal societies, rather than simply expert occupations. Although Muzio, Ackroyd and Chanlat (2008:5) argue that professionals are best conceptualised as expert personnel with "no mandatory membership or official credentials", there is a case – depending on purpose – for differentiating expert labour from more officially qualified and credentialed skilled work such as that of accountants, architects, school teachers and others who attract some form of professional recognition.

Nonetheless, despite very recent debates about whether uniformed emergency service workers such as police officers, firefighters and paramedics can usefully be seen as professions (McCann and Granter, 2019), there is no agreed definition. There is particularly strong disagreement between the views of the general public with their own value-laden interpretations of professions and academic researchers studying this field who link them more to expertise and occupational exclusivity. This disjuncture is highlighted by the quote in Box 1.1. The basic conception of professions, as outlined in Chapter 3, is also dependent on the theoretical perspective adopted (Suddaby and Muzio, 2015). Macdonald (1995) further underlines the difficulty of defining professions by noting that, outside of the Anglo-American context, the usage of the term 'profession' in certain European countries has no direct equivalent to that employed in Britain and the United States. He therefore suggests that, in using this term, it should be seen as a kind of shorthand, rather than a universally and precisely defined technical concept. Having said this, he still centrally sees professions as being contemporary occupational groups that purvey advanced, complex, esoteric or arcane knowledge, usually of a utilitarian nature related to practice. In these terms, there is a link with the past in the usage of terms like *professio advocatorum* by medieval lawyers in Europe to describe themselves, based on classical Roman sources (Brundage, 2008).

Box 1.1 Competing definitions of a profession: Lay vs. academic conceptions

Professor Stephen Ackroyd from Lancaster University Management School succinctly brings out one of the key differences between lay and academic definitions of a profession and why so many occupations seek to associate themselves with the title of 'profession':

> In everyday speech to be a professional requires only that a person is paid for their work and/or adopts a business-like approach to it. Professionalism is an attitude to work which anyone may adopt. Researchers understand professions and

professionalism differently, however. For them, professionals are members of a limited group of high-status service occupations such as medicine, engineering and law. In addition to being repositories of authoritative knowledge, these occupations have some common features: restricted entry, high-level qualifications and stringent tests of competence, together with distinctive types of formal organisation. It is because of the high status and supposed effectiveness of established professions that aspects of their outlook and behaviour are claimed for work of every type.

Source: Ackroyd, S. (2016) 'Sociological and organisational theories of professions and professionalism', in Dent, M., Bourgeault, I., Denis, J-L. and Kuhlmann, E. (eds) *The Routledge Companion to the Professions and Professionalism*, Abingdon: Routledge, p. 15.

Following the later work of Freidson (2001), and as observed earlier in this chapter, it should be stressed too that the focus in this book is not so much on professionals, but on professions. As Freidson explains, the institution of a profession is far more important in the wider scheme of things – including their influence on policy – than the individual professionals who make up their number, even if the two cannot be entirely dissociated. It is also crucial that they are not confused as there is no necessary relationship between the attitudes and behaviour of individual professionals and the institutional features of professions that engage in their regulatory oversight (Stacey, 1980). Observers might, for example, criticise professional bodies for operating self-interestedly, as in the case of the Law Society in Britain (Thomas and Mungham, 1983), while acknowledging that individual practitioners may themselves be altruistic – serving the wider public rather than their own ends (Saks, 1995). Indeed, as Anteby, Chan and DiBenigno (2016) point out, professionals may often be unaware of and/or uninterested in the associations with which they are affiliated.

Defining professions in this book

While consensus on the nature of professions is lacking, this book loosely regards them in a changing socio-political milieu in a similar manner to

Freidson (2001:2) as being based on professional associations which have various forms of monopoly in the market that provide "the economic and social organization that sustains the occupational control of work." As Millerson (1964) notes, these associations conventionally include such features as registers of practitioners, prescribed qualification, codes of ethics and interlinked disciplinary arrangements. In their most potent form, such bodies have statutory underwriting by the state, but they may also involve groups based on voluntary self-regulation based on pre-scribed qualifications and disciplinary mechanisms. These groups are to be distinguished from looser entities like study associations and research societies in particular occupations because, while their networks may be exclusive, they do not seek to qualify or otherwise anoint members.

Notwithstanding the various works of Freidson (1970; 1986; 1994; 2001) which highlight the role of expertise in the professionalisation pro-cess, there is a debate as to how far the definition of such occupational groups can fruitfully be based on knowledge *per se* given the role of poli-tics in their formation and legitimation (Saks, 2012). It is true, though, that professions have traditionally been seen in reverential terms in Britain and the United States, beginning with the classic work of Carr-Saunders and Wilson (1933) who viewed them as the bulwarks of democracy, bastions of freedom, dignity and responsibility, and one of the most stable elements of society. This is part of the earlier gentlemanly ideology of public service, which saw professions as averse to seeking profit and driven by altruistic motives (Elliott, 1972). Since the 1960s and 1970s, though, as we shall discover in Chapter 4, they have been subject to increasing challenge at every level – not least by those who, on the contrary, see them in one way or another as abusing their considerable powers to the detriment of clients and/or the wider populace (Saks, 2016b).

This observation highlights that we live in a dynamic world of shifting challenges and definitions. This world involves occupations of greatly varying size. There have been many relatively new entrants to the profes-sional arena – as, for instance, self-regulatory associations in landscape architecture, heritage conservation, family mediation and vocational rehabilitation in Britain, which have more or less lengthy histories and have reached different stages of development (Lester, 2016). These new groups are typically small in size – in this case between one thousand and six thousand practitioners in each case. They also lack significant legal underwriting, with only voluntary, not legally reserved, functions – despite possessing codes of practice and some form of qualifying assess-ment. As such, there has understandably been minimal state involvement in their establishment, even if it has taken considerable negotiation skills to arrive at the current stage, notwithstanding the significance of these relatively small occupations to their limited range of clients in the wider society.

However, according to Lester (2014) both smaller and larger professions share a common root – the Latin verb *profiteri*, to profess, which relates to making a formal commitment or vow, in this case to acquiring knowledge and skills within a given ethos. This book focuses mainly on larger-scale, formalised bodies with a more substantial membership and greater influence on business and society, within this common lineage. Such bodies of course include nationally based professions ranging from the more broadly populated field of accountancy to the classic professions of law and medicine, which have also had to adapt to the new conditions of late modernity (Dent et al, 2016). Professions like these in business and elsewhere are in an incessant state of transformation as they respond to market demands, government pressures and an increasing array of social and technological innovation that will affect both their present and future – along with the growing impact of important trends in the internationalisation of professional service firms (Saks and Muzio, 2018).

The more recent drive to internationalisation and the associated scaling up of professional projects has played a particularly key part in the reframing of narratives of professionalism (Flood, 2018). At the largest and widest international and transnational level, the professional service firms that have emerged over the past two or three decades have significantly impacted the discussion – because they exist beyond any one set of national professional regulatory parameters and interface as much with international law as with traditional professional associations in specific societies. In these terms, such firms pose major regulatory dilemmas in their operation beyond national boundaries (Boussard, 2018). In these circumstances, as will be seen, professions and professional service firms have not only shown considerable resilience, but also in the case of the latter have particularly displayed an appetite for expansionary opportunism. Accordingly, they have played a vital role in proactively defending themselves against potential interlopers, as well as promoting their brand in the face of attempts to destabilise them. Nonetheless, it should be stressed that professions can lose, as well as gain, position in a competitive marketplace, including in relation to licensure (Redbird, 2017).

By implication in this fast-changing landscape, not all professional groups are equals. As in many other areas of life, a hierarchy exists (Child, 2019) in which there is a distinct pecking order amongst those that can be counted as professional groups. This can be illustrated by medicine, one of the elite professions, alongside that of law, at the apex of this hierarchy on both sides of the Atlantic. In this profession, so-called semi-professions such as nursing and allied health practitioners like dieticians and podiatrists still to some degree trail in its wake in terms of their legitimated scopes of practice (Turner, 1995). This is not to mention even more marginalised groups like herbalists and homeopaths who tend to be excluded from mandatory legislation and at best have voluntary oversight bodies which take responsibility for such matters as accreditation, codes of ethics and disciplinary oversight (Saks, 2015a). Support workers such as health care assistants are also located down the pecking order as, while they often have some level of training or at least on-the-job experience, they are by definition not part of professional groups and are typically only loosely regulated – and sometimes not systematically governed at all (Saks, 2020c).

Adams (2017) elaborates further and more generally on the distinctive nature of national professional bodies, noting that even the frequent catch-all concept of self-regulatory professions contain many variants. In her comparison of Britain, the United States and Canada, she observes that there are variations in whether regulation occurs at a national or regional (provincial/state) level. In these three societies and other national settings, some form of regulatory oversight protects the right of those on a professional register to practice, while others have only protection of title. In some contexts too, there is a mix of forms of regulation, the balance of which may change over time. Equally, there are differences as to whether professional bodies act as regulatory and advocacy bodies as in law in Britain or whether these functions are separate, as they characteristically are in the United States. Moreover, some groups of occupations are clustered under one professional umbrella in certain societies, while in other contexts they are distinct professions. The composition of boards of professions also varies, as well as their scope of activity and the links of their qualifications to universities.

To add another layer to the above analysis, professions do not just differ in their substantive characteristics within and between societies. The nature and form of writing about them also varies between contributors depending on geographical context – as will be apparent at various points in this book. As Adams (2015) points out, for example, in European countries there is a concentration on issues of professional regulatory policy. Even though Australian and Canadian authors have also prioritised the policy dimension, this has not been emphasised in the literature on professions in the United States. Having said this, many overlapping fields of interest helpfully remain in the Anglo-American context – from gender and ethnicity in the professions to professions and organisations and interprofessional working (Saks and Brock, 2018). Internationally too this literature has heavily been based on the challenges that professional groups face at a time of rapid change (Adams, 2015). However, we should conclude this section on defining professions with reference to Andrew Abbott, one of the foremost writers on professions in the United States.

Abbott (1988) famously and helpfully sees professions as part of an interdependent system based on jurisdictions, the fluid but often prescribed boundaries between professional groups. He argues – as has been pointed out above – that some professions have full control of their activities and on other occasions their control is subordinate to those of other professional groups. Such jurisdictional boundaries between professional groups are seen as perpetually in dispute both locally and nationally in the context of wider exogenous influences. Although his work is not above criticism as, amongst other things, it can underplay both independent professional development (Macdonald, 1995) and the relationship between professions and the state (Dingwall and King, 1995), this approach centred on the relations of professions facilitates understanding of their development in terms of interprofessional politics – including in response to the vacuums created in the wake of social, cultural and technological change. It also provides wider insights into the manner in which occupational groups manage to control knowledge and skill in a competitive and challenging marketplace – in a way that necessarily involves boundary work by the various professional players concerned (Malin, 2000).

Conclusion

This framework, together with the broader consideration of the definition of a profession, acts as a springboard into the next chapter, which examines the history of professions and professionalisation – especially in Britain and the United States. In Chapter 1, therefore, an overview of the book has been set out to place this history in context. The chapter has also considered the target market for this volume and the academic provenance of the author on the professions. The significance of this monograph as an indicative guide to professional groups in the modern world, compared to the previous contributions on this subject, has also been outlined. As the reader will discern, this book is distinguished by both its comprehensiveness and coherence in a complex field. But if professions are occupational groups that have been more or less successful in modern societies in achieving high socio-political rewards and a substantial amount of autonomy, how did they become established in the Anglo-American context and beyond in the lengthy historical period up to the second half of the twentieth century – before they faced increasing challenges at the peak of their powers from the 1960s and 1970s onwards? Chapter 2 examines from medieval times the manner in which they reached such a powerful position – with all its attendant privileges – in what Brint (1994) has described as the 'golden age' of professionalism.

2 The history of professions and professionalisation

Introduction

This chapter begins by considering the transition of the regulation of work in many parts of the modern world from localised medieval guilds, which in this context are echoes of professional formation from a historic past. As such, they have some similar features to the national professional bodies that emerged by the 1960s and 1970s through the process of professionalisation. This account will focus on Britain and the United States where the development of professions will be classically exemplified primarily, but not exclusively, with reference to medicine and law, archetypical professional groups centred on ring-fenced associations supported and legitimated by legislation. It will compare the development of professions in these two rather different variants of capitalism with trends in professionalisation internationally – not least in continental Europe and the then socialist countries of China and Russia, in the latter largely before the impact of *perestroika* and *glasnost* took hold in post-Soviet times (White, 2000).

Some writers have seen professionalisation as an inevitably increasing convergent development in modern industrial societies based on the determining consequences of technological change (see, for instance, Kerr et al, 1960). This is associated with a logic of industrialisation leading countries to become ever more alike – notwithstanding national cultural differences – in terms of the rising differentiation of the division of labour, growing specialisation, and increasing skills and competencies. It is argued in this book, though, that there is much variation both within and between societies in the way that this occurs and that the particular destination ultimately reached is primarily the result of specific socio-political and historical factors. In these terms, as we shall see later in this chapter, attempts to professionalise with the support of the state can fail as well as succeed in a dynamic process in which professions may come to the fore and fall back with societal change. However, for the moment, the focus is on the emergence of guilds and how these became transformed into professions – a subject to which we now turn.

The guilds and their demise

The guilds for a range of occupations from goldsmiths and musicians to potters and shoemakers can be traced back to ancient Roman times (Epstein, 1991). Craft guilds are defined by Krause (1996:2) as "institutions created by groups of workers around their work, their skill or craft." As he notes, such guilds – alongside merchant guilds which controlled trade for particular items – came back into existence with the resurgence of trade after the Dark Ages in a wide variety of forms in European cities and towns in the Middle Ages and the Renaissance. They were probably at their height around the time of the thirteenth century (Watson, 2017). Importantly, there were no nationally based professions as we know them today at this stage, although access to the classic learned occupations of divinity, law and medicine was open only to the elite who had entered very expensive university education in places like Oxford and Cambridge (Crook, 2008). As Brint (1994:112) points out, early professionalism in this sense was based on "technical expertise, service to clients based on a trust relationship, and gentlemanly status conferred by birth and higher education."

The craft guilds were mainly based on establishing a local corporate economic monopoly for skilled artisans in areas such as baking and weaving and other aspects of daily life, although they were not always supported by the relevant local city and other authorities. They typically controlled everything from their associated raw materials to work procedures, with a stratified career hierarchy of master craftsman, journeyman and apprentice (Watson, 2017). The most successful guilds in these times established power and control in an interrelated manner over the association concerned, the workplace, the market and the state (Krause, 1996). In this context, they were based on self-government in a break from serfdom under a feudal economy and the power of the feudal lord, with guild control over the rules of entry, training, dues and disciplinary measures. As early industrial capitalism developed, such bodies established to ensure mutual aid, maintain production standards and reduce competition were led by guild masters from the richer middle class – who typically set ever higher membership fees for outsiders and enlisted jurors to adjudicate disputes amongst members (Cartwright, 2018).

Krause (1996), one of the foremost writers on the local guild power that existed before professionalisation took hold on a national basis, observes that turf battles often occurred between the male-dominated guilds in their struggle for control over territory. This potentially conflictual localised system was not generally established in the United States as this was a new society founded in the sixteenth and seventeenth century through settlement from Britain and elsewhere, along with the indigenous American population (Jenkins, 2012). However, pockets of guild activity are extant even today in occupational areas such as real estate and screen acting. Moreover, in England – as indeed in a number of centralised European countries like France – the establishment of guilds, and especially the richer guilds now known as livery companies, led to a quest for Royal Charters or wider state approval based on fee payment to give still greater competitive advantage.

Eventually, though, craft guilds in Europe for a plethora of diverse local occupational groups from retailers to milliners, sculptors and painters came under attack with the rise of industrial capitalism, as power was wrested from the aristocracy (Cartwright, 2018). It is stressed by Krause (1996) that guilds then came to have an anachronistic position as 'dead weights' for the economy. This provided fertile ground for increased criticisms of guild power because they were seen as self-interestedly working in favour of their members, as well as some elite politicians who stood to benefit financially from the payments that they made to them – as opposed to working in the common interest. In their place, free trade arrangements increasingly emerged in the early capitalist industrial period, largely unaffected by the traditional restrictions of the guilds with the rise of the modern nation state. The retrogressive effect of the guilds with the rise of capitalism is particularly indicated by the entry in Box 2.1. This underlines that while, as we shall see, nationally based professions have been widely attacked by critics in the modern neo-liberal era, the guilds which preceded them were also not immune from criticism several centuries before.

Box 2.1 The negative effect of European guilds on economic growth

From her detailed, high-level research into the development of European guilds, Professor Sheilagh Ogilvie (2019), a Canadian economist and historian, argues that the stronger and less liberal the guilds, the more they slowed down economic growth from the fourteenth century onwards. To be sure, guilds have sometimes been seen as efficient institutions during their several hundred-year histories – not least by guaranteeing quality and skills. However, as Ogilvie emphasises, they less helpfully:

- excluded competitors;
- denied apprenticeships to outsiders;
- discriminated against female and ethnic minorities;
- manipulated markets;
- drove up prices for consumers; and
- blocked innovation.

In so doing, she highlights that guilds were mainly employer organisations out for themselves and not private bodies building trust and contributing to the good of civil society.

Source: Ogilvie, S. (2019) *The European Guilds: An Economic Analysis*, Princeton, NJ: Princeton University Press.

Epstein (1991) believes that, despite the demise of the guilds which had dominated most workplaces in Europe from the eleventh to the nineteenth century, one of the most important legacies was vocational education and the solidarity they evinced amongst employers and employees alike. As far as practitioners are concerned, this is a similar hallmark of the professional bodies that have since emerged in the Anglo-American context, with one caveat – they were not local, but national in scope. Krause (1996) also makes the point that the scholars' guilds largely retained their power through universities which generated the learned professions. However, there was some international variation in the longevity of the guilds. In England, for example, he notes that active craft guilds faded from the mid-sixteenth century onwards in many regions, although they survived to the end of the eighteenth century in France and much later in Italy where there was a weaker central state to enforce economic conformity. Craft guilds even grew in power up to the mid-nineteenth century in Germany, characterised by the later development of capitalism and state centralisation.

Such guilds now have very largely died out in the modern world (Murphy, 1990), except in part in a popularly conceived symbolic sense as 'dining clubs for the wealthy'. In this respect in Britain, for example, longstanding bodies such as the Merchant Tailors and Stationers' Livery Companies still exist. They were descended from the guilds, although they now fulfil a much-reduced range of functions – mainly including charity work and education (Gadd and Wallis, 2002). More recently founded guilds have come on the scene over the past few decades such as the Guild of Beauty Therapists and the Quilters' Guild, which each have several thousand members, alongside the more extensively positioned Guild of Master Craftsmen providing, *inter alia*, marketing and insurance services for subscribers (Hoffman, 2011). These are very different from formalised professional bodies, but nonetheless provide a link with the past. So too does the wide range of technical and vocational qualifications that are delivered by the City & Guilds in London to develop skills, following its foundation in the late nineteenth century.

However, as Ogilvie (2019) points out, guilds hold a much greater contemporary significance in terms of our academic understanding of present-day institutions – not least because they provide insights into the effect of controlling markets economically through closure by the multi-stranded social networks on which they are based. These academic insights particularly apply to the monopolies they once so extensively created through restricted supply and higher pricing of services, which is of course very pertinent to the study of current-day professions. This relevance is underscored by the fact that the European guilds, which grew up from the eleventh century onwards, covered the production of many goods and services, including those provided by physicians, surgeons and other subsequently professionally anointed groups. This brings us back to the scholars' guild as a precursor to the central role of the university today in professionalisation.

Krause (1996) notes that the early European university did not have a fixed location and was made up of masters and apprentices – with instruction in Latin in the stock areas of civil or canon law, medicine and theology. The professoriate and their middle and upper-middle-class students were based in centres like Bologna, Cambridge, Florence, Oxford and Paris. England, according to Krause, is a deviant case since groups like doctors and lawyers were initially trained largely outside the universities, directly in hospitals and at the Inns of Court in London, respectively. The position on the continent and in Scotland was that there was more continuity with the role of the university in the Middle Ages. The United States began with the English model, but by the mid-nineteenth century began following the continental European approach to which England was finally to revert, in which universities held power over membership and training for the professions. Such variations highlight the difficulty of assuming a unilinear model of professional development.

The historical development of professionalisation

This observation is very apposite in evaluating the model put forward by the American social scientist Wilensky (1964). Following in the footsteps of Kerr and colleagues (1960) in advancing the convergence thesis, he famously discussed the sequential series of landmark events that he discerned in his empirical research on the history of the professionalisation of eighteen American occupations. These principally included establishing a training school, a university school, a local association, a national organisation, a licensing law and a code of ethics in that particular order. He argued in theorising the general process of professionalisation as an offspring of the guilds that one step essentially leads on to another (Sox, 2007), although he accepted that there may on occasion be variation which requires special explanation – such as that centred on power struggles and status striving amongst the occupational groups concerned.

Wilensky (1964) is not alone in his search for a unilinear model of professionalisation. There are clear affinities here with the earlier work of Caplow (1954) who proposed an even more universal account of the sequence of professionalisation, based on his study of groups like journalists, undertakers and laboratory technicians in the United States. He argued that the following slightly different steps are undertaken in forming a profession, concurrent with the growth of education and training:

- The establishment of a professional association excluding the unqualified;
- A change of name to underpin the group's monopoly and create legislative restrictions;
- The development of an ethical code to demonstrate social value, regulate incompetence and limit internal competition;
- A political lobby to gain legal recognition, limit the professional title and criminalise the unlicensed.

Although there are a number of distinctions between the two models, including in the chronological detail and the principles involved, both Caplow and Wilensky can be seen to adopt a parallel approach to professionalisation.

This kind of approach to expounding a 'natural history of professionalism' is open to extensive criticism. Abbott (1988) has been amongst those who have taken a lead in this critique. He argues that in the case of Wilensky, the sequencing of the steps, as to which event precedes another, has been artificially imposed on his large-scale American data set. Moreover, neither Wilensky nor Caplow recognise that the evolution of specific professions can and should be dealt with on a case-by-case basis, as opposed to being corralled into a more or less rigid schematic straitjacket. There is also no mention of how professionalisation links to the wider social structure and culture, rather than simply the work that professions do. Nor is there much sense of how the internal dynamics of professional groups impinges on the outcome in this process and how the nature of professionalisation itself may change in a single society over time. In these respects, it has most recently been noted that even collegiality, so often seen as a defining feature of professionalism, can in fact vary in form and extent in particular professions depending on the politics involved (Denis et al, 2019).

In addition, it is very apparent from the various attacks on professions over the past four or five decades – which will be dealt with in a subsequent chapter – that professionalisation is not inevitable and that deprofessionalisation or some other outcome such as internal professional restratification may also occur. Stalled cases of professionalisation in the United States up to the 1980s that Abbott (1988) cites include those of psychological mediums, electrotherapists and railway surgeons. There is also the further complexity that there may be amalgamations and divisions – not least historically as took place at different times between doctors and then social workers in Britain. To complete the critique that Abbott puts forward, neither Wilensky nor Caplow adequately examine the interdependence of occupational groups in the professionalisation process. As he notes, this cannot be considered completely in the abstract – as illustrated by the interface of various types of engineers, lawyers and accountants in the United States.

Johnson (2016) underlines that their accounts are unduly focused on North America, observing that professional associations generally emerged before the founding of training schools in Britain linked to the stronger anti-monopolistic culture in the United States in the eighteenth and early nineteenth centuries. This is reinforced by the historical reflections by Sugarman (1995) on the intersection between law, lawyers and accountants in England. Millerson (1964) indicates that even within a single society, like Britain, there may be different rather than convergent paths to professionalisation in both substance and time-scale. His concluding impression is that there is "individual uniqueness, tempered by an adjustment in the social and educational climate of the time" (Millerson, 1964:86). These difficulties are even more accentuated when we look at a broader range of modern societies, where there is an even more heterogeneous picture. Some of the differences are highlighted in the comparative study of health professions in the United Kingdom and Germany by Kuhlmann, Allsop and Saks (2009), who pinpoint diverse institutional pathways to professional governance and public control.

Such differences are picked up more pervasively in the systematic and much wider comparative analysis of professionalisation undertaken in these countries by Neal and Morgan (2000). They chose nineteen professional occupations in the United Kingdom, thirteen of which had more or less direct parallels with those of the nineteen professions examined in Germany – namely, that of the accountant, actuary, architect, dentist, general practitioner, optometrist, patent agent, pharmacist, physiotherapist, psychologist, solicitor, surgeon and veterinary surgeon. While there were broadly similar sequential stages of professionalisation within each country, they found that the historical role of the state in professionalisation was quite distinct. In the United Kingdom the professions played a more 'bottom-up' role in professional formation, whereas in Germany the state had taken a more 'top-down' interventionist position in initiating and administering professions. This parallels the observation by Johnson (2016) that professions in the former British colonies were a result of government initiatives rather than professional agitation.

The analysis by Neal and Morgan (2000) also includes reference to the impact of the European Union in shaping the conduct and behaviour of the British, German and other European professions – not least in relation to the effect of the European professional transparency directives on the control of education and professional regulation. The importance of the European Union in regularising professional development should not be understated, but the form of European influence will obviously change over time. In the case of the United Kingdom, for example, it will be weakened by Britain's recent departure from the bloc which will importantly affect such professionally relevant issues as free movement of labour which impinges on previously restrictive practices in the professions (O'Rourke, 2019). These considerations in an increasingly internationalised modern world underline that the approach taken by both Wilensky (1964) and Caplow (1954) is, as Johnson (2016:29) aptly comments, "historically specific and culture-bound". This critique is echoed by Henriksson, Wrede and Burau (2006) who see such interpretations as having a heavily ethnocentric American bias.

As the examples given demonstrate, therefore, we need to be wary of not only ethnocentrically based analyses, centred on examples from a single country, but also contentious interpretations of the empirical cases considered within the constraints of that society. In the Anglo-American context, as in continental Europe more generally, the nineteenth century was when contemporary professions particularly began to be born as they replaced local guilds as occupational intermediaries in the developing capitalist system (Brint, 1994). This was a time when a whole range of groups from civil engineers to university professors started to emerge in ever-greater numbers with the rise of a modern industrial society. It was a time too, in terms of this volume, when – following the founding of the first modern business school in Paris in 1819 – institutions like the Harvard Business School and the London School of Economics came into being later in the century, the former of which pioneered the now pervasive Masters in Business Administration and the latter of which served the elite in fields such as politics, public administration and commerce (Crook, 2008).

Brint (1994) classifies the various professions that emerged in politics and public life by the second half of the twentieth century into five main occupational categories that usefully map onto the Anglo-American context:

- business services (for example, financial analysts and corporate lawyers);
- applied sciences (including engineers and geoscientists, amongst others);
- culture and communications (for instance, academics, journalists, and media professionals);
- civic regulation (as illustrated by judges and government administrators); and
- human services (encompassing groups like teachers, social workers and nurses).

In a period of burgeoning professionalism in numerous fields over one and a half centuries, we should be alive to the many paths that have been taken to professionalisation in the modern world, both within and between different clusters of professions.

This is especially so because, perhaps on account of the competitive marketplace in which they interact, such developments have often taken place in a silo-based fashion without too much information sharing, including reference to lessons drawn from best practice or otherwise in adjacent professionalising space (see, for example, Allsop and Jones, 2018). What, though, does the process of professionalisation look like historically in particular instances and in different countries, after – and in some cases interlinked to – the large-scale demise of the guilds? By way of illustration of the different processes of professionalisation that have occurred, we shall now consider two international comparative case studies – that of the traditionally leading-edge professions of medicine and law in the halcyon period for professions in the Anglo-America context up to the 1960s and 1970s when self-regulatory professional groups were in their prime.

The comparative cases of Britain and the United States

The process of professionalisation will first be examined in medicine in Britain and then in the United States, before we turn to the parallel example of law in these two countries. In considering these cases, it should be emphasised that both of these societies were distinctively marked in the modern socio-political environment by the emergence of independent professional bodies with a high degree of control over their working conditions. This makes the Anglo-American analysis to some extent unique, in that this contrasts with some parts of continental Europe in which such expert groups were in effect creatures of the state bureaucracy. In the terms expressed by Collins (1990:15), such expert personnel on the continent acted "as elite administrators possessing their offices by virtue of academic credentials."

As a prelude to this analysis of the emergence of the professions of medicine and law in the Anglo-American context, the socio-political landscape in each of the interconnected liberal-democratic societies concerned needs to be briefly sketched out – beyond the period of British settlement and colonisation in the New World which ended with the War of Independence towards the conclusion of the eighteenth century (Jenkins, 2012). Despite their very distinct, but intertwined, histories, both countries in some respects share a common political template. As liberal democracies, as Newton and van Deth (2010) point out, Britain and the United States in the modern era have for long been committed to hold elections for a representative legislature and to protect the human and civil rights of their citizens – within a capitalist framework predicated on the ownership of private property and the market. Although the specifics of the political institutions differ, this ensures that there is a system of checks and balances – in which centres of private power counterbalance the state in decision making.

One main substantive difference in terms of political philosophy between these liberal-democratic countries is that there has been more comparative emphasis in Britain than the United States on egalitarian rather than libertarian values. To be sure, as Raphael (1990) notes, in the eighteenth and nineteenth centuries the national government in Britain placed a good deal of stress on a *laissez-faire* approach – in which individual freedom in a privatised economy was given higher priority than justice and welfare, with little state intervention. However, this was to change with the growing emphasis in the twentieth century, within the framework of a class-based capitalist society, on advancing equal opportunities and meeting basic needs through central welfare provision (Brown, Crowcroft and Pentland, 2018). As such, a distinctive mix between marketisation and statism emerged in modern Britain, as in several other European countries (Rothgang et al, 2010).

However, in the United States as another form of capitalist economy, while federal expenditure on health and other collective welfare areas has risen (Bradley and Taylor, 2015), much greater stress both historically and contemporaneously has been given to the 'hidden hand' of the market, entrepreneurialism and the notion of equality before the law (Greenspan and Wooldridge, 2018). Outside of the corporate system in a more ethnically diverse, class-centred and marketised society, charity is seen as the most appropriate means to address social concern (Jenkins, 2012). This has been complemented by a devolved state-based political system, in contrast to a much higher level of centralisation in Britain (Saks, 2015e) – notwithstanding the recently increased devolution of political authority to the home countries (Bradbury, 2020). Against these evolving socio-political contexts, how did medical and legal professionalisation play out in Britain and the United States?

Medical professionalisation in Britain

In early modern Britain – or, more precisely, England, on which we shall focus – there was a pluralistic health system in the sixteenth and seventeenth century with no clearly distinguishable medical profession. Self-help dominated, drawing on such folk remedies as charms and herbal preparations. The limited amount of paid health care came from groups like midwife healers and empirics with little or no formal training (Saks, 1992). In contrast to the male-dominated medical profession that was to emerge, women played a central part in health care (Chamberlain, 2010). Co-terminously, a small number of upper-class, university-educated physicians ministered to the societal elite, including royalty, who paid for heroic therapies like bloodletting and purging. With shades of a high-status guild, the Royal College of Physicians obtained a monopoly of medical practice in 1518 within seven miles of the City of London, a standing from which it continued to exercise a powerful influence on professionalisation in the British nation state henceforth (Stevens, 2003).

As Stevens (2003) relates, in parallel, the socially subordinated apo-thecaries, who were schooled through apprenticeships, established the Worshipful Society of Apothecaries of London incorporated by Royal Charter in 1617. They at first dispensed prescriptions and then became more independent practitioners with the founding of the Society of Apothecaries in the late seventeenth century and through the 1815 Apothecaries Act, which gave them the right to examine and license prac-titioners. Meanwhile, the Company of Barber-Surgeons united the Com-pany of Barbers and the Guild of Surgeons in 1540, subsequently gaining the title of the Royal College of Surgeons of London in 1800, based on varying levels of university and apprenticeship training. These two groups then came together with the apothecary-surgeons serving as general prac-titioners for the lower classes in urban areas and for wider populations in the provinces. The historic shifts in the relationship between these groups were to fundamentally shape the professionalisation process.

Surgeons, apothecaries and physicians up to the beginning of the nineteenth century competed on a more or less level playing field with rivals purveying secret remedies and other nostrums to the newly forged middle classes in a developing capitalist market in the so-called 'golden age of quackery' (Porter, 2001). In reality, there was little to choose between practitioners vying for fee payment at this time; the group of 'regulars', who were to become part of medical orthodoxy, were just as prone as the 'irregulars' to use magic and trickery in plying their trade – in their case it was based on Latin mumbo-jumbo, while the irregular hucksters often sold their mystical pills and potions in sideshows (Porter, 1995). Moreover, notwithstanding the commodifi-cation of health care under capitalism in the expanding hospital and community sectors, their level of expertise was similar and appren-ticeships were common to both. Although medical knowledge and education through medical schools expanded with the Enlightenment (Spary, 2013), hospitals were still popularly known as 'gateways to death' as their focus was on scientifically classifying, not effectively treating, disease in an era when aseptic techniques and anaesthesia were not routinely applied (Waddington, 1984).

The increasing unification of the surgeons, apothecaries and physi-cians was key to their professionalisation by the mid-nineteenth century, in the face of their own limited effectiveness and liberal advocates of a free market. Professionalisation was primarily fostered through the Pro-vincial Medical and Surgical Association (later to become the British Medical Association), which was formed in 1832 (Stevens, 2003). Partly as a result of its lobbying, a platform was laid for the standardisation of medical education and the criminalisation of unlicensed practitioners such as homeopaths and hydropaths, who were attacked as 'quacks' in medical journals and elsewhere (Saks, 2015a). As Waddington (1984) notes, a unified national medical profession was finally created in Britain for the first time through the 1858 Medical Act – albeit after seventeen bills were presented to Parliament before the legislation was finally passed. The Act established a self-regulatory profession centred on a community of equals with a statutory register policed by the General Medical Council. This enabled professional control of educational and training standards and disciplinary action by peers based on explicit ethical codes for doctors.

These standards were unified further through more integrated examinations instigated by the 1886 Medical Act. Larkin (1995) observes, though, that the 1858 Act and its successor legislation was not formally monopolistic in that it did not actually prevent the medically unqualified from practising under the Common Law. However, this state-endorsed legislation did put competitors at a significant disadvantage. It provided exclusive use of the title of 'doctor' for those with medical qualifications, which was legally enforceable and deprived competitors of their legitimacy. In addition, the unlicensed remained largely outside the publicly funded health service which increasingly developed under, first, the 1911 National Health Insurance Act and, then, the 1946 National Health Service Act. Aside from being mainly positioned in the private sector, there were other legislative exclusions for the unlicensed – not least in signing statutory documents like death certificates and, by the mid-twentieth century, in limiting claims to treat a range of conditions such as cancer, diabetes, epilepsy and glaucoma, which were legally defined as being solely within the terrain of the medical profession.

The medical profession in Britain became further established in the first half of the twentieth century as more effective biomedical treatments became available – with the shift to laboratory medicine and the introduction of therapies like radiotherapy for cancer and penicillin for infections. This trend was accelerated after the Second World War with the introduction of more complex, high-technology medicine such as open-heart surgery and organ transplantation (Le Fanu, 2011). As Stevens (2003) observes, this was linked to the growth of funded government medical research and an ever-stronger link of hospitals and medical schools to universities. In consequence, the profession of medicine became more specialised by the 1960s and 1970s. At first this included areas like obstetrics and gynaecology, ophthalmology and paediatrics, which then spread further to fields such as cardiology and psychiatry. Each of these typically became associated with its own Royal College. Even family practitioners, who formally referred patients on to specialists in the health care system, developed their own specialist body – the Royal College of General Practitioners.

These Royal Colleges, together with the British Medical Association, in turn, shaped the undergraduate and postgraduate curriculum through the General Medical Council. This was therefore a time when the profession had developed a common identity based on general practitioners and hospital specialists within a unified biomedical paradigm. Both of these were well rewarded, especially at higher-prestige consultant levels (Stevens, 2003) notwithstanding ongoing inequalities of gender, race and class within medicine itself (Saks, 2015b). The standing of the profession working primarily in the free-at-the-point of access National Health Service with some interlinked private practice (Klein, 2013) was enhanced still further in terms of jurisdictions by the professionalisation of other limited and subordinated health professions under the shadow of the medical umbrella from the latter part of the nineteenth century to the mid-twentieth century and beyond. As Allsop and Saks (2002) relate, these variously included the range of professional groups registered under the auspices of the 1852 and 1868 Pharmacy Acts, the 1878 Dentists Act, the 1902 Midwives Act, the 1919 Nurses Registration Act, the 1958 Opticians Act and the 1960 Professions Supplementary to Medicine Act.

The health professional groups to which these pieces of legislation and subsequent amendments gave rise all added greater lustre to the medical profession that had developed a much-enhanced capacity to delegate. By now, medicine had a more cohesive identity, facilitated by the growing evidence-based culture engendered by its in-house journals like the *British Medical Journal* and the *Lancet* (Bartrip, 1990). This was further reinforced by sustained attacks by the orthodox medical elite comprised of the British Medical Association and the Royal Colleges – not least through the General Medical Council – on complementary and alternative practitioners of therapies from herbalism and homeopathy to chiropractic and osteopathy, which denied them opportunities to cooperate with doctors and gain state legitimacy (Saks, 2002b). This served to create a high point in the self-regulatory professionalisation of medicine in Britain. What, though, of the process of medical professionalisation in the United States?

Medical professionalisation in the United States

The process of the professionalisation of medicine up to the 1960s and 1970s on the other side of the Atlantic took quite a different course – in part because professional licensing in the multitude of different states in the United States did not materialise until the early twentieth century. Notwithstanding its liberal-democratic credentials and significant professional regulatory state intervention, medicine in the United States has for long far been more dominated by private sector and market dynamics (Saks, 2018b). Their influence stretches back to the sixteenth and seventeenth centuries during the colonisation of the New World, especially from Europeans (Jenkins, 2012). At this time indigenous Indian medicine, underpinned by a spirit philosophy, was increasingly supplanted with the arrival of doctors from Britain and elsewhere who took on the role of generalist surgeon-apothecaries rather than that of physicians, reflecting the anti-elitist values of the settlers (Stevens, 1998).

In a difficult environment in America, plagued by devastating epidemics and with relatively few educated practitioners, those with backgrounds in law, the ministry and teaching also served as doctors from the seventeenth century onwards using imported medical texts and natural therapies such as herbalism (Duffy, 1993). More emphasis was placed on apprenticeships as medical schools and universities were not as developed as in Europe, resulting in a much smaller gap between 'regulars' and 'irregulars' than in Britain (Stevens, 1998). The large number of self-appointed doctors known as 'physicians', who operated alongside female midwife folk healers in the competitive market under this early form of capitalism, were very much against introducing the tripartite medical structure extant in Britain as it did not mesh with the anti-monopolistic culture (Abrams, 2013). Instead, the key division apparent at this time was between physicians trained through apprenticeships and those educated at the growing range of universities in Europe and North America (Starr, 1982).

As Stevens (1998) notes, by the beginning of the nineteenth century a group of better educated, mainly male physicians with loosely cast codes of ethics and a more cohesive occupational network had come on the scene – in contrast to the mainly female irregulars such as botanical practitioners in individual practice (Starr, 1982). However, as in Britain, there appeared to be little difference in their very limited ability to treat illness. It is not surprising, therefore, that the local guild-like licensing arrangements centred on medical societies, which grew up in some places, were generally ineffective in controlling the competitors of poorly rewarded regulars. This was a time of rapid growth of medical schools with varying standards when the ignorance and lack of skill of rival 'quacks' was often portrayed as endangering health (Bonner, 2000). At this point, health care still primarily took place on a self-help basis through females in the home – where life centred on exercise, fresh air, cleanliness and following oral folk traditions (Starr, 1982).

The main obstacle to medical professionalisation in this context in a predominantly fee-for-service system was the anti-corporatist philosophy that prevailed in the Jacksonian period in the 1830s and 1840s. But if this favoured free competition rather than licensing where "the knowledge ethic was aggressively democratic, anti-corporatist and individualistic" (Porter, 1992:8), the net result was that physicians adopted more moderate allopathic remedies and general hospitals were much slower to develop than in Britain. The conflict between regulars and irregulars, though, was sharpened by the fact that some of the latter, as epitomised by the homeopaths, also aimed to restrict competition (Haller, 2009). As Stevens (1998) points out, the American Medical Association founded in 1847 was the key body in moving forward medical professionalisation. Amongst other things, it gradually eased the deep rifts between groups of physicians – aided by the unifying influence of local medical societies as a growing distinction emerged between generalists and mushrooming specialties like dermatology and ophthalmology.

The main contribution of the American Medical Association, though, was to strive to standardise and raise the level of medical education, while working to exclude irregulars from federal posts and state medical societies in the second half of the nineteenth century. It also increased cohesion through the establishment of the *Journal of the American Medical Association*, which promoted scientific biomedicine and variously attacked medical sects and fairground sellers of patent medicines (Starr, 1982). A major development in medical professionalisation was the founding of state medical boards as they became transformed from being a despised monopolistic privilege to an ideological defence of certified trading rights, with a minimum of diploma-level entry from accepted schools (Johnson and Chaudhry, 2012). Despite variation in the terms of licensing in a more fragmented system than in Britain, exclusive licences for medical practice were provided everywhere by the beginning of the twentieth century, with a majority of medical society representatives on each state board (Starr, 1982). Krause (1996) characteristically sees this as expanding the independent guild power of the medical profession.

Starr (1982) observes that there was also a rising bar for accreditation of medical schools following the 1910 Flexner Report, which resulted in many closures of such establishments. In addition, the American Medical Association facilitated greater legal uniformity in the separate states – not least through the founding of the national Council on Medical Education – and gained control over the supply of physicians through the universities. Crucially too, marginalised outsiders were not only effectively policed by the federal Food and Drug Administration, but also could only practise if they gained separate state licences (Saks, 2015a). However, medical professionalisation did not go without challenge in a more privatised economy than Britain. From the early twentieth century onwards, the increasing number of corporations providing medical care through third-party insurance schemes for employees and mutual benefit societies – alongside an expanding, bureaucratised private hospital sector – drove down medical fees and threatened the independence of physicians (Starr, 1982). In this respect, physicians in the professionalisation process did not have the protection of a state medical shelter, as in the context of the medical-Ministry alliance in the first half of the twentieth century in Britain (Klein, 2013).

While the United States constitution emphasises equality of opportunity, the medical profession was operating in a setting up to the 1960s and 1970s with more unequal access to a less centralised and efficient health service than in Britain – which generally worked to the detriment of poor, ethnic and rural communities in a profession that was itself heavily stratified by gender and other forms of diversity (Saks, 2018b). The American Medical Association can be criticised for its opposition to a more comprehensive medical system in the health care market and its later related resistance in the 1960s to Medicare and Medicaid as safety nets for the aged and those on social security, respectively (Starr, 1982). However, it was active in trying to ensure the medical profession retained its autonomy and its relatively high rewards – in the face of the pressures of the escalating costs of biomedical innovations such as electrocardiography and cataract surgery, as well as new generations of drugs such as penicillin and the sulphonamides (Rutkow, 2010). The profession also helped to attract support for hospital development through such schemes as the Hill-Burton programme and federal and private funding of medical research from the mid-twentieth century onwards (Starr, 1982).

As part of this development, Stevens (1998) highlights that specialisation outstripped that of Britain, with nineteen specialist boards formed by the mid-twentieth century including in anaesthesiology, otolaryngology and thoracic surgery. This was linked to direct physician access to hospitals, with a much more fluid relationship between hospitals and the community services and a greater proportion of specialists as opposed to generalists than in the British context (Stevens, 2003). That the mainly male medical profession had reached its zenith in the United States by the 1960s and 1970s was underlined, as in Britain, by ongoing physician dominance of the increasingly licensed limited and subordinated health professions operating in areas from laboratory work and pharmacy to nursing and physical therapy in the division of labour. In addition, one of the most challenging alternatives to medicine – that of osteopathy – was by the 1960s well on the way to being incorporated through licensure into the medical profession (Saks, 2015a). But if there are both similarities and significant differences between medical professionalisation in Britain and the United States, what of the processes surrounding law in these two liberal-democratic countries?

Legal professionalisation in Britain

In England – on which this chapter on legal professionalisation in Britain focuses given the divergence between the constituent societies – lawyers had their origin in the courts of the medieval church (Brundage, 2008). However, paid attorneys and the very small closed specialist order of serjeants began to emerge as a profession with a wider brief by the end of the fourteenth century (Brand, 1992). As Burrage (2006) points out, though, they were not organised as corporate bodies at this time, even if there was regulation with sanctions for miscreants inside and outside their ranks by the King, Parliament and the courts within the precincts of London. They did, nonetheless, establish themselves in inns near the courts – hence the origin of the still surviving four Inns of Court by the fifteenth century. There is no direct lineage with the modern division of labour as, by the mid-seventeenth century, the two modern jurisdictions of barristers and solicitors were neither identifiable nor demarcated – with the main division being between London and the provinces operating in a range of business and other functions in the commercial largely *laissez-faire* market economy.

As Lemmings (2004) observes, though, the traditional rituals of the legal elite declined with the rise of an affluent middle class as the two branches of the legal profession gradually began to emerge with a referral relationship in a more competitive era. Burrage (2006) notes that the Inns of Court, along with the now defunct Chancery Inn, were independent of the state in early modern England, controlling the admission, training, certification and licensing of advocates who appeared in the royal courts in Westminster and acting as stepping stones for students who wished to join the Bar. In these terms they were an effective self-regulating force without a university underpinning, associated mainly with the landed gentry (Macdonald, 1995). Importantly, they had the collegial cohesion to withstand the attack by Parliament on lawyers during the mid-seventeenth century Commonwealth under Cromwell following the defeat of the royalists in the English Civil War. The distinctive position of autonomous self-regulating professional control was thereafter maintained by barristers from the Glorious Revolution to the 1960s and 1970s, based on a developing monopoly of pleading in the High Court and places on the bench as judges (Abel, 1998).

As Krause (1996) relates, despite their continuous history over many centuries, the Inns of Court were the main focus for guild power, as the major professional reference point – to one of which all barristers must belong. Despite the strengths of these self-perpetuating oligarchic subgroups headed by senior barristers and judges from the latter part of the seventeenth century, they could only rarely agree between themselves and resisted any far-reaching attempts at reform. Burrage (2006) notes their anomalous nature as a profession because, for most of their subsequent history, they were unconcerned about setting formal educational admission requirements; students simply needed to be accepted by one of the Inns and then spend five to seven years participating in the life of the Inn, including dining in the relevant hall on a number of occasions. Even though the Bar Council was founded in 1895, it did little to change this and did not have the power to represent barristers as a whole to the state until in 1966 the Senate of the Bar emerged out of the Bar Council (Krause, 1996).

Nonetheless, Abel (1998) observes that, even before this time, the legitimacy of the Bar was rarely challenged, given its position at the apex of the British class structure. Those who became practising barristers were typically Oxbridge graduates who used networks in their Inns to arrange a pupillage before taking the Bar final examination, following the lengthy period required of students to self-support during their apprenticeship. As Burrage (2006) stresses, this period in chambers was not open financially to many recruits beyond the sons of the propertied, which reinforced the informal barriers to entry to the profession. Even when Oxford and Cambridge did introduce degrees with legal components in the mid-nineteenth century, they were not planned with the Inns – and, indeed, it was only by the first half of the twentieth century that exemptions were allowed based on achievements in such university education. Having said this, with the widening university base by the 1970s, a growing number of institutions offered undergraduate law degrees with selected exemption from Bar finals that paved the way to the protected title of barrister.

On the other side of the coin, Macdonald (1995) observes that solicitors historically were 'officers of the court'. From this position they moved from being documentary and procedural experts to becoming exclusive gatekeepers to both the general legal process and barristers themselves. By the eighteenth century, articles were the accepted method of entry and training for attorneys. Early in the following century, though, the Law Society followed the Inns of Court in offering university graduates an exemption – in this case for three years (Burrage, 2006). As Macdonald (1995) notes, this was formalised through the 1825 Solicitors Act, which established this regulatory body of the solicitors' branch of the profession, subsequently reinforced by the Royal Charter granted in 1845. The Law Society provided the roll for a group that was inferior to barristers, but built its monopoly on the basis of uniformity of training and qualifications during the nineteenth century to one of greater, if not complete, equality with the Bar. In the case of solicitors, however, a more credentialist route was followed by the Law Society than for their elite counterparts – albeit with parallel control by practitioners themselves and a focus on practice-based, rather than university-led, training.

As Krause (1996) comments, in terms of legal professionalisation, solicitors – whose number of members was ten-fold that of barristers by the second half of the twentieth century – were not required to have a degree in law in the period before the Second World War. Rather, a five-year apprenticeship sufficed, although solicitors continued to give more emphasis to tested competence, largely through commercial crammers and correspondence courses rather than legal education provided by the Law Society. This legitimated their position more than the inherited rank and status that underpinned the standing of barristers. Burrage (2006) notes the uneasy relationship of the Law Society with universities up to the 1970s, which was to change with the subsequent expansion of university law degrees. He underlines that solicitors, unlike barristers, did not generally hold a formal monopoly over most of the legal services they provided at this time, with the main exception of conveyancing. Like the medical profession in Britain, they held a monopoly primarily derived from the protection of title rather than a legally prescribed monopoly in providing advice, as was affirmed by the 1974 Solicitors Act.

The legal profession, like the British medical profession, therefore reached its self-regulatory pinnacle in the first two or three decades of the second half of the twentieth century. At this point, as Macdonald (1995) relates, lawyers could be described in seventeenth-century terms as 'lesser governments', given their power over the functioning of the legal and judicial system. The legal profession has therefore for long served as a direct extension of the state, which distinguishes it from the medical profession in Britain – notwithstanding its close entanglement in the medical–Ministry alliance in the interwar years and subsequent central connection through the National Health Service (Klein, 2013). This did not insulate the legal profession from jurisdictional skirmishes from other professions – not least accountancy, with which battles over territory raged in the hundred years from 1850 to 1950 (Sugarman, 1995). However, the powers of the legal profession, paralleling that more extensively extant in medicine, were reinforced by growing numbers of paralegal personnel, with their origins in barristers-clerks and solicitors-clerks, to whom the profession could subdelegate (Ward, 2017).

As with medicine in Britain by the 1960s and 1970s, there remained similarly strong intergenerational familial links, ethnic discrimination and male dominance in accessing top positions in law (see, for example, Sommerlad, 2017; Sommerlad and Sanderson, 2018). This highlighted that legal professionalisation in a capitalist economy did little to reduce inequalities not only inside, but also outside, the profession – as a less good service was provided to a more diverse minority and proletarianised clientele in a largely privatised, class-based system (Fine et al, 1979). This was true notwithstanding the introduction of legal aid for the poor as a form of social welfare just after the mid-twentieth century (Moore and Newbury, 2017). Paradoxically, this in part helped bankroll the higher-status work of barristers whose operation was in ongoing tension with solicitors in a split profession (Burrage, 2006). The continuities and distinctions associated with the professionalisation of law on the other side of the Atlantic, with its greater emphasis on the operation of the market, will now be explored.

Legal professionalisation in the United States

In America, as noted in the previous discussion about medical professionalisation there, British and European settlers before the eighteenth-century War of Independence brought a democratic, anti-elitist ethos – which was opposed to such institutions as aristocracy and the monarchy (Jenkins, 2012). In this context, lawyers were not well organised, with the caveat that a wealthy elite sent their sons to be trained at the Inns of Court in Britain in a rather gender-biased manner. They had a higher status at this stage in America than in Britain (Burrage, 2006) and increasingly replaced the lay people who had worked as lawyers under the supervision of preachers, before Puritanism faded and commerce increased (Krause, 1996). While these groups of newly forged attorneys formed exclusive social networks based on background, these networks were not typically formalised – with the exception of colonies in New York, Pennsylvania, Rhode Island and Virginia. As a result, along with the absence of a centralised legal system, there was little direct pressure for reform by the revolutionary governments and only slow incremental change thereafter (Burrage, 2006).

As Macdonald (1995) relates, however, protests against lawyers did occur in post-revolutionary times, most notably in Massachusetts – while formal prerequisites and qualifications for legal practice as a counsellor-at-law were abolished in the states of Ohio, Georgia, Tennessee and South Carolina in the early nineteenth century. Although this did not stop voluntary associations of lawyers being formed, these largely collapsed from 1830 until after the Civil War because of the radical egalitarianism of the Jacksonian period, when law, medicine, religion and engineering were made open to all irrespective of qualifications and were colonised mainly by white Anglo-Saxon Protestant males. As Pound (1977:229) notes: "Distrust of things English, pioneer distrust of specialists, led to the general rejection of the common-law idea of an organized, responsible, self-regulating profession." However, as in the case of medicine, professions began to develop on the foundation of modern, practical knowledge in an array of associations with varied structures and goals in the newly established fragmentary political structure of the United States (Burrage, 2006) – with university schools of law, including Harvard Law School, gradually building their reputations by the end of the nineteenth century (Macdonald, 1995).

In this vein, the American Bar Association was founded as a regulatory body in 1868, even if, as Krause (1996) suggests, it did not have the early influence on legal education that the American Medical Association had on medicine. Abel (1989) affirms that most lawyers in the United States continued to be trained by apprenticeship until the 1940s and 1950s. Even those who did go to state law schools had not usually been to college before this and a majority of these schools only had part-time academic staff on their faculties, preferring instead to employ practitioners to prepare students for the Bar examinations. However, the American Bar Association supervised these examinations and, as a consequence of discrimination against women and ethnic and religious minorities, white males predominated amongst the graduands. According to Krause (1996), in the first half of the twentieth century two types of schools existed – elite schools with limited enrolment and high selectivity and a much larger group of smaller schools with wider recruitment. This division created a two-tier profession of a rather different kind to that of Britain – with mainly upper-class graduates from elite schools who undertook corporate work for large private law firms, and lower-class and minority lawyers from schools of lesser status who ministered relatively autonomously in solo practice to the individual problems of middle- and lower-class clients, with the poor at the margins (Abel, 1989).

Aside from educational oversight and policing the ethical codes of qualified lawyers, Rueschmeyer (1988) notes that the framework for legal professionalisation in the United States was based on the English Common Law system focused on legislation and precedent, rather than the code and general principles of continental civil law. Similarly, as in England, the profession established itself as the source of the judiciary – albeit in the United States through state and local Bar associations, alongside the consultancy role of the American Bar Association at federal level. However, not all English practices were adopted. Understandably, given the anti-elitist political culture, the traditional division between barristers and solicitors ultimately formed no part of the America legal profession – despite initial moves towards an English-style referral system in some of the early colonies (Burrage, 2006). Instead, Krause (1996) observes that legal work in the United States in the modern era was generalised, rather than being apportioned, as the profession developed in a more inclusive manner dealing with everything from legal advice to both businesses and individual clients, to representation in court cases.

As Burrage (2006) describes, there was also – perhaps surprisingly given the more privatised American socio-political context – slightly more public-funded, legal practice than in England after the Second World War, apparently mainly because of the earlier emergence of salaried public prosecutors in the United States. Interestingly, a further distinction from Britain was that practice-based training was less accentuated in the United States where greater stress as time passed was placed on university education – albeit with indirect control over university law schools through accreditation. In this way, lawyers established a precedent for other professions – namely, that professionals were exclusively made in universities and thereby played their part in promoting the world's first mass higher education system. As in medicine in the United States, supply came to be regulated by the profession through entry criteria and examinations in the universities. In the case of law, Bar examination committees, rather than law schools, oversaw these and thus exercised control over the inflow and outflow into the legal profession.

Given the prejudice of lawyers controlling local, state and national bar committees, Krause (1996) claims that a handful of segregated law schools were virtually the only source of recruitment of black students to legal practice after the American Bar Association first agreed to admit them in the early 1940s. At this stage, women and religious minorities faced parallel, if not quite so extreme, obstacles (Abel, 1989). Meanwhile, as Krause (1996) relates, the male white Anglo-Saxon Protestant elite in corporate practice in an entrepreneurial society controlled the big city Bars, the state Bar associations and the American Bar Association itself. In the period up to the mid-twentieth century, this resulted in it adjudicating most individual ethical misconduct cases against its developing codes of ethics – as corporate cases were rarely investigated at this stage (Burrage, 2006). At the same time, while delegation occurred to subordinate groups, non-lawyers were prosecuted for unauthorised practice and the profession largely repelled the monopolistic claims of competing professions in areas like accountancy and real estate in adjacent jurisdictions (Krause, 1996).

However, while the American legal profession, like its British counterpart, was at the peak of its self-regulatory powers by the 1960s and early 1970s, the challenges to its authority were also rising. Although the numbers and ratio of lawyers to the population was beginning to expand, this was the era – following the civil rights movement, anti-Vietnam activism and the rise of feminism – when the lack of sensitivity in the profession to diversity started to come under serious attack. As Krause (1996) notes, just as in the case of medicine, a growing band of university academics took issue with the lack of representativeness of the American Bar Association and the state Bar associations in terms of these and other shortcomings. The consequence of this counter-cultural movement, which swept the modern world at this time, for the legal profession and professions in general will be considered further in Chapter 4 of this book, but for the moment the direction of travel of the American legal profession up to this point – and its distinctive contours relative to the British legal profession – should now be apparent.

Professionalisation in a wider comparative perspective

The cases of medicine and law in Britain and the United States highlight the particularism of routes from localised guilds to strong national patterns of self-regulatory professionalisation in the period up to the 1960s and 1970s. As has been seen, the path and the sequence of steps taken to the destination in the formation of exclusive professional associations based on specific expertise has varied greatly not only for different occupations within a single society, but also across the two diverse, but interlinked, international contexts examined here. This variability of the nature and timing of professional emergence relates to many aspects of the journey, from the shifting importance and texture of university engagement to the influence of the socio-political milieu in which they are situated – not least through the traditional and other divisions of society at large. Detailed historical analysis highlights that it is not only the processes of professionalisation that exhibit diversity, but also the evolving dynamic form of the professions themselves. But if this renders generating simple typologies of the sort that have been considered earlier in this chapter highly problematic, this is accentuated by a wider consideration of the professionalisation of occupational groups outside of the top professions of medicine and law.

This can be exemplified by brief cameos of the process followed by pairs of relatively established professions in the Anglo-American context. In Britain, for instance, there were close parallels between the professionalisation of medicine and veterinary surgeons – at least through the Royal Charter granted to the latter in 1845 and subsequent exclusionary professional regulatory legislation in 1881 that helped to contain competition from the unlicensed (Pattison, 1984). This ultimately paved the way for the 1966 Veterinary Surgeons Act, which enabled the approximately 24,000 veterinarians to secure a broader monopoly over animal care than that for the 200,000 doctors in relation to humankind – which covered treatment, as well as the protection of title gained in medicine (Whiting, May and Saks, 2020). Some of the potential factors involved in this differential historical positioning, which has persisted despite the higher status and considerably greater pay of the medical profession in Britain (Belfield et al, 2018), are explored in Box 2.2.

Box 2.2 Historical differences in regulating the medical and veterinary profession in Britain

Dr Pru Hobson-West from the School of Veterinary Medicine and Science at Nottingham University and Professor Stephen Timmons from Nottingham University Business School explore why veterinarians gained and maintained broader powers under the 1966 Veterinary Surgeons Act in contrast to medicine in Britain. They refer to the following factors:

- Socio-economic: The decline of farming, helping to decouple animals from public health;
- Socio-political: The predominance of veterinary private practice and the lack of a National Health Service for animals; and

- Socio-ethical: The lower moral status of animals compared to humans.

  These explanations may well help to account for part of the regulatory difference in terms of the lower stakes involved in veterinary as opposed to clinical medicine. However, as even Hobson-West and Timmons acknowledge, they are contentious and may not be the whole story. Nonetheless, their analysis does highlight historical variations in the form of professional regulation, as well as the debates about the reasons for these, which will be even more apparent in the next chapter on competing theories of professions.

  Source: Hobson-West, P. and Timmons, S. (2015) 'Animals and anomalies: An analysis of the UK veterinary profession and the relative lack of state reform', *Sociological Review* 64: 47–63.

There was a similar *volte-face* in the interconnected trajectory of law and accountancy in Britain; here, accountants in the process of professionalisation went from being peripheral players to solicitors in the nineteenth century to the principal business advisers of the middle classes by the mid-twentieth century (Sugarman, 1995). Despite much internal in-fighting, the springboard to their national ascendance was not statutory regulation, but piecemeal legislation requiring services to be provided by qualified professionals registered with bodies such as the Institute of Chartered Accountants in England and Wales and the Chartered Institute of Public Finance (Macdonald, 1995). In terms of professionalisation, this contrasted with the way accountancy was transacted in the more corporate United States where lawyers continued to hold sway over providing financial services to the commercial classes (Sugarman, 1995). Moreover, on the other side of the Atlantic, accountants were historically subject to regulatory legislation – and did not indirectly gain a monopoly as in Britain through legal requirements in dealing with company accounts. This meant that companies in the United States normally had to use a member of the American Institute of Certified Public Accountants for their accounts to carry conviction (Macdonald, 1995).

Parallel professional groups like American architects also built up a regulatory framework in professionalising on a state-by-state basis. According to Freidson (1986), by the beginning of the second half of the twentieth century architects in all states formally required a licence to practise, although many worked without one and some states accepted experience in place of formal educational qualifications. In contrast, architects in Britain now have national protection of title, based on lengthy education and experience, following early nineteenth-century debates as to whether architecture was simply a creative art or profession (Kaye, 1960). As Macdonald (1995) emphasises, occupational solidarity, as in many other areas, was vital in eventually winning professional closure – as was the educational platform it established both in this country and on the continent with support from the European Union (Le Bianic and Svensson, 2008). The mainstream cases of architectural professionalisation, similarly pervaded by gender and ethnically based glass ceilings (Macdonald, 1995), further highlight the variation in the routes to professionalisation in the Anglo-American context.

Looking more widely to the comparative field of higher education – a key underpinning of much international professionalisation – lecturers and professors in British and American universities, respectively, typically required higher education qualifications for employment up to the 1960s and 1970s. In the United States, they only belonged to fairly loose non-compulsory professional associations – such as the American Association of University Professors founded in 1915 and bodies representing specific disciplines like the American Sociological Association. In these circumstances, Krause (1996) highlights that their exclusivity, with all the attendant class, ethnic and gender barriers, was traditionally centred on being hired – with or without tenure – by high-level personnel in universities, where they worked largely autonomously with prescribed freedoms and responsibilities. However, while this could be viewed as another path to professionalisation in a much wider spread of modern industrial countries, from Australia and Canada to France and Italy, this has been contested.

More specifically, Muzzin and Martimianakis (2016) see this as the zenith of the guild power of the academic profession, which has since gone into decline because of increased constraints on academic freedom in a global economy. However, building on such an academic base, the 1960s and 1970s was a time when Bell (1962; 1976) was forecasting the rise of a universally dominant professional knowledge elite, replacing social classes as a central driver of the so-called 'post-industrial society'. This paralleled the much-revered work of Perkin (1989), who elevated professions above class as a mainstream aspect of modern England. Of course, the growing prominence of professions has since been disputed because of the subsequent impact of wider institutional and organisational change on the once autonomous professions (Evetts 2006). But such arguable claims only throw into relief just how far professional groups had come as a crucial feature of society in the immediate aftermath of the mid-twentieth century – in terms not only of power, but also of sheer numbers.

By the outset of the second half of the twentieth century, Millerson (1964) observed that some two-dozen new qualifying associations were formed in every decade in England alone in Britain. In parallel, Ehrenreich and Ehrenreich (1979) commented on the rapid growth of a broad span of powerful professional groups in the United States – a rise in the number of professional associations based on certification and licensure that continued into the twenty-first century, especially in health care, law, architecture and engineering (Redbird, 2017). This was reinforced by the increase in numbers of professionals linked to the expanding range of professional groups. Goldthorpe (1982) reflected on the major growth of professional practitioners in Britain in this period, while Giddens (1981) claimed that the proportion of professional workers in modern societies had trebled in the twenty or thirty years since the mid-twentieth century, making up as much as 15 per cent of the labour force in the United States. Of course, some of this growth of professional service and technical staff should be treated with scepticism as many were not mainstream professionals like doctors, lawyers and accountants, but more menial workers such as clerical workers, waiters and porters (Kumar, 1991). However, there was no doubting the escalating numbers of professions in the Anglo-American context and their rising power, prestige and other privileges at this time (Portwood and Fielding, 1981)

Broadening further the span of countries under scrutiny in the modern world, it is worth noting the case of Sweden. Here Agevall (2016) likens the professionalisation of university teachers metaphorically to a boa constrictor, a creature able to swallow items wider than its own diameter. This was because in the 1970s a state higher education reform expanded this sector by incorporating most occupations linked to post-secondary education into the hitherto closed university system – from nursing, occupational therapy and social work to dance and music. This case is important because, as Hellberg (1990) indicates in her analysis of the development of the veterinary profession in Sweden since the eighteenth century, the state actively influenced the detailed process of professionalisation. However, as suggested earlier in this chapter, the state-led process of 'professionalisation from above', rather than the more occupationally driven 'professionalisation from within', was even more pronounced historically in Germany, not least under totalitarian Nazi rule (McClelland, 1991). Although professional groups like engineers and chemists stood up to authoritarianism at this time, German knowledge-based professions generally followed an upward trajectory based on the tradition of cooperating with the state, in return for recognition of elite status, as opposed to fighting the state for their independence.

The fragility of professionalisation: The case of socialist societies

The examination of the role of the state in professionalisation also throws up another issue – namely, that there is none of the inevitability implied by contributors like Wilensky (1964) in discussing the professionalisation of everyone with expert knowledge. This notion was systematically belied by the experience of socialist societies in Eastern Europe and the Far East up to the 1960s and 1970s. This highlighted the fragility of the belief in an automatic trend towards professionalisation – especially in Russia and China, two of the most populous countries in the world. In the early decades of the twentieth century, both of these countries at different stages implemented socialist ideologies based on the industrial working class and the peasantry, respectively, in what politically became rather different, but unmistakeably, authoritarian regimes (Koesel, Bunce and Weiss, 2020). We shall begin the examination of the implications of this in each of these countries by first considering medicine in Soviet Russia – the professionalisation of which we have focused on extensively in the Anglo-American context so far in this chapter, alongside the case of law.

As Saks (2018a) recounts, the Pirogov Society, an independent body of doctors, finally emerged at the forefront of the drive to professionalise just before the October 1917 Russian Revolution, following a long battle against the Tsarist state, which was averse to challenges to its centralised power. Despite the support of the liberal Provisional Government formed immediately after the overthrow of the Tsarist regime at the beginning of 1917, when the Bolsheviks took power Lenin and his successors in the Communist Party deconstructed the embryonic profession as physicians from previous regimes were generally seen as bourgeois class enemies. While doctors continued to receive a six-year higher education, amongst other things, their specialist medical curriculum became more broadly directed towards the proletariat, their salaries and status were substantially reduced, the market was flooded with Soviet physicians, and medical decision making came under the sway of Party officials. This led Field (1957:45) to see the spirited emerging medical profession of the early twentieth century turn into "a docile and politically inert employee group."

The state's prevention of the development of autonomous professionalisation under the auspices of a Marxist-Leninist philosophy was also mirrored in other knowledge-based occupations in the Soviet Union up to the early years of the second half of the twentieth century (Balzer, 2016). Iarskaia-Smirnova and Abramov (2016) note that incipient professional groups like architects, engineers and teachers were similarly impacted at this time – even if they too had previously ridden the waves of rigid Tsarist state control before their growing independence in 1917 was rapidly overtaken by the constraints of the ruling Communist Party in the new socialist state. As Pomeranz (2019) highlights, the case of law was no exception in the unified bloc of Russia and associated Eastern European states, in which Lenin regarded lawyers as engaging in an inherently bourgeois preoccupation. Neither under Tsarism nor Soviet rule was there an independent legislature or judiciary in Russia. Under socialist leaders like Lenin and Stalin, lawyers came under the ongoing monopoly power of the Communist Party, where the concept of an autonomous legal profession was an anathema.

A parallel pattern was also evident in China following the success of the Chinese Communist Party in taking over power in 1949 from the nationalist puppet government of the Guomindang, following the demise of the Imperial dynasties. Before this time, groups like civil engineers and architects (Rowe and Wang, 2013) had established a professional foothold through degree-based licensure in the first half of the twentieth century. However, after the Great Leap Forward of the 1950s, the Chinese Cultural Revolution took place from 1966 under the leadership of Mao Zedong (Dikötter, 2016). This resulted in millions of people being executed, tortured or publicly humiliated and 'undesirables' being sent to the countryside to be re-educated by peasants in the Great Proletarian Revolution, under the guise of 'letting a thousand flowers bloom'. These 'capitalist-roaders' included many students and intellectuals, as scholars and scientists were purged and universities closed. Professional bodies in all areas including law and medicine suffered heavily in this period, not least since the Communist Party had already prohibited their independent existence, leaving the government as the sole regulator (Hsiao and Hu, 2013).

During the Cultural Revolution, lengthy stretches of university education were abolished or radically collapsed. In medicine in China, for example, the typical three- to five-year formal education and training of physicians was reduced to a matter of months for 'barefoot doctors'. They focused on practical remedies for the most common diseases, were drawn from the peasantry and then took over the role of frontline workers in the countryside (Horne, 1971). This dramatic change under-lines that professionalisation is by no means an automatic process for groups of experts and there are, for better or worse, other ways of managing knowledge in work settings. It also provides a salutary note to the apparent premise of Wilensky (1964) that the sequence of professio-nalisation can be analysed in abstraction from the socio-political context in which particular occupational groups are situated. It is not just that some groups do not achieve success in their efforts to professionalise in liberal democracies in the modern world; in some societies, the state provides blanket resistance to autonomous professionalisation of any kind in a world of multiple modernities.

Conclusion

Notwithstanding the position in state socialist societies, professionali-sation had widely taken place in many modernised countries by the early decades of the second half of the twentieth century. Although the focus in this book is on modern societies, we should not understate the lessons that can also be drawn from the related experience of pro-fessionalisation in emerging economies. In Brazil, for instance, Cunha and colleagues (2018) intriguingly profile the various phases the legal profession has passed through since the creation of law courses in the early nineteenth century, linked to political and economic changes from its time as a Portuguese colony to the assumption of power by the military in the 1960s and 1970s. In India, Ramnath (2017) has inter-estingly analysed the post-colonial development of the engineering profession up to the mid-twentieth century, centrally examining the replacement of the substantial proportion of British by native Indian engineers in the process of industrialisation. Bonnin and Ruggunan (2016) additionally throw into relief the implications of Dutch colonial history for professionalisation in their consideration of the invidious influence of Apartheid on professions in a similar period in South Africa. These examples further highlight that professionalisation does not occur in abstraction from the broader political context, even within a single nation.

Such illustrations from the developing world therefore underline that the process of professionalisation up to the 1960s and 1970s was not straightforward and cannot be disassociated from the direction of the societies on which this book is pivoted. We have already seen in this chapter how far the pattern of professionalisation in modernised countries varied over this period across a broad span of professional groups – and, indeed, in some cases was complicated further by the professionalising claims of particular occupational groups being undermined in different socio-political regimes. The study of professions in the modern age, loosely defined as independent and exclusive national associations of expert practitioners, though, has so far been quite descriptive. This has enabled us to outline their historical development to the point where they generally reached the height of their autonomous powers in the so-called 'golden age' of professions (Brint, 1994). We shall now turn to take a more analytical approach to professions and professionalisation through a theoretical lens. This will include consideration not just of positive, reinforcing theories of the professions, but also the more critical theoretical transformation that occurred with the advent of the counter culture from the mid-1960s onward – including with the development of neo-Weberianism and associated theories which guide the remainder of this book.

3 Competing theories of professions

Introduction

Theories of professions are fundamental to interpreting their operation in the business and management field and other contexts, including their nature and role and the process of professionalisation as considered in the last chapter. After outlining historical thinking about the professions, Chapter 3 sets out the main competing theories in the field over the past few decades, again focusing primarily on the Anglo-American context. Such more recent theories include the earlier, more supportive, taxonomic approach including trait and functionalist views, which will be outlined alongside other interpretations of the activities of professional groups later in this chapter. The taxonomic approach began to be criticised from the late 1950s and early 1960s. The first critics of this rather deferential approach – aside from the longstanding resistance to professional monopolies by free market economists – came from the micro-level analysis by symbolic interactionists. Their work gave rise to the more recently generated discourse analysis based on seeing professionalism simply as an ideology used in the politics of work.

Since the 1960s and 1970s counter culture, the professions have been viewed even more critically by theorists of the professions operating at a macro-structural level – not least by Marxists, Foucauldians and neo-Weberians. The detail of these perspectives will again be given as the chapter develops. Without diminishing the value of other approaches, it is argued that the use of the concept of exclusionary social closure by neo-Weberian writers offers the most incisive basis for analysing professions. It is held to provide a more open, empirically based approach to the relationship between professional interests, the state and the market. This is especially so when employed in conjunction with a neo-institutionalist approach that accentuates the relationship of professions with wider institutional structures and, to a lesser degree, a Bourdieusian perspective that extends the analytical tools available to neo-Weberians. But before going into more detail about the nature and advantages of neo-Weberianism, which centrally informs the rest of this book, we need to place more contemporary theorising on professions in historical context.

Historical theorising about professions

In charting the deep historical roots of theorising about the professions, Dingwall and King (1995) remind us of the much-neglected work of the English sociologist Herbert Spencer on professions in the second half of the nineteenth century. Speaking of 'professional institutions', Spencer (1896) discussed the evolution and secularisation of professions both generally and specifically. In the latter respect, he did so with reference to groups like arts practitioners, lawyers, physicians, scientists, surgeons and teachers. He highlighted how such professions became increasingly differentiated in the regulation of social life in order to maintain the well-being of society. As such, specialisation was seen as part of spontaneous cooperation in the societal organism. As Dingwall and King (1995:16) note, this process "was adaptive for individuals and societies: it allowed them to prosper and gave them a more competitive edge because of the way in which it introduced more flexibility, more cooperation, and more space for innovation." Even though he did not sufficiently acknowledge the role of law in underpinning modern professionalism and arguably gave too much emphasis to the benefits of the open market, Spencer did perceive the positive role of professions in society. Crucially, he saw them in opposition to the culture of his day as humanly rather than divinely created institutions (Dingwall, 2016).

By the late nineteenth and early twentieth century, the French sociologist Emile Durkheim (1992), who is even more widely cited in the Anglo-American literature on professions, also took the view that they were a positive force in social development. This was based on his interpretation of the role occupational associations played as the societal organism strove for equilibrium against pathological and disintegrative forces. He believed that particular challenges arose in the transition from pre-industrial societies with a primitive mechanical solidarity based on shared values and beliefs, to more complex modern societies based more on organic solidarity and functional interdependence and cooperation. He was concerned that social order may be undermined in this transition by the increasing emphasis on self-interest in the modern world. For Durkheim (1964), the solution lay in the emergence of occupational associations acting as a kind of social cement with a broader territorial base than the localised medieval guilds. He saw them as providing moral authority, ensuring the continuation of a state of healthy equilibrium in the face of anarchic egotism. But if, like Spencer, he highlighted the beneficial intermediary role of professions standing between the individual and society, he is also open to criticism. In this case, amongst other things, this is because he did not place sufficient stress on the value to society of altruistic professional codes of conduct in contrast to the more abstract function of professions as intermediary groups in what otherwise might have become an anomic society (Saks, 1995).

This explicit lack of attention to the codes of conduct of professions was taken up more strongly in the period between the World Wars in the Anglo-American context by R. H. Tawney (1921), an English economic historian. He called for the expansion of professionalism into what he saw as the acquisitive environment of an industrial society. He felt the ethical role of professions would enable private interests to be more fully subordinated to the needs of the community in a functional society. Implicit in his view was the notion that professions conducted their work in a manner "designed to enforce certain standards... for the better service of the public" (Tawney, 1921:107). In saying this, Tawney argued that a Christian conscience could be revived through the professions to harmonise human discord in society in defence of the common good. What is apparent, though, in all these early landmark positions taken by Spencer, Durkheim and Tawney in theorising about professional groups is that they each share, in their own way, a positive view of professions in society. This ethos continued into what Klegon (1978) terms the taxonomic approach to professions that developed in Britain and the United States in the heyday of their self-regulatory powers in the two or three decades after the Second World War.

Taxonomic theories of the professions

In following the chronology set out at the beginning of this chapter, taxonomic theories of professions were marked by being involved in the classification of such occupational groups. In building their underlying models of professionalism, they also typically took professional ideologies on trust (Elliott, 1972). This perspective therefore reflected the widespread reverence that was culturally given to groups like doctors and lawyers in the first part of the twentieth century. In a nutshell, as Saks (2012) points out, the taxonomic approach was based on two central assumptions, namely that professions:

- possessed unique elements distinct from other occupational groups; and
- played a highly constructive role in the wider society.

The significance of this somewhat deferential approach to professions is that it not only characterised the Anglo-American literature in the period up to the 1960s and 1970s counter culture, but was also employed increasingly widely in the analysis of professions in a range of other modern societies (Adams, 2015). The perspective itself is divided into two distinct strands – the trait approach and the structural functionalist analysis of professions. We shall consider each in more detail.

The trait approach

The taxonomic account is well illustrated by the trait approach, in which its advocates set out a variety of defining features of a profession, in aiming to distinguish them from other occupational groups (Millerson, 1964). As contributors such as Greenwood (1957) and Hickson and Thomas (1969) indicate, their *ad hoc* lists characterising professional groups included items like:

- an altruistic orientation;
- systematic knowledge; and
- formal education and training.

However, there was no consensus amongst contributors to the trait approach as to what were the central features of professions; their definitions differed in terms of both the number of characteristics identified and the nature of the attributes concerned. There was also a lack of analysis of the relationship between the constituent elements put forward by trait contributors. This accentuated the weakness of the approach as it was essentially atheoretical, arbitrarily reflecting the professions' own view of themselves. In addition, the characteristics identified typically derived from the study of only a few professional groups. As a result, as Johnson (2016) has observed, it abstracted in a highly limited way professions from the wider historical and social structure – of which we have already underlined in the preceding chapters they are an integral part.

In these terms, the classificatory approach of trait writers not only provided a convenient narrative to rationalise the privileges of professions, but also paved the way for professional groups to engage in special pleading in ranking themselves in the league tables that were consequently devised (Johnson, 2016). Here both established and newly developing occupational groups were able to manipulate the criteria or selectively draw on aspects of the published social scientific literature on this subject so that they could place themselves higher up the ladder of professional standing. Saks (2016b) notes that this obscures the processes involved in professional formation which hinge on state sanction and cannot simply be viewed as a product of the traits of particular occupational groups. As will be seen, the structural functionalists, in setting out the second, more sophisticated, variant of taxonomy, were also not averse to promoting the virtues of professions – albeit usually as homogenous groups without recognising the tensions that can exist within them (Bucher and Strauss, 1961). Nonetheless, functionalists at least took a broader, more theoretical, perspective in situating professions in their organisational and societal context, including in relation to the state.

The functionalist analysis

The less narrowly conceived functionalist approach was centred on how professions met the needs of the social system. As such, it in part took its lineage from aspects of the earlier work of Spencer, Durkheim and Tawney. Its particular trademark, however, was to explain the exalted position of professions in terms of a trade-off – whereby professional groups were given high socio-economic rewards in exchange for using esoteric knowledge of great importance to society in a non-exploitative manner (see, for example, Barber, 1963; Goode, 1960). However, although it was more theoretically integrated, this perspective suffered from a similar problem to that of trait contributors in so far as it was based on the assumed positive characteristics of professions that were not normally put to empirical test – such as the concept of the collectivity orientation of professional groups (Saks, 1995). This was accentuated when conflicts of professions in organisations were discussed by functionalist writers, which tended to be reflexively seen as subverting the presumed virtuous collegial values of professions (as illustrated by Hall, 1968; Scott, 1966).

Nonetheless, despite this criticism, some functionalist writers were more subtle than others. Talcott Parsons (1952), a renowned American sociologist, for instance, based his functionalist analysis on 'ideal types' of professions. This meant that the template he employed did not necessarily represent the actual operation of professions, but normative behaviour linked to professional role expectations. Situating professions in this way in the broader social structure based on the general functional prerequisites for action systems – such as adaptation to the environment, the capacity to set goals, the integration of values and norms and institutional pattern maintenance – certainly helped Parsons to open up professional groups to empirical scrutiny. But, although he laudably goes beyond 'ground-up' trait approaches in a more open way than many of his contemporaries (Sciulli, 2009), his abstract starting point in analysing the professions is still conservative and consensual. It is hardly surprising then that his and other functionalist work has been attacked for not acknowledging interest-based conflict in driving change – including in terms of the power and self-interests of professions themselves (Saks, 1995). This brings us to more general critiques of the taxonomic approach.

The critique of the taxonomic approach

Even before the taxonomic approach increasingly emerged on the scene after the Second World War, there were of course critics in a relatively deferential culture that by and large sustained a positive interpretation of the nature and role of professions. George Bernard Shaw (1946), the Fabian playwright, is well known for suggesting in performances of *The Doctor's Dilemma* at the beginning of the twentieth century that all professions were conspiracies against the laity – not least by attacking in an English medical context the financial incentives given to doctors to engage in unnecessary surgery in private practice and questioning their infallibility. However, in the social sciences the first critics of the airbrushed imagery of professional groups embedded in the taxonomic approach were in fact the free market economists (see, for instance, Kessell, 1958; Lees, 1966). Foremost amongst these was Milton Friedman (1962), who condemned professions for forming monopolies impeding the free flow of the market in the United States. He saw this as serving professional interests as opposed to those of the wider public; in medicine, for example, the monopoly was held to stifle innovation, limit opportunities for well-qualified candidates to become physicians, and drive up the costs of medical care. The main early theoretical critique of professions in sociology, though, came from symbolic interactionists who – unlike the anti-monopolists – criticised the trait and structural functionalist theories of professional groups from a micro, rather than a macro, level.

Symbolic interactionism

In distancing themselves from metanarratives related to the professions, symbolic interactionists rejected the distinction that taxonomic contributors had made between professions and other occupational groups. Interactionists like Howard Becker (1962) saw the concept of a profession purely as a symbol employed in the politics of work, stressing that this socially negotiated label did not provide a helpful indication of how individual professionals organised and conducted their work. In other words, the notion of a 'profession' was not seen as neutral or scientific, but as "a folk concept, a part of the apparatus of the society we study, to be studied by noting how it is used and what role it plays in the operation of that society" (Becker, 1962: 33). This view was reinforced by Everett Hughes (1963) who irreverently compared the high-profile work of elite professionals such as doctors and lawyers with the 'dirty work' of such stigmatised groups as janitors and prostitutes – arguing that there were more similarities than differences between them in addressing the demands of their occupational roles. In breaking the bonds of conventional meaning, both Becker and Hughes challenged the reifications of the taxonomic approach. Indeed, Roth (1974) claimed that its advocates had been 'duped' by the professions given their reflexive acceptance of the legitimating professional ideologies underwriting their privileges.

However, while symbolic interactionism has given rise to more contemporary expression in action-based processual theories of professions (Liu, 2018) and provided a stepping stone to the less locally constrained discourse analysis which will be considered further on in this chapter, it did not displace the taxonomic approach in the analysis of the professions in the 1950s and 1960s in the Anglo-American context. Despite its freshness, there was good reason for this. In the first place, given its action-based methodology centred on the relationship between clients and practitioners, the arguments mounted tended not to be based on systematic data – certainly not sufficient to impress its more positivistically oriented rivals. For instance, Becker (1962) only drew on research from his study of a single profession in support of his view that professional practitioners did not behave with such independent authority as the symbol of professionalism would suggest. Second, the focus on the micro setting led proponents of interactionism to largely ignore broader structures of power and historical processes in explaining the success and failure of attempts by specific groups to formally professionalise (Saks 1995). Nonetheless, more critical and nuanced macro perspectives emerged in Britain and the United States with the development of the counter culture in the 1960s and 1970s, which was less enamoured with the progressive modernist narratives of the past – including those put forward by the professions (Roszak, 1995). At the front of this group of theoretical competitors to taxonomy was the Marxist analysis of professions.

The Marxist perspective

Marxist theories brought wider structural and historical analyses of professions into focus from the 1970s onwards in the Anglo-American context in a manner counterposed to the taxonomic approach. Whereas trait and functionalist contributors had seen a more amorphous and anodyne industrial society as a backcloth to their analyses, the Marxist perspective squarely places professions in a social-class-divided capitalist frame of reference. However, within Marxism there are differences over where exactly professions should be located in the classic division between the bourgeoisie and proletariat – representing capital and labour, respectively (Carchedi, 2006). In this respect, professions are rarely regarded in Marxist philosophy as part of the exalted proletarian class, which does not own the means of production and is seen as playing a lead role in the socialist revolution in overthrowing the bourgeoisie and building a classless society. One exception was Paul Baran (1973), an American economist, who claimed that the interests of professions such as physicians and scientists were opposed to those of the dominant class, as their services would be needed to an ever-greater extent under a socialist regime – unlike those of the clergy and tax avoidance specialists, for whom the demand would rapidly disappear.

Most Marxist theorists, though, take a less rosy view of the professions as a whole in capitalist societies. Poulantzas (1975) sees them as part of the petty bourgeoisie – with social workers and teachers engaging in the ideological inculcation and political repression of the working class and engineers frequently involved in their management and supervision. This has parallels with Ehrenreich and Ehrenreich (1979) who view the 'professional-managerial class' as engaging in surveillance and control for capital in the United States. In Britain, meanwhile, Esland (1980a) even sees new welfare professions like career advisers and counsellors, alongside lawyers and doctors, as agents of capitalist control – not least because, by individualising social problems which have their roots in system dynamics, they help preserve the capitalist *status quo*. Navarro (1986) goes a step further in viewing professions such as medicine as part of the dominant capitalist class, despite typically having no formal ownership of the means of production. At another remove, Braverman (1998) paints a rather different but dynamic picture of groups such as accountants and nurses becoming increasingly deskilled and proletarianised with the degradation of work under capitalism, as the owners and corporate managers of enterprises seek to increase their control of the labour process.

Despite their diversity, in considering such conflictual class-based Marxist views, we are clearly a long way from the more consensual approach of functionalist writers in the taxonomic school centred on professions meeting system needs serving the collective good. However, whatever the position taken on the variety of interpretations given by its proponents, the Marxist perspective on professions has its own fragility in rigorously providing empirical data in support of its claims (Saks, 1983). A central issue is that the theoretical arguments presented are all too frequently based on an abstracted view of the state as necessarily functioning in the long-term interests of the capitalist class. This means that the arguments by Marxist contributors about professional groups are often self-fulfilling – or at least not open to contradictory evidence (Saunders, 2007). Along with the political deconstruction of socialism in Eastern Europe in the 1980s and 1990s – and in particular that of the Soviet Union (Kenez, 2017) – Marxist theories of professions have perhaps understandably struggled to survive beyond the turn of the twenty-first century in the social sciences. What, though, of Foucauldianism, the next more critical theoretical perspective to be considered?

The Foucauldian approach

Michel Foucault was a prolific French philosopher whose work has been widely cited in the Anglo-American literature on the professions since the 1970s. His books based on the archaeology of knowledge span from intriguing historical studies of the rise of clinical medicine and psychiatry (Foucault, 1989; 1991) to a rather jaundiced commentary on the part played by the police and teachers in the apparatus of state control (Foucault, 2001). As such, Foucault provided a further critical platform for examining professional groups, in large part pivoted on applying the notion of governmentality to professions, which centred on their incorporation into state governance in the modern world. The process through which this was seen to occur was through the institutionalisation of expertise in normalising, legitimating and regulating activities – and thereby exposing apparently natural categories as social constructs (Jones and Porter, 1994). Johnson (1995) notes that Foucault conceptualised the main agency in this process, the state, as a cluster of institutions, procedures, analyses, calculations, reflections and tactics integral to governance in which professional expertise plays a key role. Accordingly, debates stemming from Foucault's work have arisen about the rationality of scientific progress relating to a range of professional groups working in such establishments as mental institutions, prisons and schools – where the policy direction taken has been challenged.

The popularity of this perspective is underscored by its application by proponents of Foucauldianism in a number of other settings such as social work (Donzelot, 1979), obstetrics (Arney, 1982), dentistry (Nettleton, 1992), general practice (Pickard, 2009) and geriatric care (Pickard, 2010). In each of these settings, the often-presumed benefits of the professional gaze have been questioned as the power and knowledge of professions have been seen to be employed to make populations governable. In spite of its skilfully crafted, counter-intuitive interpretations of the application of 'scientific' knowledge, though, the Foucauldian approach has been criticised for its high level of abstraction and for making unjustified generalisations in the face of more complex historical detail (Macdonald, 1995). This flaw can be exemplified by the universalisation by Foucault (1989) from the exceptional case of France in charting the moral origins of the 'science' of psychiatry in his book *Madness and Civilization*. In this book, Foucault makes reference to the stigmatising 'great confinement' of those unable to work at the beginning of the modern era. Yet, as Jones and Porter (1994:4) relate, while this may make sense of the French approach to handling those classified as insane in the seventeenth and eighteenth centuries, "it is not helpful for describing what was happening in other regions of Europe, including Britain, where state policy and interference in the affairs of the mad were less powerful and systematic."

Foucault's own work, therefore, has tended to be overly abstracted and, even on his own admission, he could rightly be accused of playing 'fast and loose' with the facts (Jones and Porter, 1994). Following in the footsteps of some equally illustrious proponents of the Marxist approach, he is also open to the associated charge of generating self-fulfilling statements that are not subject to appropriate empirical scrutiny. Methodologically, this is exacerbated by the conflation of professions with the state which makes it difficult, if not impossible, to separate out the distinctive role of professions and their interests in any inquiry into their actions (Saks, 2012). In addition, Foucault himself seemed reluctant to link his analysis of knowledge and power to inequalities based on features like class and gender (Jones and Porter, 1994). All of this has encouraged recent interest in the revival of elements of the symbolic interactionist strand in examining professions through the vehicle of discourse analysis (Gubrium and Holstein, 2003). Importantly, this approach shows more awareness of social divisions in society and, in contrast to interactionism, takes its analyses beyond simply the micro level – usefully extending into the meso and macro spheres.

Discourse analysis

In this regard, discourse analysis considers the way in which occupational groups like managers and supervisors use the concepts of 'professions' and 'professionalism' in their narratives in debates and discussion. Fournier (1999) provides a very helpful pioneering example of this approach; she adopts this perspective in studying fields not traditionally linked to professions such as advertising and recruitment. It is argued that appealing to the discursive resources of professionalism in newly emerging occupational areas like these can, amongst other things, act as a disciplinary mechanism for the personnel concerned in their work identities and conducts – even if it is not a perfect form of regulatory government of employees. Subsequently, discourse analysis has been applied in the literature to more established occupations operating in the private and public sectors which have been formally recognised as professions. These span from architects (Cohen et al, 2005) and auditors (Whittle, Mueller and Carter, 2016) to the client-facing caring professions in the human and social services like coaching and psychotherapy (Graf, Sator and Spranz-Fogasy, 2014).

As such, the main advantage of discourse analysis has been to enhance our understanding of professional cultures and workplace dynamics in specific settings. It has also helpfully expanded the range of occupations amenable to scrutiny as professions beyond that normally considered – widening the field of vision to include occupations which have not yet been able to formally erect restrictive legal boundaries around their work (Evetts, 2003). This potential applicability to a broader span of professional and professionalising groups than those centrally considered by the mainstream macro structural theories analysed above is certainly an advantage. However, discourse analysis has similar disadvantages to symbolic interactionism. This is because of its frequently restricted micro and meso focus on the workplace and its treatment of professionalism simply as a negotiated label (Saks, 2016b). Like interactionism, therefore, discourse analysis does not necessarily address the wider history and structure surrounding professions and professionalisation. It can, though, usefully help to analyse ideologies supporting professional claims. This is illustrated by Taylor (1995) who argues that archaeologists retrospectively invented a progressive heritage from amateurism to legitimate their own position as a profession.

Having said this, the examination of discourse can have greater analytical leverage when it is allied to broader theoretical perspectives on professions. For instance, Saks (1995) has shown that it can make an important contribution in his neo-Weberian examination of the ideologies of the medical profession in shaping state policy in response to medical innovation. Indeed, Fournier (2000) strongly allies herself with the macro structural neo-Weberian concept of exclusionary social closure in her more recent analysis of the making and unmaking of boundaries between professions and other occupational groups. This, she notes, "involves not only an occupational group appropriating a field as its exclusive area of jurisdiction and expertise, but also the making of this field into a legitimate area of knowledge" (Fournier, 2000:69). Such an association leads neatly into a further mainstream theoretical perspective that will now be outlined – that of neo-Weberianism, which is held to have many benefits in the Anglo-American context and beyond, compared to the theories of professions already considered in this chapter from the taxonomic approach onwards.

The neo-Weberian theory of professions

As indicated above, the neo-Weberian approach to professions in Britain and the United States is based on the concept of social closure and in its purest form involves the establishment of state-sanctioned monopolies in the marketplace through the process of interest-group politics. The abstract concept of social closure originated in the late nineteenth and early twentieth-century work of the German sociologist Max Weber (1968). This was in spite of the fact that Weber himself perversely never actually wrote about professions themselves because an understanding of the separate existence of these occupational groups was not embedded in his native language at the time he was writing (Swedberg and Agevall, 2016). Since the writings of Weber so centrally underpin the theoretical perspective adopted in this volume, a brief pen picture is now included as Box 3.1 to provide some background to his life, work and the key concept of social closure.

Box 3.1 Max Weber: His life, work and the concept of social closure

Max Weber lived from 1864 to 1920. He was born in Erfurt, Prussia, as part of a wealthy and well-connected family. He studied at the University of Heidelberg and the University of Berlin, where he also taught before taking up Chairs at the University of Freiberg, the University of Heidelberg and, finally, the University of Vienna and the University of Munich.

During his lifetime, he was an eminent social scientist and wrote several scholarly books, treatises and essays spanning the disciplines of sociology, history, economics, law, philosophy and political science. These covered subjects ranging from methodology, theory and religion to politics and science as a vocation.

The most substantial of his books is *Economy and Society*, where he discussed the central notion of social closure that underpins neo-Weberian literature on the professions. In his scholarship, this concept played an important part in the analysis of social stratification more generally, although it was not employed directly by him in association with the professions.

Source: Swedberg, R. and Agevall, O. (2016) *The Max Weber Dictionary: Key Words and Central Concepts*, 2nd edition, Stanford, CA: Stanford University Press.

The neo-Weberian style of theoretical approach, either explicitly or implicitly, developed from initial beginnings in the early 1970s to the present day through sociologists like Freidson (1970) and Johnson (2016), to arguably become the most prominent theoretical perspective in the Anglo-American social scientific study of professions. This was in no small part due to its advantages over rival theories. These benefits compared to other approaches relate to the way in which neo-Weberianism addresses the four main weaknesses of alternative perspectives in analysing professional groups. They can be itemised as follows:

- The neo-Weberian approach enables professions to be examined in a more open manner than the reflexively deferential taxonomic approach.
- It transcends the largely small to mid-range focus of symbolic interactionism and discourse analysis by dealing with the wider structural and historical aspects of professionalism.
- Neo-Weberianism is not limited by the self-fulfilling and rigid notions of the capitalist state frequently contained in Marxist approaches.
- Such an approach in principle enables the systematic empirical examination of professional groups without being as blinkered to evidence as some Marxists and Foucauldians.

This is not to question the value of other theoretical approaches, the employment of which hinges on the research questions being asked (Saks and Allsop, 2019). At the very least in this context they can stimulate different modes of thinking about professions. Nor is it to suggest – as will be elaborated shortly – that neo-Weberianism itself is without its own limitations.

Nonetheless, the great strengths of the approach in analysing professions at the meso and macro level should not be understated. Neo-Weberianism, though, can take different forms which are, to varying degrees, complementary to the variety of theoretical perspectives already considered. Indeed, there are clear links between Weber's original work and the other approaches we have examined. This is very apparent, for instance, in the influence of Weber's social action theory on the development of symbolic interactionism and the conception by Parsons of the social system in his structural functional analysis (Ritzer and Jeffrey, 2018). As regards the study of the professions itself, the field-breaking neo-Weberian account by Magali Larson (1977) of the rise of professionalisation in Britain and the United States draws heavily on Marxist theory in charting the historical background to this professional project. Conversely, she integrates a more Foucauldian style of approach into her later work on professions in the Anglo-American context. Here she balances her neo-Weberian focus on the market with the need to understand both the discourses employed and the relationship between the knowledge and power of professional experts (Larson, 1990).

Freidson (1970) too draws to some degree on symbolic interactionism in his early neo-Weberian study of the American profession of medicine – further highlighting the complementarity of the perspectives involved. Nonetheless, he does stress the benefits of defining a profession structurally as it liberates us from "the confusion and special pleading which permeates most discussions of professions" (Freidson, 1970:187). At another remove, Evetts (2013) has employed concepts other than social closure from the rich Weberian treasure chest in examining professions. This is illustrated by her application of Weber's notion of legal-rational authority in her model of 'organisational professionalism', in opposition to the idea of 'occupational professionalism'. In the former case, emphasis is placed on bureaucratisation, rationalisation and centralised control of professions rather than viewing such occupational bodies as being more independently constituted. As will be discussed later in the book, Evetts arguably believes there is a move towards organisational professionalism in modern societies, which textbooks on work and organisation have sometimes reiterated (see, for instance, Thompson and McHugh, 2009; Volti, 2008). However, the most common element in the neo-Weberian approach to professions drawn from Weber's original work remains that of social closure (Saks, 2016b) – most clearly exemplified in the outcomes achieved by medicine and law in the professionalisation process in the Anglo-American context, as set out in Chapter 2 of this volume.

The neo-Weberian approach centred on social closure is primarily based on seeing professions theoretically in terms of their exclusionary legal boundaries. For neo-Weberians, these boundaries derive from the relations of the market as opposed to the relations of production as in the Marxist perspective (Saks, 2010). More specifically, neo-Weberian work is centred on the process through which some occupations are able to regulate market conditions in their favour, in the face of competition. In this respect, professions are seen as limiting access to opportunities to a restricted group of eligibles – which in turn creates a group of disenfranchised outsiders. As such, professionalisation is conceptualised as a credentialised strategy to control the number and type of entrants to an occupation to underwrite or improve its market value (Parkin, 1979). There are various neo-Weberian definitions of professions in these terms. Typically, professionalisation is portrayed as involving direct market control of services through self-governing associations of formally equal colleagues (Parry and Parry, 2019). Other kinds of professional market control are more derivative. This includes that conceived by Freidson (1970) where professions are based on legitimate, organised autonomy in making technical judgements and organising work. The definition of Johnson (2016) also fits into this mould – where the producer is seen as defining the needs of the consumer and how these are to be satisfied.

Crucial to most neo-Weberian analyses is state underwriting of the legally defined territory of professions, which typically enhances the income, status and power of such groups relative to most other occupations in the marketplace. Here more fully fledged professions are based upon statutory registers of qualified practitioners in Britain and the United States (Parkin, 1979). Thus, as we have seen, the British medical profession was centred on a national system of legally credentialed registration through the General Medical Council from the mid-nineteenth century, while the American medical profession was pivoted on state boards licensing physicians from the early years of the twentieth century. As such, these arrangements enabled parallel, if different, forms of exclusionary social closure (Saks, 2015e). In Britain, these monopolies supplanted the earlier controls of local guilds of physicians, surgeons and apothecaries (Krause, 1996). As we also saw, a similar pattern occurred in law in this country with the development of the Law Society to regulate solicitors and the Bar Council to oversee barristers. This was paralleled by the creation of state bar associations providing professional market control of attorneys in the United States (Burrage, 2006). Such cases highlight the benefits of a more robust and legally formalised definition of a profession compared to the more fluid negotiated order approach of symbolic interactionists and some advocates of discourse analysis – not least because of debates over state policy underwriting professional privileges.

The advantages of the neo-Weberian approach are underlined by the greater understanding it provides of the hierarchical relationships of power and dominance between leading professions and other professional groups in the Anglo-American context, based on differential state legitimation. This is exemplified by more subordinated professional groups like nurses and teachers who are defined by Parkin (1979) as characterised in neo-Weberian terms by the notion of 'dual closure'. This means that while they possess a form of professional exclusionary closure, they are also characterised by elements of usurpationary closure. The latter is based on defensive and sometimes illegitimate unionised activities more typical of the working class. This politicised version of the factors involved in their positioning applies to a number of professional groups strategically defending their boundaries against occupations both above and below – as has also been documented by Nancarrow and Borthwick (2021) in relation to the allied health professions in Britain and Australia. This and other kindred analyses depart from functionalist conceptualisations of such interstitial groups as 'semi-professions', in which occupational station is seen as largely pre-ordained by relatively restricted skills and qualifications, in terms of meeting the needs of the social system (Etzioni, 1969).

Aside from the occupational dynamics linked to the politics of work that the neo-Weberian perspective importantly covers, its proponents have also increasingly acknowledged the rising influences on professions that go beyond the nation state (as illustrated by Olgiati, 2003). In recent decades, this has included the influence of the European Union on the mutual recognition of qualifications and transnational migration that heavily impacted on exclusionary closure in pre-Brexit Britain (Evetts, 1998). As will be seen further down track in this book, such influence has been ever more apparent in Britain, the United States and other modern societies given the expanding global scale of professional service firms (Flood, 2018) and the increasing number of transnational projects involving professions (Hasselbalch and Seabrooke, 2018). We shall now turn to set out selected examples of studies that have been conducted from a neo-Weberian perspective to give a stronger flavour of this theoretical approach. These lead us into a world characterised by politics, professional power and group interests (Saks, 1987) – not least in the illustrative case of medicine.

The distinctive profile of neo-Weberian studies: A medical illustration

This choice of illustration is based on the notion that the best way of exemplifying the neo-Weberian approach to professions in action is to take a familiar, but coherent, case study to illustrate the difference between this approach and other macro-structural perspectives considered. In Chapter 2 it will be recalled that we descriptively charted in the Anglo-American context the professionalisation of medicine, alongside law, from the early days of industrialisation up to its halcyon period in the 1960s and 1970s – when it attained unprecedented power and autonomy. In light of the macro theories outlined in this chapter, we can now ask how explanatory interpretations of this process differ and assess the relative strength of the distinctive concepts that neo-Weberians have applied in facilitating our understanding of it. We shall begin by looking at the case of medical professionalisation in Britain before moving on to consider the parallel position in the United States. In this respect, both of these cases have been comparatively analysed in depth at the macro level by Saks (2015e) – on whose neo-Weberian contribution we shall now draw.

Medical professionalisation in Britain

In the case of Britain, taxonomic writers see the professionalisation of doctors as arising from the positive intrinsic features of medicine itself, as indeed did Wilensky (1964) in his 'natural history of professionalisation' that we have already covered. Within the taxonomic approach, functionalist theory goes the furthest at an explanatory level. In this vein, Goode (1960) saw medical professionalisation as being driven by highly valued expertise, which physicians regulate in the common good in return for state-underwritten independence to meet the needs of industrial societies. In Britain specifically, Wallis and Morley (1976:11) hold that medical pluralism was overtaken by the occupational monopoly established by the 1858 Medical Act because of the impact of the Industrial Revolution on "the demand for effective medical treatment and the ability of the profession to provide it". This was seen as being functionally precipitated by the break-up of communities with growing social and geographical mobility – alongside the development of science and technology with the bacteriological revolution and the discovery of the germ theory of disease, which made medicine more effective.

Such a functionalist approach, however, empirically overstates the extent of social fragmentation linked to the Industrial Revolution (Saunders, 1986). Moreover, as was seen in Chapter 2, it greatly exaggerates the effectiveness of scientific medicine in the nineteenth century as the key pharmacological and other advances in diagnosis and treatment in medicine took place later in the next century (Cook, 2013). In addition, it underplays the serious hazards to health posed by heroic therapies such as bleeding and purging widely employed by doctors, as compared to the safer homeopathic and hydropathic treatment frequently used by their more marginalised rivals (Porter, 2002). In this light, it is hardly surprising that Marxists have taken a more politicised view of the 1858 Medical Act and its aftermath. Thus, Navarro (1978) saw the emergence of the British medical profession as driven by its contribution to capital accumulation in addressing the disease and diswelfare of a class-divided capitalist society, rather than meeting generic societal needs in the bland industrialised world conceived by the functionalists.

However, while Navarro (1976) was clearly more aware than Wallis and Morley (1976) of the counterproductive effects of modern biomedicine, he in turn oversimplifies the relationship between the medical profession and capitalism. In so doing, as noted earlier, he commits the fundamental Marxist heresy of seeing the profession as part of the ruling class, without having ownership of the means of production. Johnson (1977), though, in his Marxist phase, took a more orthodox view in seeing the medical profession in Britain as an agent of capital in the labour process – in which it fulfils the functions of capital, in contrast to those of the collective labourer. He argues that only occupations fulfilling the former role, involving control and surveillance activities in the interests of the capitalist class, can successfully engage in professionalisation under capitalism. Medicine is seen to fit into this theoretical framework by monopolising official definitions of health and legitimising the withdrawal of labour on behalf of the dominant class, which in turn is held to explain its privileges under capitalism.

Nonetheless, the interpretation by Johnson (1977) also falls foul of a number of common weaknesses in Marxist accounts. Not only does it lack detail, but it is not wholly sustained by evidence in the process of critically exploring available data. For example, by linking the professionalisation of medicine solely to its role in the class structure, he does not fully explain the continuing existence of professions like the clergy, whose standing is based on a legacy from the pre-capitalist era (Portwood and Fielding, 1981). Similar criticisms can be made of Johnson (1995) in his later Foucauldian mode, where he sweepingly sees the medical profession in modern Britain in terms of governmentality, where medicine is an institutionalised form of expertise in state formation. Both these interpretations can be seen as tautologous in Marxist and Foucauldian accounts since the profession is viewed as inevitably following structural imperatives for the state – without any apparent need for supporting or contradictory evidence. What, then, of the distinctive neo-Weberian approach to conceptualising and explaining medical professionalisation in Britain?

The starting point for neo-Weberians here is that medicine in Britain is based on a national system of exclusionary social closure in the market, beginning with the 1858 Medical Act. In this vein, Parry and Parry (2019) view the coming together of physicians, surgeons and apothecaries to obtain legally sanctioned registration arrangements as an act of 'collective social mobility'. In his neo-Weberian phase, Johnson (2016) endeavours to account for such medical professionalisation as a form of institutional control won through interest-group politics. He argues that this goal is most likely to be achieved when consumers form a heterogenous group, which enables producers to assume greater power over them. He observes that this condition was present by the mid-nineteenth century in Britain with the emergence of an urban middle-class market for medical services with industrialisation. This broke the hold of upper-class patronage that had characterised medicine in pre-industrial Britain (Saks, 2002a). The growing homogeneity of the medical profession itself also added to its bargaining power, along with the increasing high-class recruitment to medicine and its network of aristocratic and other elites. Although more evidence needs to be explicitly adduced for such claims in Johnson's neo-Weberian analysis, other contributors have provided this (see, for instance, Waddington, 1984). Johnson's analysis therefore clearly provides insight into the main contours of the neo-Weberian approach in practice.

Importantly, Berlant (1975) further exemplifies the distinctive nature of neo-Weberianism. He contended that the furthering of medical interests through professionalisation in the Anglo-American context stemmed from both its tactics of competition and the prevailing socio-economic conditions in the market. Organised medicine in Britain was thus able to progress its position by shifting its ideology to ride liberal attacks on corporate monopolies in the nineteenth century. This step, which resonates with discourse analysis, is accentuated by its ideological emphasis on the General Medical Council controlling the performance of doctors and protecting its medical title in a *de facto* monopoly. This emphasis recognised that excluding unregistered practitioners, whose practice was underwritten by the Common Law, was strategically best avoided. However, in examining medical professionalisation on both sides of the Atlantic, Berlant is open to the accusation of being gender blind, although this has subsequently been addressed from a neo-Weberian perspective by the work of contributors like Witz (1992) – who highlighted the influence of patriarchy on the development of the largely male medical profession in Britain. But if Berlant needed to give more attention to this aspect of the British socio-political context, Saks and Adams (2019) underline this by calling for greater use to be made of Weber's original concepts to enable us to examine the much-neglected 'black box' of the internal workings of the state in understanding the dynamics of medical professionalisation in Britain.

The discussion to date – while critical – helps further to highlight the distinctive texture of neo-Weberianism. This includes its analysis of the competition between the medical profession and outsiders, which plays a key part in explaining how the medical profession managed to gain, maintain and extend its position of exclusionary social closure in the period up to the 1960s and 1970s. Within a neo-Weberian perspective this has tended to be seen as based primarily on the pursuit of professional group interests, although there are sometimes tensions with the common good. Given the need for more empirical evidence on these potential tensions in some neo-Weberian accounts, Saks (1995) has developed a methodology for examining the extent to which professional groups subordinate their self-interests in enhancing their own income, status and power to the public interest. In operationalising the theoretical concepts involved, he was able to demonstrate that, in the response of the British medical profession to acupuncture in the nineteenth and twentieth centuries, the public interest had been compromised by professional self-interests in a predominant climate of rejection. Much neo-Weberian work has since been conducted on the more general historical interplay of medical interests, professionalisation and different forms of complementary and alternative medicine in Britain (see, for instance, Saks 1996; 2003a; 2008). We shall now exemplify how neo-Weberians have deployed their approach to explain the rather different route to medical professionalisation in the United States, as against other macro interpretations.

Medical professionalisation in the United States

In exploring the drivers of medical professionalisation in the United States, the functionalist variant of the taxonomic approach has run into similar difficulties to those in Britain. Notwithstanding the comments already made about Wallis and Morley (1976), their functionalist perspective seems to stand up better in the United States than in Britain in relation to the scientific drivers for professionalisation in meeting system needs. This is because professionalisation based on state-by-state licensing took place half a century later, at a time when there was less medical deployment of heroic medicine, aseptic techniques and anaesthesia were more widely applied, and there had been greater technological advance (Ramsden, 2013). While Stevens (1998) supports this view about medical professionalisation meeting the public interest at this stage, it is important to exercise caution as the application of the scientific method was still at an early stage in the early twentieth century and most significant developments in surgery and other medical fields came several decades later (Le Fanu, 2011). In explaining the professionalisation of medicine in the United States, therefore, it is understandable – just as in Britain – that more overtly politicised accounts have come to the fore.

Here the Marxist account of Navarro (1976) again overstates the historical contribution of medicine to capital accumulation. Aside from not sufficiently problematising the role of medicine in the class divide between capital and labour, Starr (1982) notes that Navarro more generally overrides the complexity of the relationship between medicine and capitalism in the United States. However, some Marxist theorists have a more subtle interpretation. Thus, McKinlay (1977), for example, recognised that American physicians had some autonomous control over their domain, although it was restricted by the interests of industrial and financial capital. Nonetheless, even his account does not give enough credence to the more open political structure of Anglo-American liberal democracies. This is also true of the Foucauldian analysis of Johnson (1995), who precludes the connection between the state and the medical profession from being operationally examined because of their inextricable entanglement in the institutionalisation of expertise (Saks, 2003b). What, then, of neo-Weberian explanations of medical professionalisation in the United States? What shape do they take and are they more persuasive?

The neo-Weberian analysis of Johnson (2016) seems as good a fit in the United States as it is in Britain. His conception of medical professionalisation as a type of institutional control in a pluralistic social order is endorsed by Starr (1982). Notwithstanding the greater degree of specialisation of American physicians compared to British doctors under the biomedical umbrella, Starr noted the increase in both the fragmentation of medical clientele and upper-class medical recruitment in the United States. His neo-Weberian analysis can in fact be aligned with the seminal account by Freidson (1970), who claimed that medical professionalisation occurred in the United States as a result of broad public support in the market – as well as sponsorship by strategic elites which led to growing state sanction. The work of Berlant (1975) again well illustrates the neo-Weberian approach. He stressed the *de jure* nature of the exclusionary closure surrounding medicine in the United States based on the legal control of practice, as opposed to the *de facto* monopoly in Britain. From his comparative examination of these two societies, he also argued in classic neo-Weberian style that in the more devolved American system, the medical profession won and extended its monopolistic standing by using the political rift between national and local economic interests to its benefit. In a strong antitrust climate, state medical licensure therefore was a measure to protect local economic interests against large-scale corporations.

As in Britain, there is also a lively neo-Weberian literature on the pursuit of professional self-interests by American physicians in attacking unlicensed practitioners of alternative therapies through bodies such as the American Medical Association and the Food and Drug Administration (see, for instance, Boyle, 2013; Kelner et al, 2003). In the course of these neo-Weberian analyses, as we shall see on both sides of the Atlantic, not all the battles to exclude rivals were successful – such as in relation to osteopaths and chiropractors (Saks, 2006). However, there are some difficulties surrounding such neo-Weberian explanations of American medical professionalisation. Freidson (1970), for instance, errs in not explicitly identifying the strategic elites to which he refers in promoting the autonomous professional control of medicine (McKinlay, 1977). Proponents of neo-Weberianism in the United States, like those in Britain, may need also to give greater attention to gender and other aspects of social closure related to inequalities in explaining the form of professionalisation (Tang and Smith, 1996). This leads on to further brief consideration of neo-Weberian work outside of the medical arena to illustrate its broader application.

A wider range of illustrative neo-Weberian work

The detail provided in the Anglo-American medical case study above has hopefully been instructive in highlighting the distinctive features of neo-Weberianism in operation. This will now be followed by further examples of its application, without contrasting it so systematically with other macro structural perspectives, in the two societies concerned to a range of other professions. In the broader health field, for example, a neo-Weberian approach is again well represented by Freidson (1970), who explored how officially underwritten professional standing was obtained by comparing optometry and pharmacy in the United States. He found that they both had the same minimum period of training and similar degrees of specialisation and abstract knowledge. Yet, while in most American states the trained optometrist could legally diagnose and prescribe, the trained pharmacist could not. This comparison serves as a further riposte to the unilinear interpretation of professionalisation set out in the taxonomic work of Wilensky (1964) considered in the last chapter. It also reinforces the distinctive neo-Weberian fascination with the socio-political aspects of professionalism, In this case, it may be concluded that power and rhetoric is of greater significance than knowledge and training because the subordinated profession of pharmacy has historically been more strongly subject to medical dominance than the limited profession of optometry.

Moving on to the treatment of non-human animals, neo-Weberians have also recently explored the creative interplay between professional self-interests and the public interest in explaining patterns of professionalisation – as illustrated by the case of veterinary medicine in Britain (Whiting, May and Saks, 2020). Importantly, as Saks (1995) has argued, professional self-interests and the public interest are not necessarily polarised concepts, but can coalesce as well as work against each other in securing exclusionary social closure. For neo-Weberians who steer a closer path to that taken by Weber (2011) himself, their interaction needs to be resolved through careful empirical inquiry and not simply read off or dogmatically imposed upon particular situations – as often happens with other approaches. The example of the professional altruism debate in law is instructive in showing how neo-Weberians provide such an evidential base. Here Halliday (1987) in exemplary fashion examined the archives of the Chicago Bar Association and a national survey of bar legislative and judicial actions in the United States. On the basis of this research, he concluded that the quest for monopoly was more public spirited than self-interested as it was oriented towards the improvement of law and the legal system. Despite the 'civic professionalism' of American lawyers, though, the Bar Association was found to have at times acted vigorously in its own interests, but its overall operation served the common good.

Occupational success in a competitive marketplace for neo-Weberians, however, ultimately hinges on the state being persuaded that professionalisation is a desirable outcome. From a neo-Weberian platform, Macdonald (1995) has shown that it was crucial for accountants and architects to put forward acceptable political objectives for state officials for them to professionalise in Britain. In this process, modern states and societies have usually been more receptive to the case of minority groups in relation to professions, notwithstanding strong resistance to their claims in earlier periods (Hearne, Metcalfe and Piekkari, 2012). Nonetheless, minorities have not always achieved the positive outcomes that might otherwise be anticipated; Bolton and Muzio (2008) found from their neo-Weberian analysis of professional projects in law, management and teaching in Britain, for instance, that – while these produced greater opportunities for women – gendered patterns of exclusion, segmentation and stratification persisted. Parallel gender restrictions were discovered by Kuhlmann and Annandale (2012) in a variety of contemporary health professional fields. And, as Saks (2015b) has noted, in both Britain and the United States, inequalities within and between professions can invidiously impact on inequalities without – leading to further forms of social exclusion amongst their clientele based on gender, as well as class and ethnicity.

Other neo-Weberian contributors have written extensively not just about development in single, silo-based professions as set out above, but also interprofessional working across occupational groups in a variety of fields including education, housing, nursing, the police, social work, and youth and community work (Barrett, Sellman and Thomas, 2005). This highlights that there is more to the analysis of professional groups for neo-Weberians than simply instrumental turf wars between professions and other occupational groups over jurisdictions (Abbott, 1988). Some neo-Weberian theorists of professions recognise that collaborative ways of working can be more helpful than not for the wider society (Leathard, 2003). Such contributions, of course, have also had their critics, including those drawn from the counterposed perspectives outlined above. As more general criticisms of the neo-Weberian approach to professions have not yet been considered, this chapter now turns to consider the critiques to which existing neo-Weberian analyses can be subjected within this perspective. This picks up on some of the weaknesses we have already touched upon in the examination of medical professionalisation from a neo-Weberian perspective on both sides of the Atlantic. The response to such critiques is also presented in defence of this approach. It is vital that we understand this retort because – as the favoured theoretical framework employed by the author – it is used extensively to consider the issues examined in the remaining chapters of this book.

Criticisms of the neo-Weberian approach

Despite the undoubted value of studies conducted from within the neo-Weberian perspective on professions in comparison with other theoretical approaches, it can be criticised on a number of counts. Although he is a major proponent of neo-Weberianism, Saks (2010) has outlined three areas of criticism of the application of neo-Weberianism to the study of the professions in the Anglo-American context at different stages of his academic career. These are as follows:

- The approach has often been implemented without due empirical rigour.
- Many of the claims of its advocates have frequently been unjustifiably negative.
- Its proponents do not sufficiently link their work to the broader division of labour.

We shall now examine each of these specific areas of criticism in turn, with reference to further publications by neo-Weberian writers on professional groups, before going on to highlight why these do not constitute fatal flaws in its implementation.

The first criticism is that the neo-Weberian theoretical framework has too often been operationalised without adequate empirical scrutiny (Saks, 1983). Johnson (2016) illustrates this well by giving no evidence for his claim that the emergence of the professions auxiliary to medicine in Britain was based on the way in which doctors defined their own roles and consequently resulted in an 'irrational' utilisation of resources. Similarly, Perrucci (1973) does not provide any justification for stating that in the United States the public interest is always subordinated to professional self-interests, when the two conflict. Such neo-Weberian contributors instead seem to have been swept along by the more radical climate of opinion about professions that followed in the wake of the 1960s and 1970s counter culture – which we shall consider in more detail in the next chapter. As a result of their unguarded comments on the nature and role of professions based on the exercise of power, interests and exclusionary social closure in the marketplace, such neo-Weberian accounts go little beyond the now much-challenged assumptions of taxonomic writers – instead substituting reflexive negativity for knee-jerk positivity.

This leads on to a second related criticism of the neo-Weberian approach. This is that the claims of its proponents about professions have been prone to be rather too adversarial (Saks, 1998). The neo-Weberian work of Johnson (2016) can again be taken as a key example in so far as he simply asserts that lawyers and other professionals do not act in the public interest because of the lack of relevance of their services to black and feminist groups. Beattie (1995) makes similarly critical claims about the negative consequences of professional tribalism in British health care. This unsubstantiated view of professions flies in the face of the need to reconstruct, rather than simply to deconstruct, the operation of such groups (Saks, 1998). We must of course avoid unthinkingly viewing professions as a virtuous occupational group like many trait and functionalist writers. Nonetheless, we should also recognise that they can be humanising, as illustrated by contemporary analyses of nursing and midwifery (Borsay and Hunter, 2012; Bourgeault, Benoit and Davis-Floyd, 2004). And although lawyers have sometimes been lampooned by neo-Weberians – not least by using the metaphor of 'vampires' to highlight their pursuit of financial self-interest (McGillivray, 2004) – this should be tempered by acknowledgement of the *pro bono* work undertaken on behalf of the disadvantaged by legal and other professionals (Granfield and Mather, 2009).

The third criticism of the application of neo-Weberianism to professions in the Anglo-American context is that its advocates do not sufficiently connect their work on professions to the wider occupational division of labour (Saks, 2003b). To be sure, a broad span of professional groups has been examined by neo-Weberians – from social workers (Lymbery, 2000) to actuaries (Collins, Dewing and Russell, 2009). However, the work of neo-Weberian writers has been rather too focused on a small band of occupations like medicine and law that have achieved full exclusionary social closure. As a result, the relative position of newly professionalising groups like complementary and alternative practitioners to doctors has frequently been given far less attention than due in Britain and the United States (Saks, 2015a). This is even more pronounced in the study of the relationship between health professions in general and the broader constituency of support workers – where, despite forming the majority of the health workforce, the latter have become the invisible providers of health care (Saks, 2020c). Accordingly, explanations of the relative success and failure of professional projects and depictions of the comparative ascendance that professional groups have obtained in the division of labour have been incomplete.

Moreover, in examining the processes involved in professionalisation in the division of labour, neo-Weberians have all too often overlooked the fact that marginalised groups themselves have interests and power (Cant and Sharma, 1996). Analysing these aspects of the interaction between such groups and more dominant professions, though, can be fundamental in understanding outcomes. This is best exemplified by the way in which American physicians allied with the homeopaths in the late nineteenth century to overcome the antitrust resistance to professionalisation (Saks, 2015e). It may have only been through this mechanism that the medical profession was able to gain state licensure across the United States – following which the homoeopathic training schools were completely decimated in the critical medical reviews in the aftermath of the 1910 Flexner Report (Haller, 2009). In terms of the wider occupational division of labour, neo-Weberian contributors have also commonly been guilty of considering the features of top professions without examining how distinct they are compared to groups that have not professionalised. This is illustrated by Svennson (1999) who examined public trust in a number of professions from economists to veterinarians, without external occupational comparators. How do we know that these groups are held in higher regard than non-professionalised, skilled occupations like car mechanics and carpenters? This is a significant question for state policy in the vindication, or otherwise, of particular patterns of professional closure.

In defence of neo-Weberianism, though, these three broad areas of criticism relate more to the operationalisation of this theoretical approach than a fundamental flaw. Many of the issues can be addressed by simply developing more balanced and thoroughgoing evidence-based understanding of professions within this perspective. In addition, more extended holistic research engagement in the division of labour would effectively counter arguments that neo-Weberian studies to date have been rather too myopic – as well as opening up new occupational vistas for its proponents. This undermines the argument by Evetts (1998) that the approach has limited relevance because its focus on exclusionary social closure excludes the analysis of engineering and other knowledge-based occupations in Britain. In fact, it does not matter that certain occupations currently lack full exclusionary closure in the Anglo-American context as they can still usefully be examined both singly and comparatively by neo-Weberians. As Evetts describes, engineers are normally employed in technical work with a degree in science, mathematics or engineering itself and may or may not have chartered status with protection of title in a highly diverse and specialised field. Nonetheless, it remains an interesting question for neo-Weberians as to why engineering has not fully professionalised in Britain as in a number of other professions and modern societies, and what its prospects are in so doing in the future.

Following on from the discussion about the alleged limitations of neo-Weberianism in Britain by Evetts, the claim by Sciulli (2005) that the neo-Weberian approach to professions is restricted because social closure is largely confined to the Anglo-American context is also flawed. Of course, as seen in the previous chapter, there are fewer classic professions in neo-Weberian terms in continental Europe (Collins, 1990), where Evetts (2000) notes that parallel occupations are often embedded in government bureaucracies and other public sector bodies. Against this, though, many professional bodies are based on exclusionary social closure in countries from Australia and New Zealand to Canada (Allsop and Jones, 2008). In European societies too, neo-Weberian scholars can gain important insights by analysing occupations across the regulatory spectrum – from independent lawyers in Germany with full social closure (Rogowski, 1995) to doctors in contemporary Russia still striving to gain autonomous profession standing following state-induced deprofessionalisation in Soviet times (Saks, 2018a). Having said this, it should be underlined that in this chapter we have focused on considering mainstream theories of professions – culminating in the more detailed examination of the preferred neo-Weberian approach. We shall now examine two less prominent theories of professions which have the potential to complement the neo-Weberian focus in this book.

Other complementary theories to neo-Weberianism

The first of these perspectives is based on the work of the French social theorist Pierre Bourdieu, which has begun to be cited increasingly in the Anglo-American literature on professions. His profile in this area is set out in Box 3.2. Perversely, Bourdieu himself questions the utility of employing the concept of a 'profession' and even discredits it (Bourdieu and Wacquant, 1999). Nonetheless, some neo-Weberian contributors like Noordegraaf and Schinkel (2011) believe that Bourdieu's theoretical concepts may illuminate the evolution and practices of professional groups. In this respect, they argue that his work – which has also been associated with Marxist theory – may be especially useful in synergy with neo-Weberianism in analysing professionalism as a kind of 'symbolic capital', linked to prestige, reputation and renown, which is challenged and subject to ongoing struggle and negotiation in power-driven contexts. In their eyes, this makes it particularly suited to interpreting the development of new professional fields and conflicts within and between professions. Here professional groups may be seen as engaged in what Bourdieu views as a general 'field of power'. Spence, Voulgaris and Maclean (2017) view such an approach as the key to understanding class cultural cleavages in professional groups, while Suddaby, Cooper and Greenwood (2007) have seen professionalism in this framework as a legitimated way of acting. This can be linked to notions employed by Bourdieu like the 'habitus', which expresses the manner in which individuals develop attitudes and dispositions in engaging in specific political practices (Medvetz and Sallaz, 2018).

Box 3.2 Pierre Bourdieu, Weber and the professions

Pierre Bourdieu, a highly influential French social scientist, was born in 1930 and died in 2002. He taught and held Chairs at the Universities of Paris and Lille, as well as a number of other prestigious Parisian research centres. He contributed to an extremely broad range of areas in an interdisciplinary manner – from cultural and gender studies to anthropology, philosophy and sociology.

Interestingly, throughout this time, Bourdieu did not believe it was important to affiliate his work with particular schools of thought, but he nonetheless acknowledged the writings of Max Weber, along with contributors like Karl Marx and Emile Durkheim, as landmarks that structured theoretical space and perceptions of this space.

This was not the only link to Weber. As has been seen, Weber never wrote directly about the professions, but contributed an important theoretical legacy to the neo-Weberian analysis of this group. Similarly, Bourdieu – while dismissive of the concept of professions – assembled a body of work that, in conjunction with neo-Weberianism, has greatly assisted our understanding of such occupations.

Source: Webb, J., Schirato, T. and Danaher, G.
(2002) *Understanding Bourdieu*, London: Sage.

The Bourdieusian view of the professions highlights the constantly evolving theories about them, as well as providing a potentially synergistic perspective on professions to neo-Weberianism. In this sense, Bourdieu has applied his theory to fields such as the arts, education and journalism and takes seriously the ideas of neo-Weberian contributors such as Larson (1977) and Freidson (1970) in understanding how professions emerged (Bourdieu and Wacquant, 1992). He sees the resources in the struggle to secure power as forms of capital. In education, for instance, he refers to the 'scholastic mode of reproduction' in which children from the upper class are systematically advantaged in attaining societal rewards because of inherited cultural capital (Weininger and Lareau, 2018). These forms of capital underpinning professional and other forms of group dominance include economic and social capital centred on social networks and relationships (Bourdieu, 1985). However, as Webb, Schirato and Danaher (2002:1–2) note, in terms of the French analysis of the professions, "Bourdieu's status is far more peripheral than that of Foucault, with whom he shares so many theoretical interests and inclinations". This is changing, but it is disconcerting in a neo-Weberian context that he should connect the word 'profession' primarily with its normative origins in the work of Durkheim and the functionalists as a social category positively maintaining society. This leads him to see the concept of a profession methodologically as a pre-constructed category based on stereotypes that excludes as much as it includes as an analytical tool (Olgiati, 2010). In this light, we need to be careful about seeing the ideas of Bourdieu even now as a mainstream complement to neo-Weberianism.

While the work of Bourdieu and his associates will occasionally be introduced in the remaining chapters of this book, more important as a complement to neo-Weberianism in the theoretical and empirical analysis of professions is neo-institutionalism. The recent development of the neo-institutionalist approach is linked to the growth of interest in professions in business schools alongside the social sciences. As such, it has focused most recently on locating professions theoretically in commercial and public sector settings, not least in the context of institutional logics in organisations and of multinational professional service firms. Here Suddaby and Muzio (2015) view the neo-institutional perspective on professions as seeing them as one institution struggling with others for survival in an ecology of institutional forms. This drives the study of professions further towards the analysis of wider structures in exploring their role in building economic, political and social institutions. In these terms, professionalism is seen as playing an important part in the broader process of institutionalisation, including in understanding the influence of professional groups. In the neo-institutional approach, the significance of institutionalisation for professions has been considered both generally (Scott, 2008) and in relation to specific groups (Goodrick and Reay, 2011). Although there can be tensions between neo-institutionalism and neo-Weberianism (Muzio, Brock and Suddaby, 2013), the neo-institutional approach is drawn upon where appropriate in the remainder of this book to augment the neo-Weberian theoretical framework for studying professions.

Having said this, some words of caution are in order. Proponents of neo-institutionalism typically adopt an ecological perspective where professions are conceptualised as competing for jurisdiction and social position symbiotically with other professional groups and different institutional forms, spanning from transnational corporations to nation states. This is illustrated by the more recent work of Abbott (2005) and is centred on the premise that professions have their own internal ecologies and are situated in complex environments linked to other ecological systems, including universities and governments. In this respect, the theory of neo-institutionalism can be criticised for its ecological premises related to animal and plant behaviour (Dingwall, 2016). Here there has been extensive theoretical debate about the importance of socio-biology in shaping human evolution based on biological determinism (Baxter, 2007), as against politics and power (Perreault, Bridge and McCarthy, 2015). In using this approach, therefore, the implications of social Darwinism in reinforcing racial and other forms of inequalities through the eugenics movement (Bergman, 2020) clearly need to be avoided. If its ecological underpinning is seen purely as a metaphor, neo-institutionalism can provide a useful and complementary way of viewing the professions alongside neo-Weberian theory. Its value is demonstrated by Faulconbridge and Muzio (2012) in developing a transnational neo-Weberian perspective on professions, which highlights the need to place professions in a wider socio-political context.

Conclusion

We have now therefore reviewed a range of mainstream and other related theories of the professions – most centrally including neo-Weberianism, which acts as frame of reference for the rest of this book. These have moved us from a simple description of the historical development of professionalisation to a more incisive analysis of the whys and wherefores of professionalism. Mention of metaphors in relation to the ecological underpinning of neo-institutionalism (Suddaby and Muzio, 2015) as an allied perspective to neo-Weberianism is also a reminder of their significance in interpreting the nature and role of professions in society. While not theories in themselves, metaphors reflect, and act as a stimulus to, theoretical development. Although once disparaged as going beyond scientific understanding (Cornelissen, 2005), their value is reinforced by Liljegren and Saks (2016) in their book *Professions and Metaphors* who note how such devices can greatly add to our comprehension of professions, not least by borrowing concepts from one domain and applying them to another. This has already been highlighted in this and previous chapters with reference to concepts such as a 'boa constrictor' swallowing greatly increased numbers of occupations linked to university teachers (Agevall, 2016), 'vampires' to caricature avaricious lawyers (McGillivray, 2004), and 'turf wars' to depict jurisdictional conflict between professions and other occupational groups (Abbott, 1988).

In subsequent chapters the use of metaphors will be amplified further within a neo-Weberian perspective by the employment of concepts like 'zoos, circuses and safari parks' to indicate the different stages of development of professional regulatory policy (Saks, 2014) and 'crabs-in-buckets' to depict professional status competition (Stringfellow and Thompson, 2014). In terms of what is to come, though, an understanding of the competing and complementary theoretical approaches so far outlined provides a very helpful platform for the next and subsequent chapters. This particularly applies to neo-Weberianism, but other approaches referenced in this chapter will also be introduced where relevant in the spirit of eclecticism that underlies this book – since even very different approaches may on occasion intersect and/or promote further thinking on professionalism (Saks, 2016b). In Chapter 4 we look primarily through a neo-Weberian lens at what happened to professional groups in the Anglo-American context and beyond after reaching their high-water mark of autonomous self-regulation in the 1960s and 1970s. As will be seen, at this point they came under growing attack with the rise of the counter culture, which created an increasing climate of negativity about the professions. The implications of this for subsequent professional development in modern neo-liberal societies are then outlined – before we turn to focus on business and management issues specifically related to the professions in Chapter 5 and their possible future manifestation in Chapter 6.

4 Attacks on professions
Professional deconstruction?

Introduction

As noted at the end of the previous chapter, we shall now document the increasing attacks on professions from the 1960s and 1970s onwards. Of special interest is their effect on the highly independent and well-rewarded elite professions such as medicine and law at this time in Britain and the United States, along with other neo-liberal capitalist societies. This is explored primarily from the neo-Weberian perspective on which the rest of the book is centred that highlights the impact of the more critical climate for professions from several directions – not least from the vantage point of clients, citizens, the state and corporations. First, though, we discuss the rise of the counter culture some five decades ago which seriously began the challenge to the public deferentialism to professional groups embedded in the taxonomic perspective on professions – and arguably their significant deconstruction in late modernity. As will be seen, this deconstruction has been exacerbated by increasing public scandals involving the professions, the postmodern 'war on expertise' and the existence of an ever-stronger group of free marketeers.

Before we do so, it should be stressed that there was some counter-cultural resistance to mainstream professional authority in the preceding century in health care and other areas. This is illustrated by the substantial involvement of the public and practitioners in alternative medicine in Britain in these years when the latter were frequently consulted in opposition to the newly emerging biomedical orthodoxy. However, as has been documented, the use of such unorthodox practitioners from herbalists to homeopaths progressively decreased under medical pressure in the years up to the mid-twentieth century (Saks, 2015e). In law in the United States too, the National Lawyers Guild – a progressive public interest association of lawyers, as well as law students and paralegals – was initially founded in the 1930s to protest against the exclusionary membership practices and conservatism of the American Bar Association (Flam, 2019). This stands in a long tradition of earlier more general resistance to conventional practice within professions themselves (Brint and Levy, 2002). Nonetheless, the scale of the challenge to professional groups rapidly ramped up thereafter – as the shining star of mainstream professions became tarnished. This was reflected in a greater number of radical caucuses developing within a wider range of professional groups, as dissent increasingly arose from without (Perrucci, 1973).

The growing critique of professions

The counter-cultural challenge

In this respect, the counter culture that swept the modern world from the 1960s and 1970s challenged materialistic values and the technocratic solutions that were being put forward to address societal problems. In so doing, it demythologised conventional views of scientific progress championed by professional groups and led to the exploration of alternative lifestyles to counter the apparent loss of spirituality in modern societies (Roszak, 1995). Associated with this popular revolt were new hippy fashion styles and experimental psychedelic drug usage based on a desire for a more natural existence. Aside from the high-profile links of the counter culture with meditation and mysticism – as exemplified by the Beatles' links with the Maharshi Yogi (Saks, 1997) – there was a push for greater public empowerment and self-help. This widespread reaction against accepting conventional authority increasingly led to the questioning of professional experts – not least architects and urban planners who, as Gans (1972) pointed out, were heavily criticised for designing for communities without engaging with the people who actually lived there.

One of the fiercest critics of professions in modern societies at this time was Ivan Illich (1973a), who saw their operation in the modern world as a form of imperialism that exploitatively worked to the prejudice of the wider society. As such, Illich provided a radical critique of the professional establishment, which led to many global dialogues between himself, the public and the professional parties concerned. While he did not endear himself to everyone – including the Church establishment, of which he was a part – he had very wide popular appeal. His general approach symbolised the counter culture. His personal background and approach are summarised in Box 4.1.

Box 4.1 Ivan Illich: Professions as a form of imperialism

Ivan Illich was one of the icons of the counter culture. He was born in Vienna in 1926 and died in Bremen in 2002. Having gained his doctorate at the University of Florence, he was ordained in Rome and practised as a Roman Catholic priest, following which he became Vice Rector of the Catholic University of Puerto Rico.

He then moved to Cuernavaca in Mexico, where he founded a famous intercultural centre that became a free university, which acted as a magnet for intellectuals from the Americas and internationally. It was from here that he launched his attack on professions as a form of imperialism, alongside other institutions associated with so-called 'scientific progress'.

The basic philosophy on which his ideas were based is perhaps best expressed in his book *Tools for Conviviality*. Here he railed against the institutionalisation of specialist knowledge – claiming that we need to overcome professional monopolies in such areas as agriculture, health, home-building and learning, and restore practical knowledge to the citizen in modern industrial society.

Source: Illich, I. (1973b) *Tools for Conviviality*,
New York: Harper & Row.

Illich believed that, once industrial enterprises expanded beyond a certain point, they become counterproductive as they started to threaten society itself. The theme of counterproductivity was classically reflected in his first book on *Deschooling Society*, in which he argued that compulsory universal education had reached a watershed whereby it was becoming a danger to society (Illich, 1971). Schools and the teachers within them were held to be not only disproportionately expensive in financial terms, but also based on the illusion that learning was synonymous with teaching. In fact, according to Illich, formal schooling undermined individual independence and deflected attention away from other key social institutions like work, friends and the family, which had their own educational roles. Rather than serving as a marker of progress, therefore, he saw increasing levels of schooling as intellectually emasculating and urged that schools be disestablished.

In tune with the counter culture, Illich (1976) made parallel arguments in *The Limits to Medicine* about the role of physicians. In this book, drawing on a wealth of qualitative and quantitative data, he claimed that high-technology health systems had grown to the point where they too were counterproductive at a variety of levels, including:

- producing clinical damage which far outweighed the benefits of professional intervention;
- increasingly abrogating patients' rights to care for themselves and infringing their privacy;
- alienating people with illnesses by repressing pain and extending sick life; and
- turning the population into passive consumers as opposed to autonomous producers.

Drawing on Greek mythology, these various layers of iatrogenesis were depicted by Illich as a 'medical nemesis' in which society was held to be receiving retribution for striving to be god-like – in other words, for pursuing the dream of gaining immortality unchecked by reasonable self-restraint. One of the reasons why this book made such a dramatic impact was because it went beyond the influential anti-psychiatry movement at this time that had endeavoured to expose what it saw as the brutal treatment by institutional psychiatry of mental health (see, for example, Laing and Esterson 1973). Instead, Illich hit right at the heart of medicine by addressing its negative effects on physical, as well as mental, illness.

This attack on the medical profession – like that on schools and their teachers – struck some chords, but was of course open to challenge on several counts. He certainly hit the mark in terms of the damage wrought by such medical interventions as the prescription of thalidomide in pregnancy and the excessive use of radical mastectomies by doctors as a treatment for breast cancer in the 1960s and 1970s (Saks, 2000). However, Illich's arguments about the ineffectiveness and destructive side effects of modern medicine seemed even at that time to fly in the face of many of the improvements made in biomedical treatment. As Horrobin (1977) pointed out, such benefits were greater than those brought about simply by advances in sanitation and diet. The interpretation by Illich was also challenged by Marxist commentators like Navarro (1976) who argued that the divisive social-class aspects of modern medicine under capitalism were given insufficient emphasis in his account. This paralleled the critique of Illich's analysis of education by Bowles and Gintis (1976) who felt he downplayed the invidious role of the education profession in class reproduction in a capitalist society. Whatever the merits or otherwise of Illich's arguments, therefore, the views of the Marxist critics underlined the highly critical views on professions that emerged in the counter culture.

The exacerbation of the counter-cultural critique

As we shall see later in this chapter, this critical climate was further exacerbated in the period following the counter culture as a consequence of a series of public scandals surrounding the professions involving malpractice that threatened the wider society. One example of such malpractice was the shocking case of serial child sex abuse by priests linked to the Vatican, which still rumbles on (Keenan, 2012). This and other recent instances of deviance in professions has underlined the frailty of the practice of individual professionals and the failings of professional bodies themselves – including in adequately using their hard-won self-regulatory powers to police insiders. Such deviance inflamed the attacks on them arising from the heady counter-cultural ideals aimed at transcending the more conservative socio-political environment of the first half of the twentieth century. However, two subsequent attacks have perpetuated and extended this critique of professionalism. One of these is the emergence of a nihilistic postmodern ideology about professions and the other is the growing political support for a free market approach which sees monopolistic professions as adversely interfering with the balance of supply and demand, to the detriment of the public. Leicht (2018) has concisely outlined both these contemporary critiques and it is to his work that we now turn.

Regarding the first recent critique of professions, Leicht (2018) speaks of a 'war on expertise'. He notes that this term has been expounded by Nichols (2017) who has called for democratisation in the campaign against established knowledge – such that everyone's opinion is of equal value, irrespective of expertise. The use of Google and other search engines on everything from heart surgery to global warming seems to have accelerated the currency of this view. Leicht (2018) equates it with postmodern scepticism – which is a latter-day response, building on the counter culture, to the modernist narratives of science and the ideology of progress that had earlier provided a philosophical foundation for the professions. The aim of this more sceptical movement, based on the work of Lyotard (1984) and Bauman (1992), is to restore difference, dialogue and diversity in a world crushed by rationality and scientism. Since professional work has traditionally imposed uniform solutions from above, by extension professions themselves have become an increasingly endangered species. To be sure, this postmodern approach has been critiqued both generally (Harvey, 1990) and in specific fields (Scambler and Higgs, 1998) – not least for its destructive anti-intellectual thrust and minimising the attention given to the iniquitous class structure of capitalism (Harvey, 1990). As Friedman

(2019) indicates too, professions can counter the threat of such populist views by:

• directly labelling them as fake news;
• adjusting their practice to reduce their impact; and
• adopting the bywords of the protagonists into their own repertoire.

However, no matter how far professions emphasise their morality and passion, there is no doubt that the thrust of the war on expertise has put them on the backfoot.

According to Leicht (2018), the second challenge to self-regulatory professions over the past few decades is the rise of neo-liberal political and economic ideologies favouring a free market, rather than leaving professions to be arbiters of our destiny. This has created a tension between the traditional emphasis of professions on autonomy, ethics and collegiality, and an approach centred on enhancing market efficiency through the New Public Management in more privatised economies and societies with stronger public services. This tension is well illustrated by Cummings (2011) who discusses the different implications these counter-posed approaches hold for the legal profession in relation to the concept of justice. As Leicht (2018) observes, in the longstanding professional model, professions know best, with credentialing as a quality assurance tool and client and public-facing codes of ethics. In contrast, in the neo-liberal consensus model, consumers are at the hub and markets determine what is right – naturally rewarding those who behave in the interest of consumers without formal professional intercession. The underlying belief that professional monopolies are simply protective devices in competitive markets to raise prices for their services and restrain trade recalls the earlier work of Friedman (1962), outlined in the last chapter. Like postmodern scepticism, the free market model has also been powerfully criticised – including, as Leicht (2018) notes, in the light of the 2008 financial crash, which can be seen as the direct result of an excessively deregulated market. The main point here, though, is that both these challenges have added to the contemporary attack on professions.

This is an appropriate stage to consider how, and to what extent, the critique of professions from the 1960s and 1970s has impacted on their actual operation and destabilised them, from the viewpoint of the neo-Weberian concept of exclusionary social closure. In the light of the previous reference to consumers and the wider public, we should also be clear about the nomenclature of clients and citizens used here. It is important to note that there can be a conflict between a client-serving and citizen-oriented approach. To give a simple, but topical, example, it may be in the interests of all citizens that an individual suspected of having Covid-19 goes into quarantine because of the risk of infection, but the person themselves may not consider their interests are best served because of the impact on their social life. This conflict is apparent in the codes of ethics of professions, which vary in the extent to which they emphasise one or other or both of these approaches. Saks (1995) found in his review of the ethical codes of a wide range of Anglo-American professional bodies, from architecture and engineering to pharmacy and veterinary medicine, that the codes in the more privatised United States tended to place greater stress on service to clients rather than the general public – as opposed to collective interests in the more state-driven British economy. This threat from clients and citizens to the professions will be considered next, followed by the challenges posed by the state and corporatisation in an organisational context.

Professions, clients and citizens

From a neo-Weberian perspective, the challenge to professions from clients and citizens and their implications for service users in the Anglo-American context has grown since the counter culture. As Tonkens (2016:45) points out, users have increasingly sought to be empowered through "the extension of choice and voice", while there has been ever-greater recognition of citizen expertise. She notes that this has diminished professional authority, while clients and citizens have become more respected, in contrast to being stereotyped and objectified with imposed professional definitions of their needs. There are several ways in which this has been increasingly apparent in recent decades in relation to the citizenship rights and responsibilities of users. These can perhaps best be considered through the categories that Tonkens outlines of:

- deliberation – public engagement with professional bodies;
- choice – the involvement of individuals as consumers; and
- responsibilisation – people taking responsibility for their own situation.

Although, as we shall see, the activities undertaken under these headings have not always produced as positive an outcome as might have been expected for clients and citizens, they will each now be examined in more detail, focusing primarily, but not solely, on the illustrative case of professional involvement in health care.

Deliberation

Deliberation involves public engagement in the growing number of forums related to the provision of professional services. Here there has been increased user participation in such areas as citizens' juries, governance committee activities and evaluation projects, which has been facilitated by the growth of the internet and the expanding number of organised groups of users (Tonkens, 2016). In health care this is exemplified by rising public engagement in the previously sacrosanct area of medical research through such bodies as INVOLVE, which officially supports public involvement in the National Health Service in Britain, and the Patient-centred Outcomes Research Institute in the United States (Synnot and Hill, 2019). Both of these bodies have developed in the wake of the counter culture to combat the perceived elitist positioning of independent, self-regulating professions and improve their public accountability. Nonetheless, some professional groups have sought to manipulate this form of citizen engagement to their own advantage in health care and elsewhere – not least by legitimating their own decisions by creating the appearance of democracy (Milewa, 2004). However, in the social care field this has been partly counteracted by the rising influence of service users and the growing effectiveness of their training (Carr, 2007). As Liljegren, Höjer and Forkby (2014) note in their analysis of child protection systems in Sweden, though, it is important to differentiate the involvement of lay people in governance in a consultative and executive capacity.

This executive aspect of deliberation has recently helped to further challenge professions. It has involved increasing client and public representation on decision-making boards and councils, which has sharply expanded of late, as broader stakeholder regulation has increased. In Britain, for instance, the General Medical Council has been significantly reformed by being reduced from its traditional 104 members including a very small minority of lay representatives to 12 members with 50 per cent lay representation from 2012 onwards – along with an independent complaints system (Roche, 2018). In the United States too, lay members increasingly sit on many of the medical boards, thereby enhancing public protection (Horowitz, 2013). Similar trends have also been apparent in other professional fields such as law, including the oversight of the Legal Services Board of the Bar Standards Board and the Solicitors Regulatory Authority in Britain, which has diminished their self-regulatory powers (Sommerlad et al, 2015). Parallel patterns have emerged in cognate fields in the United States, Canada and a broad span of other countries (Adams, 2017). Nonetheless, as Tonkens (2016) observes, there may be further to go in terms of gender and ethnic representation in such groups and the extent of professional control over who is selected. Even when lay people have representation, moreover, they are frequently ill-equipped to make expert comment on technical issues and may only be involved in setting up, not implementing, professional projects. Their experience may also be used to legitimate professional decisions already made – rather than acting as a corrective. For all this, though, increasing lay representation on professional boards and associated committees has helped to limit the autonomous professional power once held before the 1960s and 1970s (Saks, 2016a).

In addition to enhanced formalised public engagement, there has been increased citizen empowerment in deliberative decision making in the face of professional dominance through informal interaction between professionals and their clients. Here Sennett (2003) argues that in United States health care each party brings a different kind of expertise to the table, based on technical knowledge and the experience of living with illness respectively. Tonkens (2016) observes that this recognition has enabled an associated shift in power with the growing self-adjudication of problems by users, especially as more information becomes available online and is accessed before professional engagement. She notes that in medicine this has led to more negotiation and power sharing with professionals over diagnosis and treatment, except where clients are more vulnerable in health terms or lack the necessary literacy and computer skills. As Muzio and colleagues (2016) point out, in a wider range of professional activity including accountancy and law, giving in to the client's wishes has actually imperilled professions further as client capture, in which the user becomes sovereign, is sometimes a factor in professional misconduct cases. The challenge is greatest when users avoid orthodox professions altogether by consulting directly with marginal practitioners like complementary and alternative medical therapists in health care. However, this is less common and threatening than strategically employing alternative therapies where health professionals have not successfully treated conditions (Saks, 2006). To further muddy the water, some forms of complementary medicine – like chiropractic and osteopathy – have now gained professional standing through statutory regulation in neo-Weberian terms on both sides of the Atlantic, albeit not on an entirely equal basis in terms of payment for procedures by insurers and other official health providers (Saks, 2015a).

To add to the challenge to professions from clients and citizens through deliberation, growth is also apparent in more organised lobbying by citizen groups – although this tends to be more localised and narrowly focused in the United States (Horowitz, 2018). In Britain, such lobbying has been facilitated by organisations such as Community Health Councils, which were formed in the 1970s within the National Health Service to allow for health consumer representation, and their successor bodies, the Patient Advocacy and Liaison Services, now established in every trust (Klein, 2013). As Dingwall and Hobson-West (2006) point out in the health area, patient advocacy has also involved increasing litigation through the courts. In Britain, this has spanned from actions based on individual cases of medical negligence to collective action. The latter is exemplified by the lawsuit taken out by some one thousand parents, before it was withdrawn in 2003, against the three main manufacturers of the MMR (measles, mumps and rubella) vaccine. This was feared to have highly unsafe side effects for children, despite support from leading members of the Royal Colleges. In the United States, such legal action has been even more common, with American physicians coming under pressure from patients to undertake extra tests and practice reviews. Some of this activity has been focused on ensuring health rights in fields like informed consent and access to medical records. Such intensified legal action may have paradoxically meant that doctors – even with medical insurance – do not always act in their clients' interests because of their fear of intervening as a result of the risks of litigation (Saks, 2000).

Choice

According to Tonkens (2016), a second major challenge to professions from clients and citizens since the counter culture in modern neo-liberal societies like Britain and the United States is from individual choice-making consumers. In this challenge, the demands of consumers have been inserted more centrally into the service relationship with professions. Initially, as she relates, governments sought to make consumers passive in what were effectively command systems in which professions dominated the decision-making process. However, in the more critical climate that has emerged in relation to professions there has been a shift towards commodification based on markets and responsiveness to consumers. This was pivoted on the introduction of more transparent performance measures for professions to enable greater freedom of choice by consumers. As Evetts (2011) observes, professions and professional service organisations have consequently been involved in converting themselves into enterprises in which relationships between clients and professionals are transformed more into those with customer relations departments, where consumer demands in the market are paramount.

This trend can again be illustrated through the health professions in Britain, where there is the growing use of 'big data' in gauging the performance of doctors and other professional personnel in the National Health Service and private health care (Kirkpatrick and Veronesi, 2019). Importantly, these data are now selectively and transparently available not only to managers, but also to members of the public. They include everything from clinical indicators such as mortality rates to patient survey results based on assessments by groups like inpatients and those attending accident and emergency departments. As Klein (2013) relates, this built on the position in the 1990s when performance indicators were first used as a tool of managerial control and then became a means of giving the public information about the health service to assist them to make informed decisions about their care. However, at this point it was top-down consumerism as it was local, regional and central managers who ultimately made contracting decisions. This was to change, though, in succeeding decades when more information was made available about such areas as general practice so that users could make informed choices in a patient-led National Health Service – in which money followed patients choosing services from their personal doctor to referral providers.

In the United States, consumers have also been involved in redressing the power of medicine in an increasingly informed manner – not least in their attempts to contain growing medical expenditure, such as through the once popular Health Maintenance Organizations acting on their behalf, with a proportion of consumers on their boards (Saks, 2015e). As Horowitz (2018) notes, in recent years – following the bankruptcy and subsequent mergers of many of these bodies – the Consumers Union has become a more prominent player in facilitating choice on the other side of the Atlantic. This has occurred as it has turned its attention from general consumer issues in rating goods like cars and washing machines to opening up parallel information on health care. In this way, it has looked to make patients stronger consumers by increasing access to data on doctors, as well as on hospitals, to inform choice. The Consumer Union has also formed the Patients Safety Action Network, which has called for more medical board transparency to improve the position of patients *vis-à-vis* physicians in the marketplace. Some parts of professions have more strongly embraced lobbying than others. A case in point here is that of American cause lawyers who have sought more democratic relationships with clients. They have done so by embracing civic agendas through transgressive lawyering that has challenged existing power structures over issues like race and gender inequality (Flam, 2019).

While commodification has amplified the attack on independent self-regulating professional groups, as Tonkens (2016) observes, it has not passed without criticism for limiting democratisation and replacing voice about human concerns with the arguably shallower concept of consumer choice in the market. Nonetheless, as the work of Freidson (2001), one of the leading neo-Weberian writers on professional groups, has implied in differentiating the logic of professionalism from that of the market, as well as the state, this still represents a threat to professions as classically defined. He conceives professions in ideal typical terms as being more focused on the welfare of clients and citizens than simply following market preferences or pressures from the state that may undermine their autonomy. As if to underline such distinctions, in her study of health and social services in England and Sweden in terms of marketisation, Fotaki (2011) found that pro-market policies did not meet the perceived needs of users of individualised public services. Instead, they were more likely to promote new types of volatile and fragile partnerships with professionals, creating a subordinated user who has no choice but to 'choose' services over which they have little control. As a result, in practice, Tonkens (2016) believes that, while the exercise of increasing consumer choice has impacted negatively on professions as service providers in terms of trust by clients and citizens in a competitive environment, its main effect may actually have been to create more regulatory red tape.

Responsibilisation

For Tonkens (2016), the third element of the attack on professional groups by clients and citizens over the past fifty years is that of responsibilisation. As she says, this may be as much a consequence of individualisation as collectivisation. In health care it is manifested in clients becoming increasingly responsible for their own wellbeing as citizens, including by fostering networks for social support. The impetus for this has grown in other fields too such as those related to architecture and engineering, with the enhanced public desire for practical self-sufficiency (Strawbridge and Strawbridge, 2020). There may of course be issues of public safety, which have led to legal limits on what actions it is permissible to undertake in place of a professional. This may not be problematic in straightforward matters like maintaining a healthy lifestyle – as has occurred through healthy living movements based on self-help in Britain and the United States in the historic past (Saks, 2015e). The trend to want more individual and community responsibility, though, has intensified as time has gone on.

In these terms, as Tonkens (2016) notes, it is important to recognise the two forms such responsibilisation may take. These are:

- 'top down', where professional experts devolve responsibility to clients; and
- 'bottom up', in which clients on the ground demand more responsibility.

Self-help in modern societies may now be becoming more bottom up than top down. However, to first illustrate the top-down approach in health care, experts acting either independently, or on behalf of government, may ask citizens to enhance their wellbeing by social distancing as they have recently done in response to the threat of Covid-19. In the current context, this may also involve, for instance, stopping smoking, and reducing obesity by dieting and exercising as part of a public health drive (Baggott, 2011). Top-down responsibilisation is therefore far more likely to return professionals to the paternalistic roles for which they were so heavily criticised in the 1960s and 1970s (Tonkens, 2016). As a result, it may not encourage new forms of citizenship as it reinforces professional power in a Foucauldian manner, accentuating the tendency to discipline and dominate through governmentality (Ilcan and Basok, 2004).

Bottom-up responsibilisation, however, may at least prompt professionals to engage in more of a negotiating role with clients. In this sense, in health and social care and other professional fields, self-help and/or the use of informal care in the community may involve co-production between clients and professionals (Fotaki, 2011). This is exemplified by clients with diabetes who wish to take more responsibility for their use of medicines in association with the practice nurse to whom their oversight is typically sub-delegated by doctors (Childs, Cypress and Spollett, 2017). However, there may be intrinsic limits on the level of empowerment that is possible within the biomedical paradigm based on objectified scientific knowledge (Saks, 2002a). Medical domination may also be reinforced rather than subverted by the growing pattern of self-medication and unpaid care from family and friends that align with biomedical parameters (Kelleher, 2006) – particularly in relation to bodies like the Ileostomy Society and the Society for Skin Camouflage that health professionals themselves have played a part in setting up (Saks, 2000). This may also apply to those who use complementary and alternative medical remedies for a restricted range of conditions within the prevailing medical paradigm. An example is that of patients who access acupuncture *in situ* for pain centred on orthodox neurophysiological theories, such as those linked to the release of endorphins. This is very different to using acupuncture at a distance as a general panacea based on the *yin-yang* principles of traditional Chinese medicine (Saks, 2006).

Bottom-up approaches, though, may not always lead to cosy and cooperative relationships with professions. More challenging situations may occur when informal social networks of clients are locked into subversive subcultures opposed to conventional professional practice. In the health field in the Anglo-American context, there are several oppositional self-help groups, such as the animal rights movement opposed to medical laboratory experimentation (Elston, 2006). As Saks (2000) notes, other concrete illustrations of adversarial self-help groups range from the Association of Victims of Medical Accidents in Britain to the National Women's Health Network in the United States. A classic example most strongly linked to the counter culture in both countries is the long-standing Boston Women's Health Collective (2011). Its philosophy has clear feminist roots and is driven by an attack on sexism towards women as consumers of orthodox medical services in a patriarchal modern society. It seeks to establish alternative service provision with limited input from health professionals – with the aims of demedicalising women's lives and demystifying modern medicine through the promotion of practices such as natural home births. Supporters of alternative therapies like homeopathy – based on the principle antithetical to biomedicine that the lower the dilution of a drug, the greater its potency – are perhaps most in tension with the medical profession. Although homeopaths have been much maligned in recent years in the face of the resurgence of scientism, they represent a potential oppositional threat to the medical profession's interests in neo-Weberian terms in maintaining and extending its income, status and power (Saks, 2015a).

Professions and the state

Aside from these three dimensions of challenge from citizen and client engagement, a second strand of endangerment to the lofty self-regulating position that professions had attained in the 1960s and 1970s in Britain and the United States has come from the state. This is rather paradoxical for neo-Weberians because, as has been seen, the state underwrites the exclusionary closure on which professions are classically centred in such neo-liberal societies (Saks, 2010). However, the state in this context can serve as something of a double-edged sword. This is because the state as an entity cannot be seen as completely separate from the wider public as many of its actions are at least overtly undertaken on behalf of the welfare of citizens. As Peeters (2013) has commented in his study in The Netherlands, for instance, governments use political techniques to influence citizen behaviour to entice, persuade and otherwise nudge citizens to take responsibility in producing public value. Several examples of this type of action which have threatened professional groups over the past five decades have already been indirectly referenced in the discussion about professions, clients and citizens in the Anglo-American context above – underlining that these areas are interlinked to state action.

However, the focus now turns to considering the more direct and arguably more detrimental influence of the state on professions in the period of late modernity as the neo-liberal state has increasingly intervened in the regulation of professions (Reed, 2018). This is particularly well illustrated in the more public sector-oriented case of Britain, which will now be extensively documented. Here the threat from the state to the professions began in earnest under Margaret Thatcher's government from 1979 onwards – which was committed to giving greater emphasis to market forces, although not at the expense of a strong state. In a rarely cited University of California working paper, Burrage (1992) highlights the attack on professions during the Thatcher period. He recounts that this was translated into:

- changing their working practices;
- reducing their powers; and
- increasing regulation.

He argues that this was part of the implementation of an often implicit, but nonetheless real, anti-professional ideology. This resulted in more attention being given to organising, monitoring, incentivising and punishing professional groups for their actions. He illustrates this with reference to elite civil servants, whose training – like barristers in pupillage – was heavily centred on work experience, following careful selection into this exclusive administrative class. Over the period of Thatcher's government, they were subjected to an aggressive efficiency campaign aimed at disrupting their carefully protected independent professional service ethic and increasing their attachment to the state.

This attack on professionalism was paralleled by the government's termination of the solicitors' conveyancing monopoly in 1983 to secure greater consumer choice and reduce the price of services (Burrage, 1992). It also introduced a new group of licensed conveyors in direct competition with solicitors, which is still in operation today through the Council for Licensed Conveyancers that now offers optional qualification and further challenge to solicitors through the licensing of probate practitioners (Ward, 2017). As Burrage (1992) points out, since solicitors were so reliant on income from conveyancing, the end to this monopoly also led to pressures on barristers as solicitors sought new markets for their services in a divided profession – not least in terms of the right of audience in the High Court and the crown courts. In addition, the Thatcher government removed legal aid from the administration of the Law Society, the solicitors' professional body, while some of the discretion of magistrates' courts and their clerks was taken away by the growing centralisation of state control. Abel (2003) describes this period and the ensuing decade as one of the most tumultuous for the legal profession in which the state endeavoured to promote cheaper, higher quality services, with greater responsiveness to complaints. But this was not the end of the state reforms – in 2007 the Legal Services Act established the lay-dominated Legal Services Board as an independent authority overseeing the regulatory bodies for different branches of the profession (Adams, 2017). Having said this, there were limits to state encroachment as the two branches managed to fend off government attempts to remove the long-established notion of self-governing professions in a climate where public confidence in this arrangement was waning (Burrage, 2006).

Burrage (1992) notes that the profession of school teaching – which was also differentiated, albeit by the level at which teaching took place – was affected too by the state assault on the professions. In the 1980s, the Thatcher government introduced mandatory appraisals and excluded teachers' representatives from high-level discussions about the curriculum and assessment, as well as abolishing standard pay and conditions. Aside from enhancing consumer power over professions by giving parents greater choice over the schools their children attended, it subsequently allowed parents to vote for schools to opt out from local authority control too and imposed a national curriculum on schools – thereby limiting the scope of teachers' professional judgement. Moreover, by introducing a teacher licensing scheme, the government broke the monopoly of teacher training colleges on the admission of teachers to the profession. This subversive stance in relation to professional authority was largely mirrored by its reinforcement of the need in higher education for stronger corporate management by university Vice-Chancellors. Such strictures reducing academic professionalism were put forward alongside government recommendations for the adoption of comparative university performance indicators and state action to limit the independence of universities through greater funding control. This was additionally to apply to colleges of further education and the then polytechnics in an era of increasing marketisation (McCaig, 2018).

Meanwhile, as Burrage (1992) recounts, the health professions came under further attack from successive Thatcher governments. The first step was dissolving the opticians' monopoly on the sale of spectacles in 1980 to provide greater consumer choice and reduce the artificially inflated price of glasses. The next was to put in place Sir Roy Griffiths, a director of the Sainsbury's supermarket chain, to launch an inquiry in 1983 into the running of the National Health Service, in which doctors and other health professions had hitherto operated relatively autonomously. His subsequent report called for greater general management of professional groups at every level of the National Health Service – resulting in tighter and more detailed contracts regulating their conditions of work (Klein, 2013). An analogous management regime was also applied to nurses, who – while not as autonomous given their typical line reporting to consultants and general practitioners – had similar professional characteristics. In addition, nurses were hierarchically regraded, damaging their traditional professional collegiality. It is not surprising that Burrage (1992:9) says that, by the end of the Thatcher period in the National Health Service, "rational bureaucratic pyramids of control and accountability had been superimposed on the host of professional... enclaves and communities". Although doctors were offered a way out of state medicine from 1989 when they could join independently funded hospital trusts or fundholding practices, and while many took up managerial positions within the state-run health service (Saks, 2015e), this could not mask the diminished position of medical and other professional groups in a climate increasingly critical of professions.

Burrage (1992) observes that professional bodes were almost uniformly hostile to the reforms under Margaret Thatcher. He highlights three main responses as being to:

- try and mobilise public opinion to have the reforms amended or abandoned;
- negotiate amendments during implementation of the reforms to limit or sabotage them; and
- take up a defensive, adversarial stance in the workplace to resist reform on the shop floor.

The latter position sometimes involved union-style politics by professions – such as in the case of the industrial action taken by nurses in response to the introduction of general management and their regrading. While a little exceptional for professions at that time, this was very resonant with the neo-Weberian concept of dual closure based on exclusionary closure and usurpationary action more typical of the working class. However, for all their demonstrations, mass advertising campaigns and other strategies, the professions so affected were unable significantly to roll back the changes made by the state. Indeed, the reforms were to become even more hostile to the professions after the Thatcher era, as the case of medicine clearly exemplifies. The new Conservative government under John Major brought in some limited changes in the first half of the 1990s with the Patients' Charter aimed at advancing consumer rights, but this was not very far reaching and did little to press the medical and other health professions further (Allsop and Saks, 2002). But the impact of state reforms on the professions was greater still from the time when New Labour came to power in 1997 with a remit and resolve to modernise the health service.

The background to this was a series of high-profile public scandals in the aftermath of Thatcherism that did not reflect well on the health professions. As Allsop and Saks (2002) document, these began with the unacceptably high mortality rate for child heart surgery at Bristol Royal Infirmary and the removal of deceased children's organs without consent at Alder Hey hospital in Liverpool. These were followed by the case of the nurse child murderer Beverley Allitt and, most significantly, that of Dr Harold Shipman, the mass serial killing general practitioner who is known to have ended the lives of over two hundred of his patents over several decades without detection by the General Medical Council. Such cases spurred the new government led by Tony Blair and then Gordon Brown in the period up to 2010 to undertake major reform of the medical profession – in a manner that has now been implemented and has cascaded to other health and care professions. In this process, the state introduced such reforms as the mandatory revalidation of qualified practitioners and the introduction of independent disciplinary procedures to ensure fitness to practise (Roche, 2018). Perhaps most significantly a meta-regulator overseeing the regulation of the health care professions was established by law in 2002. This has had several name changes, from the Council for Healthcare Regulatory Excellence to the present Professional Standards Authority for Health and Social Care (Allsop and Jones, 2018). However, despite its shifting title and powers, its establishment led to the medical and other health professions losing their independent self-regulated powers in the transition to a position which may now be best termed as 'regulated self-regulation' (Chamberlain, 2015).

The reform of the health professions, therefore, continued into the period under the subsequent Coalition and Conservative governments that took up office from 2010 onwards. It was accelerated by more public scandals including those related to poor standards in the Mid Staffordshire NHS Trust, which resulted in a very low quality of patient care and higher than expected mortality (Roche, 2018). The implementation of the previous state regulatory framework for the health professions was now accompanied by more formal efforts by the government to break down the barriers between health and social care – not least through the establishment of localised Health and Wellbeing Boards and more devolved Clinical Commissioning Groups. These changes have been metaphorically depicted by Saks (2014) within a neo-Weberian perspective in terms of a shift from zoos to circuses and then to safari parks in the more critical professional climate. These metaphors can be itemised as follows:

- The concept of zoos refers to the classic self-regulatory framework of the professions, enclosed by cages they themselves had built in an exclusionary manner.
- The notion of a circus refers to the move to a more regulated environment in which a ringmaster, representing the state, makes the professions perform to an accepted standard.
- The concept of a safari park refers to the shift to a position where selected professions are encouraged to operate together across boundaries in a more open terrain.

This chronology interestingly follows the successive phases of animal management in the wider society where animal rights have become more significant. However, in the case of the professions, the shift underlines the contours of the assault on their independence by the state. While there has been some resistance by doctors to the reforms in practice (see, for example, Tazzyman et al, 2020), the winds of change have had a substantive effect on their operation.

This metaphorical depiction of the changes that have now been imposed on almost all of the health professions since the 1960s and 1970s through state action can also be applied to certain other professions. This includes academics in higher education in Britain, considered earlier in this section. Here the increase in state direction and relative decline of university independence has been overlain by the encouragement given through government research funding councils and other state bodies to expand cooperation between universities (Saks, 2015d). As Muzzin and Martimianakis (2016) point out, this has been replicated in other modern societies, with the growth of national as well as international collaboration in this field. Although the United States is based on a more commercialised system, where there is greater private funding for university endowments, they still argue that the power of academics has waned because of state rationalisation – not to mention the effects of receding state financing in an era of massified public higher education (Brint, 2018). In this respect, the United States has to some degree followed in the footsteps of not only Britain, but also Australia and Canada (Muzzin and Martimianakis, 2016). Krause (1996) agrees – noting that, while the American federal government is not directly involved in higher education except through research funding, individual state governments can starve academic programmes through the process of appropriation.

However, for all the resulting decline in their influence in decision making in the universities and their loss of tenure, Muzzin and Martimianakis (2016) say that professors and other academics have successfully fought to retain their 'bounded niches' and academic freedom in the face of actions by the state and university authorities. Nonetheless, the decline in the privileged position of professions as a result of government policies remains apparent – as illustrated by the legal profession in the United States which, like that of its British counterpart, has also suffered at the hands of the state. Following the civil rights movement in the 1960s and 1970s, Spangler (1986) observed that the public practice of law became more routinised under state control, with more rationalised workplaces and closer administrative oversight. Krause (1996) argues too that – especially with the Reagan cutbacks in the 1980s – government legal work with the poor became even less well paid. Moreover, paralleling state action in Britain, the American federal government and state supreme courts have reconsidered the monopoly of lawyers in some areas. This step, in conjunction with allowing attorneys to advertise in the mass media, increased competition between them – leading to the greater use of paraprofessionals and further fee reductions. In addition, as Abel (1986) has documented, in some states the regulation of lawyers has been taken over by state-appointed bodies in part because the legal profession has not shown itself to be sufficiently adept at policing unethical behaviour (Arnold and Kay, 1995). More recently too, greater government oversight has been applied to American lawyers, alongside accountants, in the wake of a number of financial scandals (Adams, 2017).

Of course, there are variations across societies in the degree to which the state has reduced professional privilege. As has already been seen in Chapter 2 of this book, independent self-regulating professions were never fully established in countries like China and Russia because of the antipathy of the socialist state towards such previously elite occupations – with all the implications for the subsequently suppressed income, status and power of such groups (Iarskaia-Smirnova and Abramov, 2016). However, the attack by the state on professions since the counter culture in other modern neo-liberal societal contexts has also occurred, albeit with different overlays. This includes in such European countries as France and Germany where professional groups have retained significant socio-economic rewards and privileges, but are typically more integrated with the functioning of the state (Krause, 1996). In Canada meanwhile, some provinces have established governmental oversight bodies above a number of self-regulating professions (Adams, 2017). However, as in the case of medicine, despite federal as well as provincial/ territorial oversight of physicians, the autonomy of such professions in the Canadian context continues to prevail through the system of Colleges, centred on the classic neo-Weberian model of exclusionary social closure (Ahmed, Brown and Saks, 2018).

The overarching trend for at least some emaciation of professional powers in the Anglo-American context and beyond seems to have also influenced the developing world with a colonial past, especially in Asia, South America and Africa – where countries in these continents have tended to take on regulatory patterns mirroring those of their colonisers (Muzzin and Martimianakis, 2016). It should be stressed, though, that the notion of a less trusting and persecuting state is more relevant to some professions than others, even in neo-liberal countries. As Krause (1996) notes, engineering in the United States is mainly based in the private sector and has sketchy links with the state in terms of qualifying associations, deriving most of its income in the public sector from the military-industrial complex. For engineers and many other American professions, therefore, the main source of pressure over the past few decades in a more commercialised society has come from private corporations, which direct the market, rather than the state. We shall now address in the next section this corporate dimension of the attacks on professional groups within different organisational settings in the modern world.

Corporatisation, organisations and the professions

Far from being seen as inextricably linked to the state in the governance agenda, as in the Foucauldian approach, professions have increasingly been viewed as burdens on the state that need to be controlled (Adams, 2017). Paradoxically, though, while the state in Britain has been highly challenging to professions, it has also largely provided a public sector market shelter for their privileges in a manner distinct from the United States (Saks, 2015e). Against this, American professions have more strongly retained their state-underpinned independent self-regulatory powers despite the aforementioned political pressure on the professions. Adams (2017) suggests from a neo-Weberian perspective that this difference may be explained by the more unified nature of professions and the lesser commitment of state actors to change the *status quo* in the United States compared to Britain, where a higher media profile has arguably been given to scandals involving professionals. But, whatever the interpretation of the reasons for the difference, it certainly has not protected professional groups from the debilitating effects of corporatisation in the more privatised American context. As will be seen, this is very evident in contrasting the fate of the medical profession in these two societies – notwithstanding the more resilient positioning of elite specialisms, like cardiology, in the health care marketplace of the United States (Saks 2015e).

In the United States, the general effect of corporatisation on physicians in a system centred heavily on private health insurance has been striking, as health care expenditure has spiralled over the past few decades. As Starr (1982) has documented, the decline of the traditional fee-for-service system in the United States led a growing number of private corporations to make medical care arrangements for their workers, in addition to individual subscriptions to private health schemes. The various private health insurance companies involved have managed to reduce medical fees for individual procedures to the pecuniary advantage of their corporate owners and shareholders, thereby diminishing the income, status and power of doctors. Although physicians made an initial financial killing when the federally funded Medicare programme for the elderly and the state-supported Medicaid scheme for the poor were introduced in the 1960s (Saks, 2015e), this gave way to an era when cost containment became the highest priority in both public and private sectors – hence, amongst other things, the rise and fall of the once fashionable, more cooperative Health Maintenance Organizations, which at one point seemed to offer a way forward (Coombs, 2005). As Saks (2018b) points out, a key element in this process was standardised fee setting through Diagnostic Related Groups, which escalated the long-established fear of physicians of subordination to bureaucracy. However, in Britain in the more protective environment of the National Health Service, through which most health care is still delivered, the effects of corporatisation on medical interests have had less impact – despite the parallel implementation of the New Public Management, focused on enhancing service efficiency (Dent, Chandler and Barry 2004).

As Brooks (2011) notes, the effects of the private corporate environment in the United States have also been strongly felt in law – where the largest law firm employs quadruple the number of attorneys as twenty years previously and there are now ten more firms of similar size. Krause (1996) underlines that larger law firms doing corporate work are typically more bureaucratic than smaller mass practice firms, where contracts from clients are often individually made. One consequence of cost-saving measures in more sizeable firms is that much American legal work is undertaken by personnel other than lawyers, such that Bar associations have on occasion had to prosecute for the unauthorised practice of law. This American corporate law model had spread to much of Europe by the 1990s (Olgiati, 1995) – not least in Germany where the expanding numbers of corporate lawyers became a distinctive professional legal group based on exclusionary social closure (Rogowski, 1995). Solicitors and barristers in Britain also became ever more enmeshed in the corporate net as their clients increasingly changed from individuals to large private, as well as public, organisations (Flood, 2018). As such, British lawyers are more likely today to be working in-house in a closely controlled environment that may reduce their autonomy. This trend has also indirectly depleted the power of lawyers in neo-Weberian terms by escalating their long-standing conflict with accountants over business law, as they vie for custom in more substantial market settings (Burrage, 2006). Concerns over cost – as in medicine – have also become paramount in legal practice in the private and public sectors in Britain. Abel (2003) in fact contends that it was the high costs of the administration of justice that prompted more stringent regulatory changes to the legal professions.

The cases of law and medicine highlight how the majority of professionals are now employed in corporate organisations, which are imposing controls from above and undermining independent authority. As Flood (2018) observes, the discourse of enterprise has readily become the dominant narrative based on performance reviews, hierarchy and audit. With the New Public Management, such a narrative is aimed at greater efficiency, with cost economies. Autonomous self-regulating professions with rigid scopes of practice may therefore be excessively expensive in a situation where more flexibility is required. The tension between professionals and their managers in terms of what can be seen from a neo-institutionalist perspective as competing institutional logics has increasingly been acknowledged at all levels of the organisation (Kirkpatrick, 2016). Freidson (1994) claims that the level of conflict depends on the degree to which organisations conform to Weber's ideal type of bureaucracy and the amount of discretion professionals have over their work. This said, managers in organisations nonetheless pose a novel challenge to professions in modern societies. This has led Evetts (2013) to argue that we have now moved from occupational to organisational professionalism, the ideal typical elements of which are set out in Table 4.1.

The first column of Table 4.1 based on organisational logic is centred on rational-legal authority with growing standardisation and performance monitoring in organisations, while the second column based on professional logic involves independent self-regulatory collegial authority. However, even with increasing corporatisation, the end result is not necessarily an emaciated group of professions. This is because occupational professionalism may still be completely in evidence on the ground based on expertise and other factors, notwithstanding arguments for growing patterns of organisational professionalism. The depletion of professional autonomy may also not occur because of hybridisation – a now widely employed concept related to the manner in which opposed managerial and professional principles can come together in organisations (Waring, 2014). This concept is discussed more fully in the public sector in the neo-Weberian account of Noordegraaf (2018), who provides the most cogent outline of the forces at work.

Noordegraaf (2018) argues that hybridisation is relevant to a wide range of public sector professionals – including doctors, nurses, police, judges, teachers and social workers. He notes that, particularly since the 1980s, the corporate capture of such professionals in modern neo-liberal regimes intensified with the rise of the New Public Management.

Table 4.1 Two different professional types – organisational vs. occupational professionalism

Organisational professionalism	Occupational professionalism
Discourse of control used increasingly by managers in work organisations	Discourse constructed within professional groups
Rational-legal forms of authority	Collegial authority
Standardised procedures	Discretion and occupational control of the work
Hierarchical structures of authority and decision making	Practitioner trust by both clients and employers
Managerialism	Controls operationalised by practitioners
Accountability and externalised forms of regulation, target-setting and performance review	Professional ethics monitored by institutions and associations

Source: Evetts, J. (2010) 'Reconnecting professional occupations with professional organizations: Risks and opportunities', in Svensson, L. and Evetts, J. (eds) (2010) *Sociology of Professions: Continental and Anglo-Saxon Traditions*, Göteborg: Daidalos, p. 130.

He believes that this has diluted the purity of such occupational groups because of the increasing conflicts in neo-institutional terms between organisational and professional logics (Reay and Hinings, 2009). Noordegraaf and Schinkel (2011) have argued that this might be alternatively conceptualised within a Bourdieusian perspective as a contest between managerial and professional fields over symbolic capital, while Olakivi and Niska (2017) believe it is best conceived as an amalgam of overlapping discourses. However the relationship is conceptualised, though, there are real conflicts. In the most extreme scenario, the organisations in which professionals are employed may seek total obedience from subordinates in relation to managerial goals, while professionals themselves may expect to be totally self-directing (Thompson and McHugh, 2009).

According to Noordegraaf (2018), these conflicts do not have to be so starkly counterposed and can lead to three ideal typical situations. As such, organisational and professional logics can:

- co-exist in separate ways under the same roof;
- combine to gain the best of both worlds; and
- become hybrid so that professions behave in new ways.

There is a fourth possibility, which is not mentioned by Noordegraaf, that professions become completely dominated by organisational imperatives. However, this is unlikely to occur as there would be little value in paying a high price for professional services without anything other than legitimatory benefit for organisational activities. Unsurprisingly, therefore, Noordegraaf argues that hybridisation is the most realistic outcome in entrepreneurial settings. He contends that organisations may not otherwise be able to deliver the accessible, effective and high-quality services needed in terms of the concept of a market-based performance logic – notwithstanding debates about whether hybrid professionalism may be an exceptional rather than a dominant outcome (Breit, Fossestøl and Andreassen, 2018).

Noordegraaf (2018) notes that what ultimately emerges will depend, amongst other things, on the strength of the profession concerned. Professional groups like teachers and social workers are held to be weaker as they have more external legal demands and constraints compared to doctors, who lie towards the stronger end of the spectrum. However, the situation may be a more complex than this. Freidson (1994) argues that the degree of conflict between professions and organisations may diminish where there are legal restrictions on the provision of professional services, such that only particular professions are authorised to undertake specific bodies of work. This is well illustrated by the professional remit of accountants in auditing in the United States – and in Britain where their monopoly is sustained by the Companies Act and schedules of other legislation, rather than a statutory register (Macdonald, 1995). Here professionals will most forcefully be able to defend their independence against the managerial logic of employer control, alongside democratic, market and other logics (Blomgren and Waks, 2015). While professions in public and private sector organisations can protect their professional logic or otherwise ensure that this is kept apart from other logics, the challenge to professions from their increasingly corporatised settings are plain.

It is not surprising, therefore, that the interweaving of logics through hybridisation has been widely discussed at a general level in the current literature in relation to both public and private sector organisations (see, for instance, Denis, Ferlie and van Gestel, 2015; Noordegraaf, 2015; Skelcher and Smith, 2015). In all this, it should be acknowledged, as Noordegraaf (2018) has observed, that silo-based professionalism centred on one profession is diminishing in this context with pressures to engage collaboratively in co-responsible professional teams and networks. Having said this, hybridisation has been widely analysed empirically in a number of specific professions in modern neo-liberal societies. This focus on single professions is at least partially justified by Bévort and Suddaby (2016) who found in a Big Four accounting firm that competing logics are interpreted more according to individual cognition and interpretive subjectivity than inter-subjective interactions. In their study of stand-alone professions, Miller, Kurunmäki and O'Leary (2008) examined hybridisation in accountancy in managing risk through the New Public Management in a range of settings, including the microprocessor industry and medical care. Lander, Heugens and van Oosterhout (2017) have also explored the way in which tension between profits and professionalism is resolved in relation to commercial/managerial and professional/trustee logics, in a wide span of Dutch law firms.

Interestingly, in terms of the claim by Evetts (2013) about the shift from occupational to organisational professionalism, Faulconbridge and Muzio (2008) found that, in modern large-scale globalising law firms operating primarily in the private corporate sector, a sensitivity to professional values and interests still prevails. Moreover, Jonnergård and Erlingsdóttir (2012) showed systemically that professional strategies were more significant than organisational reforms in adopting quality enhancement in medicine in Sweden. Carvalho (2014) also argues that, even when hospital funding was reduced by the state in Portugal and new management norms and values were introduced, the traditional professionalism of nurses survived – albeit in hybrid form in which their longstanding norms and values were incorporated and reconfigured within organisational parameters. There is evidence too that professional co-option can play back to change the very nature of the institutional logics themselves (Andersson and Liff, 2018). Not all is lost for professions, therefore, despite the novel organisational and other challenges to their traditional autonomy and associated rewards that professional groups have faced over the past few decades through corporatisation.

In this respect, to summarise, the assault on the independence of professions in modern neo-liberal societies since the 1960s and 1970s has taken three distinctive forms that have been considered in this chapter. The first has come from clients and citizens. The second has derived from the state. The third has been launched from the growing organisational corporatisation of professions. It should be apparent that all of these challenges are synergistically interconnected to a greater or lesser extent. This leads on to the debate about deprofessionalisation, which overviews the implications of the foregoing discussion and ties the various threads together – not least by drawing explicitly on some of the theoretical strands considered in Chapter 3 of this volume. In this regard, there is in particular a theoretical debate between neo-Weberians and Marxists who differentially conceptualise the potential trends as being 'deprofessionalisation' or 'proletarianisation', respectively – in light of the move away from the autonomous and well-rewarded position of the professions in the 1960s and 1970s.

The debate about deprofessionalisation

As has been seen in the previous chapter, within Marxist theory, the American writer Braverman (1998) argues that the professions are being inexorably proletarianised in advanced capitalist societies. He links this to the development of capitalism in which a number of middle and high-ranking occupations, including a wide span of professions, are reduced to the position of the proletariat in the labour process. He holds that this comes about as a result of the routinising and deskilling of work by managers in tasks ranging from engineering to teaching, as costs are driven down under capitalism through the application of the principles of Taylorism – based on scientific management – and succeeding managerial philosophies, such as the human relations approach. According to Braverman, to increase management control by seeking greater efficiencies in this way, the planning and conceptualisation of work is separated from its execution. He uses the development of nursing, as well as other selected occupations, to illustrate this trend. Staying with examples from health care, other Marxist writers such as McKinlay and Arches (1985) have argued that a similar process is also occurring in medicine with the increasing polarisation of the capitalist economy – even if physicians have been in a stronger position to postpone or minimise the effects.

Along with Fordism – centred on replacing skilled staff with machinery and recruiting unskilled workers to run the machinery (Malin, 2020) – such a perspective has been heavily criticised. In part this is because of the more general issues that plague Marxist accounts which were considered in the last chapter – including their frequent disregard for empirical evidence and their polemical long-term visions of the revolutionary future. In this vein, the arguments by Braverman (1998) have been attacked by Adler (2007) for implying that capitalist production necessarily leads to the deskilling of workers, although Thompson (2007) disputes the evidence he provides of skill upgrading. The grounds for this challenge, though are contentious. In the case of nursing in Britain and the United States, for instance, the most recent trend has been for them to not so much be proletarianised as to become upskilled through ever growing specialisation (Saks, 2015e). Indeed, this has happened to some, if not all, professional groups with the arrival of more sophisticated technology and the information economy (Susskind and Susskind, 2015).

The account by Braverman (1998) has also been questioned for depicting the worker as an inert player and for minimising emphasis on worker resistance (Brooks, 2011). This is perhaps explained by the fact that political activism in the workplace in the United States, on which Braverman's account is focused, has characteristically been less prevalent than on the other side of the Atlantic (see, for instance, Slaughter, 2007). However, this is a weakness in relation to professions in Britain given the interest-based resistance to attacks on them since the 1960s and 1970s. This is underlined by barristers and solicitors taking to the streets in 2014 in protest against cuts in legal aid, which had direct implications for their income, and tens of thousands of junior doctors going on strike in 2016 because of the attempted imposition by government of an adverse seven-day week medical contract (Malin, 2020). However, one charge that is frequently made which does not wholly stick is that Braverman over-romanticises the past in painting a picture of the idyllic multi-skilled autonomy of those performing craft work in earlier times (Littler, 1982). While this might apply to some more working-class trades as in the early construction of motor cars, this claim can scarcely be levelled at professions in the Anglo-American context given their relatively independent existence up to the mid-twentieth century.

Against this, it must be said that some neo-Weberian contributors such as Haug (1973) have given a similarly bleak picture of the decline in the fortunes of autonomous professional groups including doctors, albeit through the conceptual lens of deprofessionalisation rather than proletarianisation. For Haug, the main drivers were not those of capitalism, but rather those of increasing bureaucratisation involving ever more process controls and performance measures. This inter-pretation gives greater credence to the notion expounded by Weber (1968) of the ever-increasing iron cage of bureaucracy that he felt would envelop modern industrial societies. In her parallel account to Marxist contributors like Braverman (1998) centred on the United States, Haug (1973) saw such deprofessionalisation as being indicated by such trends as diminished autonomy in work performance; and declining authority over clients. This was held to be accelerated by the development of information technology and rising public education levels, in a more critical climate placing greater stress on peer review and cost containment. Similar trends have been portrayed more recently by neo-Weberians in areas such as law in which Brooks (2011) argues that the work of American attorneys has been downgraded as far as part-time and temporary assignments are concerned. However, it is very important – just as in the case of Marxist theories – that a more open approach is adopted in drawing on evidence. This is despite Haug (1973) putting up a straw man to counter the views of those, at the time, arguing for the increasing professionalisation of occupational groups in society.

It is encouraging that, several years later, Haug (1988) restated her general argument about deprofessionalisation, but on this occasion more judiciously placed greater emphasis on the insufficiency of evi-dence to either accept or reject the deprofessionalisation thesis. This is resonant with a more subtle neo-Weberian perspective, paying greater attention to critically evaluating such a proposition. Throughout this chapter, it has been seen that discussions of this nature are, of necessity, very complex. The struggle of professions against demoralising depro-fessionalisation parallels worker resistance in other fields in the face of increasing management control – from sabotage (Mars, 1982) through to strikes and work to rule (Salaman, 1979). However, professions – with a strong tradition in modern societies of having higher job satisfaction than clerical and manual workers further down the line (Blauner, 1964) – have usually exhibited greater resilience to such attacks (Brooks, 2011). As has been seen, for every blow struck by clients and citizens, the state or corporate organisations, professions have typically managed to ride the waves from a self-interest perspective – retaining a strong sense of authority and protecting their privileges in myriad ways despite ongoing changes.

Of course, some professional groups have lost out more than others in the recent critical climate for professions. In the United States, for instance, as previously indicated, the standing of many doctors seems to have become diminished with growing corporatisation (Saks, 2015e). Equally, with the adoption of different hiring policies, some lawyers in American corporate law firms have ended up undertaking rote and standardised tasks, in this case in such areas as wills and uncontested divorces in family law (Brooks, 2011). This has also happened to a wider range of professional groups in the neo-liberal age of austerity following the 2008 financial crash (Malin, 2020) as epitomised by the increasing use in Britain of teaching assistants in education (Sharples, Webster and Blatchford, 2016) and the growing employment internationally of support workers in health and social care as a substitute for health professional personnel (Saks, 2020c). Moreover, according to Thompson and McHugh (2009) there seems to have also been a backward shift in the job security of professional workers in the Anglo-American context over the past few decades.

This is not to suggest that there have been no other modes of professional adjustment in the face of such trends as escalating pressure from users, growing marketisation, increasing state intervention and rising corporatisation. One of these modes of adjustment has been through restratification, as exemplified by Calnan and Gabe (2009) in British heath care. Here the power and status of general practitioners rose from the 1990s at the expense of hospital consultants with increasing government emphasis on the importance of primary care. More recently, Adams (2020) too has highlighted the emergence of restratification, alongside hybridisation, amongst Canadian engineers, with adverse consequences for professional unity (Adams, 2020). Reprofessionalisation also remains a possibility – especially, and most broadly, in former socialist countries like Russia where there is a lobby to restore independent professional associations (Saks, 2018a). This may also form part of a defensive reaction by professions in response to attacks. One example of this is the case of law where Muzio and Ackroyd (2005) argue that more intra-occupational stratification has been created to protect the privileges of those at the top of the profession in Britain at the expense of those lower down the hierarchy.

Finally, it is vital going forward to recognise the methodological issues involved in judging the extent to which deprofessionalisation – or alternative modes of professional adaptation – has occurred in any particular professional field. While there may be macro trends in one or other direction, as we have seen, there is no necessary convergence between modern societies. We therefore need to clarify at a minimum:

- which countries are being examined in making claims;
- what professional groups are under investigation; and
- which indicators are being used to assess degrees of deprofessionalisation.

In choosing indicators to evaluate the extent to which deprofessonalisation has or has not taken place, it is critical that they are both consistent and relevant. In the example of the medical profession, Elston (1991) provides a range of benchmarking criteria that might be employed, from the degree of control of medical education and client influence over doctors to the level of skills required in medical practice, the encroachment of non-medical practitioners and the unionisation of doctors. More general indicators might embrace increased workloads, lowering of employment standards and reduced morale – especially when a growing number of employees, professional and otherwise, are held to have been plunged into precarity, with low wages and job insecurity (Standing, 2011).

Although there are debates about such indicators (Johnson, 2015), it is also important to define the timescale over which the evaluation of deprofessionalisation has occurred (Light, 1995). In addition, tricky comparative methodological issues need to be addressed if cross-national research is involved (Burau, 2019), as well as wider considerations of the use of qualitative, quantitative or mixed methods in making any assessment of trends (Saks and Allsop, 2019). To be positive, in the face of attacks over the past few decades, professions should not simply be examined in terms of having to defend their occupational privileges against a potentially downward spiral of deprofessionalisation. It is also vital to be open to using tools that recognise increasing opportunities for enhancement for some specific professional groups in the Anglo-American context and beyond. This may be particularly apparent in the case of new and emerging professional groups – such as in executive remuneration and executive search – which are considered in more detail in the next chapter on business and management and the professions.

Conclusion

Whatever research methodology is employed, though, it is very apparent from the foregoing analysis in this chapter that there is already sufficient evidence to suggest that some deprofessionalisation has occurred in modern societies like Britain and the United States – countries where exclusionary professional closure has been most strongly in evidence from a neo-Weberian viewpoint. This certainly seems to be the case even though professional resistance has in part defrayed and, in some cases, deflected the contemporary threats to the income, status and power of professions. In this latter respect, it is very interesting, for example, that, for all the market-oriented policy reforms that have taken place, general practitioners in The Netherlands still have a self-image of themselves as autonomous professionals (Hendrikx, 2018). The objective preservation of a large degree of autonomy also seems to have been the case in a number of other professions in a range of different modern neo-liberal societies, despite the rapid transformations that are self-evidently taking place (Dent et al, 2016).

As has been discussed in this chapter, the period from the 1960s and 1970s to the present day has seen many changes to the nature and form of professions in the increasingly critical climate generated by the counter culture, the war on expertise and the political desire to subject them to the rigours of the market. Having examined in some detail with illustrations in Chapter 4 the effect of these forces on the at least partial deconstruction of professions through clients and citizens, the state and organisational corporatisation, we now turn to consider in more depth in Chapter 5 business and management issues related to the professions. In this complementary chapter we shall, amongst other things, have the opportunity to explore the broader international business context of professions – as well as to analyse further more business-facing themes in organisational settings including the position of managers and other professional groups, together with their changing place in the pecking order. This will again be undertaken by selectively drawing on the theoretical perspectives we have already outlined in the previous chapter – but especially that of neo-Weberianism.

5 Business and management issues and the professions

Introduction

This chapter focuses on key issues specifically linked to business and management in modern societies. Some of these concern questions linked to the previous chapter – as, for example, the existence of hybrid professions in organisations responding to competing institutional logics in the private and public sector. Chapter 5 begins, though, by considering from a neo-institutional perspective the internationalisation of professions, including in relation to transnational engagement. It also explores in more detail the nature of multinational professional service firms in fields such as law and accountancy and their interlinkages with more nationally based professions in an increasingly entrepreneurial environment. In addition, it examines from a largely neo-Weberian perspective the long-running issue of whether management can be seen as a profession, more established business-oriented professions, and new and emerging professional groups in this area in modern societies. It concludes with some words on interprofessional issues in business in a competitive marketplace.

One of the questions to be considered – as discussed in previous chapters – relates to diversity in the professions. This chapter will continue to address this in an integrated manner where appropriate, especially in relation to ethnic and gender dimensions of social closure in the professions in a commercial context. This context for the operation of professions has become increasingly entrepreneurial in both the private and public arenas in neo-liberal countries in late modernity (Saks and Muzio, 2018). Reihlen, Werr and Seckler (2018) point out that little research has been conducted into such changes, particularly regarding professional service firms. Following Venkataraman (1997), they define entrepreneurship as the way in which opportunities are discovered, created and exploited in order to bring future goods and services into existence.

This equates with seeing entrepreneurship as opportunity seeking, manifested either through the creation of new professional service firms or through more established mechanisms including the activities of professions. The identification of this changing setting is very important as a backdrop to business and management issues linked to professional groups.

It should be noted that there may be some tension between the notions of entrepreneurship and professionalism, as Table 5.1, contrasting the ideal typical features of each, plainly demonstrates. As Table 5.1 indicates, these ideal typical concepts cover a range of aspects from the value of the work undertaken and the type of authority involved to the primary body of knowledge and the mode of organisation. The notion of professionalism that is contrasted with entrepreneurship is helpfully based, from the viewpoint of this volume, on a neo-Weberian interpretation of professions, centred on social closure in the marketplace. While presented as polar types, this is not to say that these characteristics of entrepreneurialism and professionalism cannot come together in some way in practice. This is especially possible in professional service firms – as will be discussed in more detail in the following section on the international context of professionalism.

Table 5.1 Opposing concepts – Entrepreneurship vs. professionalism

	Entrepreneurship	*Professionalism*
Value	Change and innovation	Professional standards and discretion
Type of authority	Entrepreneurial: based on the ability to make change happen	Professional: based on expert power
Primary body of knowledge	Pragmatic: anything that works	Academic: science and technology
Market conditions	Open and free market	Social closure and sheltered positions in the marketplace
Mode of organisation	Emphasises autonomy and innovation: entrepreneurial model – start-ups, corporate entrepreneurship, business incubators, innovation ecosystems	Emphasises autonomy and self-governance: professional model – professional partnerships and professional associations

Source: Reihlen, M., Werr, A. and Seckler, C. (2018) 'Entrepreneurship and professional service firms: The team, the firm, the ecosystem and the field', in Saks, M. and Muzio, D. (eds) *Professions and Professional Service Firms: Private and Public Sector Enterprises in the Global Economy*, Abingdon: Routledge, p. 112.

The international context: Professions, transnationalism and professional service firms

In the neo-institutional approach, outlined in Chapter 3 on theories of professions, there is a focus on the international context of professions – a subject on which we have only touched lightly at this point in the book. This broader approach to professions has become ever more important for understanding professional groups with growing patterns of globalisation, especially in relation to business and management (Saks and Muzio, 2018). This trend regarding professional service firms stretches beyond modern neo-liberal societies to include contemporary socialist countries like China. Li (2019), for instance, has recently reported that Chinese law firms are becoming increasingly cosmopolitan. Here it is argued that the majority of such firms have endeavoured to expand overseas by creating international offices and referral networks – within a trajectory shaped by a combination of pragmatism, entrepreneurship and state direction.

Savoldi and Brock (2019) meanwhile highlight the broad span of networks of international professional service firms in law in Europe, which may also apply to other internationalised professions. They note that these are very varied in composition and can be categorised into seven types – loose, constricted, focused, friends, exclusives, monogamous and isolated. In this typology:

- *loose* refers to networks of disconnected actors, with exchange mainly based on referrals;
- *constricted* describes referral-based networks with exchange flows and cooperation;
- *focused* indicates networks aimed at a specific sector or specialty;
- *friends* relate to informal and non-exclusive networks;
- *exclusives* depict formal alliances or cooperative relations;
- *monogamous* refers to well-established, broad, longstanding, close relationships; and
- *isolated* indicates project-related alliances of limited duration.

It is very important to understand the heterogeneity of such firms as they will have differing impacts on business and management, depending on the ways in which they are set up.

As will be seen, the kind of engagement of professions in such larger-scale institutionalised bureaucratic structures and relationships can have a range of consequences. As an indication of this, Covaleski, Dirsmith and Rittenburg (2003), for example, argue, in examining jurisdictional disputes amongst the biggest accounting bodies on the international stage, that professional work has become increasingly commodified with growing globalisation. Such insights on a global stage represent a sea change from the more traditional interpretations of business-oriented professions within a single nation state. While linked to neo-institutionalism, with its complementary association to neo-Weberianism, the article by Covaleski and colleagues also has distinctly Marxist overtones from a theoretical perspective. This highlights how we should be open eclectically to a whole spectrum of approaches whatever their relative overall merits (Saks, 2016b). We shall now examine two aspects of the interface of professions in business and management with the international agenda – first, transnational professional activities and, second, the nature of professional service firms themselves.

Transnationalism and the professions

The significance of examining professions on an international platform is underlined by Seabrooke (2014). Drawing on the work of Abbott (2005) on linked ecologies, he focuses particularly on their transnational dimensions. These go beyond, say, a high-level international summit to discuss trade matters in specific societies, which is primarily motivated by the interests of individual countries; the term transnationalism instead transcends boundaries and borders – even if it is sometimes difficult to separate from an international perspective. Within a transnational framework, Seabrooke discusses the way in which professionals strategically play off different forms of knowledge to provide policy solutions through a process of what he calls 'epistemic arbitrage'. This enables them to generate global rather than domestic markets for their services, favouring their specific field of knowledge or expertise. In this setting, transnational professionals are seen to have distinct careers, while operating across international networks. They aim to induce deference in the parties with whom they work to dominate decision making – in some cases acting as double agents in brokering change in law and fields such as investment banking and business consultancy based on their personal stature and the interests they represent (Dezalay and Garth, 2016).

By way of illustration, Seabrooke and Tsingou (2015) have applied the linked ecologies approach to the emergence of new actors and issues in transnational work on fertility by medical experts, demographers and economists in modern societies. Here they note how such professionals used their authority positively to promote policies, as well as to prevent unwelcome changes from occurring. Equally, Thistle-thwaite and Paterson (2016) describe how professionals established new transnational environmental and social standards in green accounting through the creation of standards boards in Britain and the United States. They did so by employing epistemic arbitrage between professional bodies, non-governmental organisations and major accountancy firms. A further example outlined by Eskelinen and Ylönen (2017) concerns the way in which business professionals used their expertise to defend Panama against anti-tax haven measures adopted by Argentina and Columbia. They did so with reference to international tax law overseen by the World Trade Organization. At the same time, the professionals involved helped the Panamanian authorities to 'have their cake and eat it' by promoting tax avoidance activities in Panama that were within the law.

Hasselbalch and Seabrooke (2018) have also analysed professional strategies in enterprising transnational environments at a more general level. They argue that to establish markets for their skills, professionals need to some degree to decouple from their domestic environment. As such, they must establish themselves as arbiters of relevant professional knowledge and know how to leverage institutional and organisational fields as they pursue their own transnational projects. They also need to frame strategies – by telling actors what they are considering and why it matters – in order to build coalitions around them. This may comprise:

- dealing with disruptions to an organisational field, as with the introduction of e-cigarettes;
- contests where moves and counter-moves are made by participants in the disrupted field; and
- normalisation in which professionals settle the disruption to favour of their skills and services.

The process of epistemic arbitrage may sometimes involve the creation of neo-colonial hierarchies based on inequalities of power, as in the case of some international management consultancies which benefit financially from devolving work to developing countries (Boussebaa, Morgan and Sturdy, 2012).

The projects in which the professionals involved are so engaged could involve liaising internationally with bodies at a wider level, spanning from the European Union (Evetts, 2000), to more localised groups of lawyers in Latin America (Dezalay and Garth, 2002). In scaling up the scope of neo-Weberian analyses of this activity of professions beyond the nation state, Faulconbridge and Muzio (2017) note that most of the interaction involved takes place and must be viewed through the lens of globalised professional service firms. In this regard, such firms do so by acting primarily in their capacity as economic agents (Boussebaa and Faulconbridge, 2018). We now turn to consider the role of these multinational firms, albeit without losing sight of the importance of more limited trans-local professional projects (Blok et al, 2018), alongside the broader transnational agendas (Hasselbalch and Seabrooke, 2018).

International professional service firms

Within the neo-institutionalist perspective, there has been a particular focus on the mushrooming range of professional service firms at international level with millions of employees worldwide (Adams, 2017). Recent research shows that they operate mainly in law and accounting (Saks and Muzio, 2018), although they are also occasionally involved in areas such as engineering (Malhotra and Morris, 2009) and can and do apply their expertise to governments on a consultancy basis in health and other fields (Klein, 2013). Boussebaa and Faulconbridge (2018) see the following international professional service firms as prime examples:

- Anglo-American Big Four accountancy firms, including Deloitte & Touche, Ernst & Young, KPMG and PricewaterhouseCoopers;
- United States-based strategy organisational consultancies, such as Booz Allen & Hamilton and McKinsey; and
- British-based Magic Circle law firms, such as Allen & Overy and Clifford Chance.

Flood (2018:37) comments that the push for these international firms that have recently changed the professional landscape came from finance and business, based on a desire "to exploit the fixity of labour, as against the mobility of capital, often to the detriment of labour." Consequently, professional service firms have outsourced as much work as possible to places like India, the Philippines and South Africa to reduce costs and sustain profits. One of the consequences of this driver in competition between professional service firms has also been for some firms to grow from smaller roots into giant conglomerates through a process of colonisation – a trend which has particularly affected already large accounting firms. This has allowed them to migrate to, and dominate, particular areas of work such as law, tax, management consultancy and forensic accounting in expanding into, and encroaching on, other jurisdictions. As Taminiau, Heusinkveld and Cramer (2019) highlight, central to this process has been for such firms to develop legitimising strategies to justify themselves in the new markets that they enter.

Given the heterogenous nature of the firms involved (Malhotra and Morris, 2009), it should not be surprising that the literature on this subject has in part been centred on the taxonomic approach. As such, it parallels previous work on national professional bodies – even though the classic, if arguably diminishing, concept of autonomous professions is quite removed from the notion of corporate best practice embraced by these largely globalising firms (Reihlen, Werr and Seckler, 2018). Taxonomic contributions on the latter have endeavoured to define their main characteristics – from knowledge intensity to low capital requirements, along of course with the possession and oversight of a professionalised workforce (von Nordenflycht, 2010). Such lists have been put together in a variety of ways – not least to include features felt most likely to engender the highest performance (see, for example, Empson and Chapman, 2006; Hitt et al, 2006) at a time with outsourcing and offshoring when there are real challenges to their quality, speed and reliability (Flood, 2018). Nonetheless, the categorisation of the mainstream attributes of professional service firms – just like the taxonomic perspective on professions itself – has led to significant disputes over the key elements to be incorporated, in this case from particular human resource practices to ownership types (Brock, 2006).

In this light, it has become ever more apparent that such firms may be best conceptualised in modern societies not as some kind of taxonomic abstraction, but as enterprising business corporations. Given their growing global significance, attention has shifted from examining the controls exercised by professions to the intricacies involved in running large-scale international firms (Cooper and Robson, 2006) – which themselves dominate transnational governance structures, including those of the World Trade Organization (Arnold, 2005). This trend has also been underscored in recent times by the desire of such international professional service firms to standardise the conditions of their operation – not least by ensuring a convergence of accounting standards, which was encouraged by the ill-fated International Standards Board that helped to precipitate the global financial crisis of 2008 (Brooks, 2018). In these terms, Suddaby and Muzio (2015) argue from a neo-institutionalist and neo-Weberian perspective that professional service firms should be viewed as elitist players in global economic markets that capitalise on a gendered and stratified labour force in generating financial surpluses. They claim that this more politicised approach is more fruitful than merely aiming to classify the structure and function of these firms along the lines of trait and functionalist theorists.

In so doing, and linking back to the theories of professions set out in Chapter 3, the interest-based discourse of professionalism also remains important in the analysis of the operation of these private corporations, including in managing and motivating employees (Dent and Whitehead, 2002). Reed (2012) claims too that such elite organisations play a central role in underpinning and reproducing the institutions of global capitalism centred on neo-liberal economic policies. As such, professional service firms often link professional projects to their aims as multinational corporations, which stretch beyond the nation state (Dezalay and Garth, 1996). This means that both professions and professional service firms can be seen as agents of institutionalisation (Suddaby and Viale, 2011) – as exemplified in neo-liberal societies by the legitimating role played by auditors in the public and private sector on behalf of major accounting firms (Power, 2003) and by human resource professionals in promoting equal opportunities (Dobbin, 2009). Having considered the nature and role of international professional service firms, we shall now examine in a more detailed way some of the factors involved in their success (or otherwise) in fostering entrepreneurialism.

Entrepreneurial success and professional service firms

Successful entrepreneurial practice in international professional service firms lies at the heart of the rationale for their establishment. In terms of entrepreneurialism, Reihlen, Werr and Seckler (2018) argue from their research that:

- the motivational dispositions of professionals are a fertile ground for new initiatives;
- the locus for innovation is in service delivery in interaction with clients and colleagues; and
- the relationship networks in their markets enable entrepreneurial opportunities.

However, there are complexities. They stress that there are two distinct types of professional service firm – namely, the regulated professional service firm as in accounting and law and the neo-professional service firm which lacks a clearly defined knowledge base. In this sense, classic professional service firms with well-defined standards laid down by professional associations with credentialing can be contrasted with neo-professional service firms based on activities like management consultancy, where commonly accepted standards of professional practice may be lacking (Clark and Fincham, 2002).

Innovation is consequently more bounded, with less discretionary freedom, in classical firms including accountants and lawyers as compared to the newer types – where there is greater opportunity for creative problem solving. As such, management consultants may be less likely than accountants to be accused of cooking the books when they make novel interpretations of the rules. As Greenwood and Suddaby (2006) point out, though, with reference to accountancy, regulated professional service firms do not necessarily or always stay within professional limits; amongst other things, they can push the boundaries of innovation by taking on leadership roles in professional bodies to effect change through the upgrading of standards. For Reihlen, Werr and Seckler (2018), this leads on to a discussion of the entrepreneurial team itself within professional service firms. Successful teams comprise personnel with knowledge and expertise, frequently operating across disciplines and organisational silos, who endeavour creatively to address client-defined problems. According to Reihlen and colleagues, their work involves breaking down barriers in an interactive climate. This includes barriers relating to the self-interests of the professionals involved as they may risk exposing their knowledge and/or their ignorance – both of which may threaten their income, status and power in neo-Weberian terms.

It is further argued by Reihlen, Werr and Seckler (2018) that entrepreneurialism in the team will be encouraged the more that the professional service firm:

- engages in new venture management linked to start-ups and spin-offs;
- offers support for the development and embedding of new practices;
- adopts patterns of governance that steer away from standardised approaches; and
- gives more attention to financial incentives rather than pay for seniority alone.

In addition, they indicate that entrepreneurialism will be promoted by taking a wider ecosystem approach – in which all key actors are incorporated in the network, including lead clients, professional bodies, universities, other external stakeholders and those offering complementary expertise. Finally, such institutional entrepreneurialism is seen as requiring sensitivity to developments in emerging and maturing, as well as established, organisational fields if it is to successfully come to fruition.

As part of this, Kvålshaugen, Hydle and Brehmer (2015) claim that the degree to which international professional service firms innovate will depend on taking up different learning opportunities from their past and present provision of services. This includes understanding customer needs and knowledge accumulation, alongside having a capacity to expand. But if there are potentially rich interest-based opportunities for entrepreneurship in professional service firms – which may or may not be realised – research by Harrington (2017) has also shown that such opportunities may be enhanced by applying the Bourdieusian concept of the habitus. The habitus, as will be recalled from Chapter 3, expresses how individuals develop attitudes and dispositions to engage in specific practices. In this frame of reference, Harrington found from her study of wealth management in eighteen countries that the practice of the firms was improved when professionals avoided certain behaviours in interaction with clients and peers, brought rather different work experiences to the table, and enhanced the client's cultural capital by giving access to high-status, exclusive activities like dinners and exhibitions. Indeed, somewhat surprisingly, the latter seemed more important to clients than increasing their economic capital alone.

To complement this finding, Mors, Rogan and Lynch (2018) note, from their study of a consulting company, the significance of internal and external boundary-spanning ties to the success of professional service firms. Malhotra and Morris (2009) also show how differences in professional service firms in knowledge, jurisdictional control and client relationships can impact on team working, organisational form and pricing structure in the entrepreneurial process. Moreover, Olsen, Sverdrup and Kalleberg (2019) underline the importance for professional service firms of retaining their most valuable staff. They found in a professional service firm hiring lawyers, auditors and management consultants based in Norway that some employees – and particularly non-certified employees in auditing – are more vulnerable to leaving. This is because of their client contacts and transferable skills, as these provide alternative job opportunities that may provide more job satisfaction. Faulconbridge and Muzio (2013) also point out from their analysis of professional service firms relocating to Italy that the geographical location of such firms is another factor in the entrepreneurial opportunities available.

The regulation of international professional service firms

While these various contributions help to provide greater insight into enhancing the entrepreneurial performance of international entrepreneurial work in professional service firms, there are other issues. One major area of ongoing concern is that of their regulation. This is very apparent in terms of gender diversity where Bolton and Muzio (2008) argue that the mass entry of women into the professional labour market in areas such as law and management has not yet enabled them to manage to break any glass ceilings. However, as Ballakrishnen (2017) points out, there are exceptions to this rule in international professional service firms. More specifically, she found amongst India's elite litigation, transactional law and consulting firms that in terms of employment women were viewed as best suited to transactional tasks, in contrast to male traditional lawyers who were not typically seen to possess this skill set. Nonetheless, despite opening up a promotion track, this example still smacks of patriarchalism and may serve retrogressively through female stereotyping of jobs to ghettoise women based on problematic gender assumptions.

This view is underlined by Sommerlad and Ashley (2018) who note more generally that, in law and accountancy in Anglo-American professional service firms, staff are segregated both horizontally and vertically on gender lines – with women less likely to be partners and to be as well paid as men in these firms. Other recent international research, though, suggests that there are less silo-based pathways open to ethnic minorities at the elite level. This is certainly indicated by the extensive high-level statistical study by Cameran, Campa and Clerissi (2020), which showed that fees for non-Anglo-Saxon partners in the Big Four accountancy firms in Australia were set at a comparable level to those of Anglo-Saxon partners. This was in contrast to their findings in smaller, less prestigious firms where there was significant differentiation of fees to the detriment of minorities. This is partly explained by the greater effectiveness of the implementation of equal opportunities legislation in the more bureaucratised environments of larger firms. This highlights that more intensive regulation of this sphere at all levels may help move equality concerns further forward in the future.

However, there is another major global regulatory dilemma for professional service firms. In the international rescaled political space, the key question remains of who actually oversees such firms as they are not legally recognised or certified by any single country. In this sense, professional bodies govern local practitioners in geographically bounded markets (Adams, 2017) – and are therefore not well equipped to regulate professions working internationally in professional service firms with offices in many countries (Suddaby, Cooper and Greenwood, 2007). Despite their complex regulatory environment comprised of a mosaic of different national and international regulations (Quack and Schüßler, 2015), this does not of course mean that the larger firms are averse to undertaking boundary work in defence of their own jurisdictions – including by endeavouring to manipulate national professional regulations to their own advantage. More broadly, in the case of global law firms, they strive to navigate and at times evade local regulations to serve their mainly commercial clients and to maximise their own autonomy (Flood, 2011).

Against this context, and without blanket legal recognition or certification by nation states, Boussard (2018) shows that transnational social closure still does occur, albeit primarily at a normative level. She illustrates this in the area of mergers and acquisitions in Britain, the United States and France where, in defining their jurisdictions, the global firms concerned:

- gain recognition of the symbolic and social boundaries by establishing a knowledge base;
- shape and master a professional ethos to reinforce these boundaries; and
- populate their territory in an exclusionary way by establishing professional legitimacy.

It should be noted that this analysis dovetails with the recent trend at national and international level for large professional service firms, such as those in accounting, to move towards what has been termed 'entity regulation'. As Adams (2017) describes, this typically involves a shift away from prescriptive rules governing behaviour to a focus within specific entities on principles and outcomes, including access to justice.

Although this form of regulation is regarded by its advocates as modern and innovative in transforming the nature of professional practice in a more client-friendly manner (Adams, 2017), it may have its own pitfalls as we shall shortly see in the financial sector. This is in part because it involves professionals regulating each other – albeit in a corporate context (Coffee, 2006). As such, entity regulation is another type of self-regulation based on social closure, which is also being considered for adoption by professions in national and other local contexts, including in law in Canadian provinces (Adams, 2017). Having indicated the more complex and novel regulatory overlay for professional service firms at international level and how these are negotiated, we shall now focus on considering their impact on individual business-related professions at a national level. Professional occupations in the latter sphere are typically more readily legally delineated through the traditional process of neo-Weberian professional social closure – even if the national and international domains are not entirely distinct (Saks, 2016b).

The impact of international professional service firms on national business professions

The interlinkage between international and more local levels in the business and management field is well illustrated by the influence of global corruption cases. In this regard, it should first be restated that the mainstream focus of professional service firms on the needs of their corporate clients, rather than the broader interests of citizens, can lead to client capture (Dinovitzer, Gunz and Gunz, 2014). This, as has been seen in the previous chapter, may create a greater prospect of professional misconduct (Muzio et al, 2016) – notwithstanding the increasing capacity of legal and other firms to tailor regulatory demands to local circumstances (Aulakh and Kirkpatrick, 2018). Gabbioneta, Garnett and Muzio (2020) have exemplified the process through which this can occur in the case of auditing in Britain. They note that, in business settings, criminality is most likely to take place amongst professionals with lower status and less experience – as reflected in some of the recent financial scandals that have cast doubt on the extent to which business-related professions have robust codes of ethics (Adams, 2017). However, this lower, rather than higher, level misconduct was not so much in evidence in the dramatic collapse of Enron, the large-scale American energy corporation, in the early 2000s. This case highlighted the synergies between international activities and locally circumscribed professions, given its seismic implications for the latter.

Merino, Mayper and Tolleson (2010) urge that professional misconduct is more firmly situated at the corporate level rather than the individual professional level in the wider commercial environment. In this respect, Adams (2017) relates that the bankruptcy of Enron strongly implicated Arthur Andersen, one of the world's largest accounting firms, in wrongdoing. The actions of the auditors and attorneys in relaxing their standards at this then Big Five firm led to it surrendering its Certified Public Accountants licences and ceasing to trade. This in turn resulted in changes in regulatory oversight in many nation states – including the introduction of various company law and audit liability reforms in the United States, Britain and parts of the rest of Europe (Armour and McCahery, 2006). To illustrate the specific national ramifications for the professions of the collapse of Enron in the United States, the aftermath of this scandal brought legislative change that gave the United States Securities Exchange Commission the right to regulate the behaviour of lawyers with whom it interacted. It also stripped the accounting profession of much of its independence – not least by subjecting it to standards set by a non-professional body (Adams, 2017).

Although some commentators did not think that the resulting reforms went far enough (Armour and McCahery, 2006), the case was followed on an even larger scale by the 2008 global financial crisis, prompted by the bursting of the American housing bubble and excessively risky lending by the banks, culminating in the bankruptcy of Lehman Brothers (Bernanke, Geitheiner and Paulson, 2019). The financial crisis had a considerable impact not only in creating the deepest worldwide recession since the Great Depression, but also on the limits and opportunities open to national professional bodies. Whittle, Mueller and Carter (2016) highlight this with particular reference to Britain where the Big Four audit firms came under scrutiny from a House of Lords Economic Affairs Committee in light of their apparent failure to adequately audit the banks. The audit profession subsequently faced severe challenge from the Competitions and Market Authority, including the charge that it had improperly acted in a self-interested manner to prevent, restrict or distort competition. In the wake of this challenge, a series of regulatory changes were put into place. These included introducing mandatory tendering to open up the market to accountancy firms beyond the Big Four in the public interest.

Perhaps less strikingly in light of the import of these two big-ticket events, Harrington (2015) underlines more generally how international professional service firms can influence business professionals in specific countries. As she notes from her data from a dozen-and-a-half countries in her study of globalised localism, national professions can often become agents of such firms or other transnational organisations. Her research is particularly powerful in showing how local practices can develop more widely in this way in the field of international finance. In this vein, Kipping, Bühlmann and David (2019) argue that large professional service firms can control and even capture fledgling professional associations in specific countries, such as in management consultancy and executive search. Humphrey, Loft and Woods (2009) similarly show in the case of auditing that national regulatory sites cannot be seen as existing in a vacuum, outside broader international corporate pressures.

However, it is important to acknowledge that this international/national relationship is not simply one way. As Harrington (2015) points out, individual agency and everyday interactions between professionals, peers and clients in these organisational environments can also reciprocally bring about institutional and other changes, including to broader strategic imperatives at a more global level. Nor indeed should it be assumed that the translation of transnational regulatory oversight into national contexts is in any way automatic; rather it is dependent on such factors as the capacity and desire of governments to interfere with the operation of professional associations. Such professional bodies may also themselves resist, as Suddaby, Cooper and Greenwood (2007) point out in accountancy. Now, however, we move to consider business and management professions in a more focused manner, predominantly in national settings – to the extent that they can be dissociated from the international framework in which they are enmeshed.

Business and management professions in national settings

In analysing the operation of such national-based professions in the business arena from a predominantly neo-Weberian perspective, we begin with the much-debated question of whether management itself can be seen as a profession. We then turn to look at the position of more established business-oriented professions like accountancy, law and human resource management in modern neo-liberal societies. Finally, we examine the situation of an illustrative selection of new and emerging business-linked professions that either have entered or are entering the fray, from executive remuneration consultants to project managers. We consider as part of this, in neo-Weberian fashion, the need for such groups to deal with their own interests in the market – before moving on in the next section to assess how far interprofessional collaboration has now become an increasingly essential part of business.

Management as a profession

It should be emphasised that, while managers are often viewed as standing in opposition to professions in organisations, as we saw in analysing their role in the resolution of competing logics within organisations in the previous chapter, there is a long history of debate as to whether managers should themselves be considered be a profession. Johnson (1973), for instance, spoke of the tendency of managers to call themselves professionals. He noted that, to sustain this interpretation, long training courses based on a complex body of knowledge had been put in place by a wide span of European and American management and business schools (Kaplan, 2018). In parallel, bodies like the British Institute of Managers, now the Chartered Management Institute, were formed, pivoted on the existence of such an educational base. Leicht

(2016b) says that this tendency towards knowledge-based operation has become accentuated in modern neo-liberal societies with the expansion of management autonomy, especially at the top level of organisations. This may run counter to claims that the professionalisation process has been captured by the most powerful firms, with the aim of creating corporate-dominated labour markets run by high-level managerial groups (Kipping, Bühlmann and David, 2019). The key issue here, though, is whether managers just possess the self-constructed window dressing of a profession or whether they are actually beginning to take on the substantive features of professionalism themselves.

Recently Heusinkveld and colleagues (2018) have described managers as corporate professions liaising with traditional professional groups in a business environment. In this respect, there are many advantages for managers to be viewed as a profession – not least from the standpoint of recruitment, pay and legitimation of their decision making (Thompson and McHugh, 2009). Additional credence is given to the notion of managers being a profession by the existence of transferable managerial skills drawing on classical management theories, ranging from scientific management to the human relations approach (Pascale, 1990). According to Leicht (2016b), in the United States this led to the Carnegie, Ford and Rockefeller Foundations placing management education at the forefront of their activities, which produced a semi-closed, credential-driven labour market for managers. Moreover, the increasing financialisation of the economies of the modern neo-liberal world have added further weight to management claims to be a profession in view of its key role in responding to economic shocks and growing scrutiny by external stakeholders. Others meanwhile might argue – looking forward – that a stronger link to the ethical codes of professions would only benefit managerial decision making in the public interest in the commercial world (Saks, 1995), notwithstanding the growing commitment of companies to corporate social responsibility (Hopkins, 2016).

However, against this, Child (2011) has challenged the concept of management being a profession, on the basis that this is only plausible if managers actually implement a uniform and generalised body of knowledge. In addition, aside from limited standardisation across managerial tasks, Thompson and McHugh (2009) point out that this position is scarcely sustained by the ethical behaviour of managers in practice – whose actions may be even more questionable than more conventionally defined professions. There are also questions about how far such groups have in practice attained social closure in a fully-fledged neo-Weberian sense without benefitting from the historic conditions for professionalisation in neo-liberal societies of classic professional groups like lawyers (Kipping, Bühlmann and David, 2019). Although there are bodies like the Institute of Management Services in Britain (www. ims-productivity.org) which have codes of ethics and encourage further qualification, membership is voluntary and they have no statutory basis. Having said this, Leicht (2016b) believes that managers are moving in a professionalising direction, as they increasingly engage in interpreting and creating markets and providing financial services to their corporate employers. It is also possible to see managers as a profession from a Bourdieusian perspective, as highlighted by Box 5.1 – even if the professional project of managers is not necessarily mapped on to discrete occupational groups (Ashley and Empson, 2017).

Box 5.1 Are managers a profession? A Bourdieusian perspective

Professor Matthias Kipping from York University in Canada and Dr Felix Bühlmann and Professor Thomas David from the University of Lausanne in Switzerland provide an interesting viewpoint on whether managers are a profession by drawing on the theory of Bourdieu to suggest an alternative way in which professionalisation may be seen as occurring in stratified occupational fields.

This involves employing the Bourdieusian notions of symbolic and social capital to map the growing prevalence of intra-occupational careers through the professional service firms that provide access to privileged positions in firms operating in parallel in the business area.

Based on their study of former McKinsey consultants, it is argued that this not only may be seen as constituting a form of social closure, but also facilitates collective social mobility in a manner resonant with the neo-Weberian approach to professions. This is a fascinating attempt within a neo-Weberian framework to square a difficult circle, while moving a little away from the concept of legally bounded exclusionary closure that neo-Weberians typically argue underpins the professions.

Source: Kipping, M., Bühlmann, F. and David, T. (2019) 'Professionalization through symbolic and social capital: Evidence from the careers of elite consultants', *Journal of Professions and Organization* 6 (3): 265–85.

Whatever position is taken on whether managers are a profession, they still need to work with a range of professional groups, with management so often involved in mediating the competition between them. This discussion of the other key mainstream groups involved in business begins with a consideration of accountants, who are now also most likely to take up high-level managerial positions in the Anglo-American context. Here, management accountants tend to rule the roost despite competition from other professions. As Thompson and McHugh (2009) remind us, and as will be underlined later in this chapter, while engineers have dominated management in Germany, they are not currently a high-profile profession in Britain and the United States on which this book is pivoted. This is because in these latter countries they have found it difficult to maintain a monopoly over the practices of control that are normally carried out by finance. We shall now turn to discuss more fully the case of accountants who have taken centre stage in the coordination and control of middle managers, as well as aggressively encroaching on the territory of lawyers and other mainstream professions in the business sector (Sugarman, 1995).

Established professions in business: The case of accountancy

As noted in an earlier chapter, there are many national and international accountancy bodies – not least being the global Association of Certified Chartered Accountants initially founded in 1904. One example focused on Britain is the Institute of Chartered Accountants in England and Wales (Macdonald, 1995), which regulates many tens of thousands of practitioners in this country and beyond and has a regulatory board, of which at least half of its members are non-accountants. Such regulatory bodies that have taken root in both Britain and North America have typically claimed to serve the public interest (Everett and Green, 2006). Thus, the Institute of Chartered Accountants in England and Wales on its website (www.icaew.com) claims "to act as an independent regulator to protect the public interest by making sure our firms, members, students and affiliates maintain the highest standards of professional conduct." It does so in traditional professional mode through such devices as disciplinary mechanisms, a code of ethics and achievement of the requisite training standards.

As part of the professionalisation of accounting in the nineteenth century, Brooks (2018) relates that Queen Victoria granted Royal Charters to the Edinburgh Society of Accountants and the Glasgow Institute of Accountants and Actuaries in Scotland in the nineteenth century. In addition, the merged accounting institutes south of the border were awarded a Royal Charter later in the century. However, he argues that this early esteem was not completely followed through. In some cases, actions by accountants only reflected the public interest at the ideological level as the profession developed. He believes this was accentuated when the big accountancy firms ventured across the Atlantic by the end of the century to what was then the world's largest economy. In the United States, the prudence of certified public accountants, with their increasingly demanding training and examinations on par with their British counterparts and other mainstream professions, was badly needed given the poor state of financial bookkeeping there at this time.

Nonetheless, the public interest claims of accountants are challenged on both sides of the Atlantic. Brooks (2018) argues that, while the double-entry bookkeeping of accountants facilitated international trade and the rise of capitalism, its seemingly rational neat ledger entries sometimes concealed serious wrongdoing. This was initially manifested in its use in the slave trade with its huge human costs before the cataclysmic 2008 financial crisis, when accountants were trusted under the guise of professionalism to self-regulate in the auditing process. Despite claims by the firms involved in the latter case to be providing professional services to the banks and others, they did not protect the public from the devastating effects of the ensuing bankruptcies and the wider recession. Moreover, Brooks contends that their meta-regulators such as the Financial Reporting Council and the Financial Services Authority in Britain failed to firmly tackle the issues raised in the aftermath of the crisis with sufficient force. Indeed, Bierman and colleagues (2019) argue that various forms of law and other regulation enacted by governmental entities have also had little impact in the parallel case of the United States.

Brooks (2018) documents many examples of the accountancy profession, or what he derisorily calls the 'bean counters', misleading the public thereafter. One major issue that he highlights – as part of the numerous contemporary instances he showcases of formal government approbations of the profession for misbehaviour in both Britain and the United States – is the conflict of interests that accountants frequently face on a national stage in signing off accounts, while being 'fattened on fees' in what he regards as an unhealthy situation of client capture. In a manner resonant of earlier neo-Weberian critiques of professions, Brooks argues that this has resulted all too often at best in special pleading and at worst in dereliction of duty and criminal conduct; for him, the Enron scandal in the United States and all that has since followed in the twenty-first century was just the tip of a large iceberg of accounting misdemeanours that have continued to ripple across the globe – from the Western European countries of The Netherlands and Spain to Russia and China in the East.

However, although according to Brooks (2018) some accountants have also been complicit in facilitating internationally tax avoidance schemes and other toxic arrangements, there is also the need for navel inspection by specific national associations. This is well illustrated by the accountancy profession in Ireland. This has been depicted by Canning and O'Dwyer (2018) as obstructing efforts by both the state and wider global forces to implement stronger regulation of its monopolistic governance and commercial freedoms. In this respect, the profession is reported to have done little to increase accountability in terms of the public interest it claimed to serve – in the face of significant professional malpractice and a weak disciplinary process. They relate that this was very apparent in the widespread frauds incriminating members of the Irish accounting profession in the late 1990s – after which the self-regulating profession failed to take proportionate disciplinary measures. Moreover, it allied with the major international professional service firms in accounting at this time in opposing further regulatory reform undermining its commercial freedom, while at the same time playing on its own expertise and ideological claims to public service.

As Canning and O'Dwyer (2018) note, an oversight body was eventually formed in response to the ensuing public outcry, paralleling the Public Company Accounting Oversight Board in the United States and the Professional Oversight Board in Britain. This body, the Irish Auditing and Accounting Supervisory Authority, was established on a statutory basis in 2005, but it only gained interventionist powers on a similar basis to its international contemporaries in 2016 after pressure from the European Union and the Irish government. Canning and O'Dwyer contend that the largely ineffectual nature of this oversight body can be explained by the specific historical, social, cultural and economic traditions of the society in which it was introduced. A significant aspect of this in Ireland was the lack of state involvement in setting up and running the oversight body, including in making appointments to the regulatory board. This was also evident in its initial legislative underpinning, which sheltered it from government intrusion. An underlying driver in neo-Weberian terms was the self-interested resistance of professional accountants themselves to preserve their own independence.

To be fair, the pursuit of professional self-interest in accountancy has at times coalesced with performing its public duty (Lee, 1995) and some contributors have argued that the scandalous behaviour exhibited by the profession is overstated and only occasional (Byrne, 2018). Indeed, even the harshest critics of accountancy accept that there has been positive reform of the profession in recent years – including in Britain and the United States – even if this is not felt to have gone far enough (Brooks, 2018). The reforms are exemplified by the changes made in Britain to the actuarial profession in the wake of the introduction of the Financial Services Authority, the predecessor of the current Financial Conduct Authority, which formally aimed to make financial markets work fairly, honestly and efficiently in relation to businesses and consumers. After conducting interviews with senior actuaries and accountants, Collins, Dewing and Russell (2009) concluded that this had saved the actuarial profession from its own failure to reform itself, at least in the short term. However, the cost to actuaries was that they have now come under the regulatory structures of the accountancy profession. In this sense, Collins and colleagues encourage us to see the actuarial profession from a neo-Weberian perspective, with its present manoeuvres forming part of a dynamic socio-historical professional project.

Finally, it should be noted that the significance of interests in the accountancy profession is also apparent at mid-tier and small-firm level, where its members can still sometimes operate to the prejudice of clients. Lander, Koene and Linssen (2013) more generally highlight the potentially adverse impact on professional identity and strategy that can arise with shifts from trustee to commercial logics. At the small-firm level meanwhile, Stringfellow and Thompson (2014), who studied local accountants in Scotland, found that they were too busy fighting amongst themselves over status and other issues to properly serve their clients. Drawing on micro-level perspectives of status sense-making, they labelled the accountants concerned as engaging in metaphorical 'crab antics' – where crabs fight each other rather than collaborating to escape from the buckets that contain them – in the struggles involved in negotiating macro and micro status hierarchies. This leads us on to further consideration of the legal profession, the history and contemporary operation of which has been more fully dealt with in neo-Weberian terms in earlier chapters of this book, albeit not always in a business context. The operation of lawyers in this context is examined as part of the selective illustration of established business-related professional groups, alongside the less prestigious and not quite so long-established case of human resource managers.

Other established professions in business: Law and human resource management

In relation to law, Brooks (2018) claims that lawyers, like accountants, are not exempt from responsibility for misdemeanours related to the financial crash and its aftermath. In his eyes, attorneys in the United

States and lawyers in Britain can scarcely be said to have always acted as pillars of society internationally in the lead up to, and fall out from, this pivotal event. This should not be too surprising given their ever-greater organisational entanglement with increasingly large corporate bodies, as discussed in Chapter 4. However, just as in the case of accountants, we should be prepared to see their activities in the round – even in the face of their severest critics – in terms of the public interest. In law this public interest orientation is most fully expressed in their growing involvement in *pro bono* work at the local level. This is positively illustrated in the United States, where uncompensated provision of legal services to poor people forms a substantial part of civil legal assistance, at a time of rising costs and shrinking federally subsidised law services in the market (Sandefur, 2007).

The focus here, though, is on the involvement of the legal profession in business. Sommerlad and Ashley (2018) highlight some of the current issues in corporate law in the Anglo-American context. Law firms in this context have typically restructured over the past few decades based on a more commercial logic, in part as a result of the need for new forms of legal regulation and financial instruments with a boom in corporate business. As Esland (1980b) points out, in the late twentieth century one of the most significant resulting growth areas has been corporation law, especially in the United States. He relates that law students henceforth had a major emphasis in their curriculum on different aspects of business law, while the legal profession even at that time had become a major servant of business and profit. In this sense, some partners felt they were losing the capacity and status of an independent legal profession – with a loss of control over their knowledge and the application of their intellectual skills compared to previous times (Smigel, 1964).

In this respect, the corporations and law firms in Wall Street and elsewhere became heavily dependent on each other – with lawyers sitting on the boards of corporations and participating in business decisions in relation to such issues as minimising tax liability, expanding forms of credit and industrial case law (Esland, 1980b). As such, the interests of lawyers could be impugned for becoming so closely intertwined with those of the profit-oriented corporations. Since then, though, lawyers have increasingly – but not totally – been squeezed out of the market for economic and financial advice by accountants (Flood, 2018). This growing marginality in the corporate world can be exemplified by the loss of the monopoly by lawyers of their previous positions of power in the big German banks, with a halving of their occupancy of management positions in the final three decades of the last century. Where lawyers do still retain influence at the highest echelons, though, they can have a real impact on business dealings, unlike the mass of insurance lawyers who practise on the ground in a divided profession in Germany (Hartmann, 1995). Brock, Leblebici and Muzio (2014) have argued that both lawyers and accountants in these positions are important economic actors, who arbitrate, regulate and support national and international exchanges in commerce.

From a gender perspective, as Sommerlad and Ashley (2018) note, female representation in the legal profession in England and Wales has laudably grown ten-fold since the mid-1980s, with almost fifty per cent of solicitors now being women – which has closely followed patterns in the United States and other modern neo-liberal societies like Australia. As they point out, accountancy has not been far behind, with one-third of British accountants being female, compared with almost twice that proportion of accountants and auditors in the United States. In law, as in accountancy, however, women are less likely to be partners in firms and more likely to be paid a lower salary, with these trends accentuated in the more prestigious corporations. Moreover, the negative effects of gender in the legal profession are further accentuated amongst black and Asian minority solicitors – who typically work in lower-status and less profitable parts of the profession. Historically, in accountancy too, ethnicity – as well as social class – may detrimentally affect women's experiences (Hayes and Jacobs, 2017). As Edgley, Sharma and Anderson-Gough (2016) argue, in the Big Four firms in accountancy, notwithstanding the increasingly emerging social media image of the diverse accountant as an aid to the recruitment of talent in Britain, the United States and Canada, there is still an attachment to traditional commercial discourses and motifs.

Following on from this, as Sommerlad and Ashley (2018) underline in law in Britain, despite the apparently more egalitarian expansion of the numbers of women lawyers – alongside those of accountants – archaic structures and discourses continue in such fields. These include patriarchal ideologies of the 'natural' role of femininity, homemaking and motherhood that are used to justify women's exclusion from positions in corporate law and other sectors of the legal profession. Such ideologies may transmit themselves to clients, as Bogoch (1997) discovered in her analysis of the influence of the control of discourse, interruptions, topic control and challenges in reinforcing the dominance of male lawyers over female users of their services. As Sommerlad and Ashley (2018) report, the resulting inequalities within the profession are not helped by two potentially discriminatory practices in elite firms in Britain in corporate law:

- the long working days in continuing to offer an infinitely responsive service to commercial players; and
- the time-honoured 'tournament' in which professionals compete for promotion, under the threat of being forced to leave the firm.

In the latter, a minimum requirement is that professionals exceed their targets in billable hours and engage in the aggressive pursuit of profits. In consequence, profits per equity partner in the corporate legal sector are reported by Muzio and Flood (2012) to have recently grown by 150 per cent over a fifteen-year period – albeit at the cost of further progress in terms of diversity.

Aside from the mainstream classical professions of law and, indeed, accountancy, there are other long-established professional groups that have not yet rivalled them in terms of importance. Personnel management can be taken as one of these, alongside areas like marketing, which is particularly growing in significance in professional service firms (Clark and Nixon, 2015). Like law and accountancy, this is also a largely female-populated profession with a glass ceiling when it comes to senior posts – as Webber (2019) has shown in Britain, where there is also a parallel lack of minority ethnic representation in the upper echelons of the profession. However, although Watson (2017) refers to the way in which personnel managers have embraced the symbolism of a profession to further their own occupational interests, this has not enabled them to insert themselves into a dominant position in the business professional pecking order. This may be a function of a profession that is more than three-quarters populated by women (Webber, 2019) in a patriarchal society – thereby mirroring the fate of the many female-dominated professions that have preceded it (Witz, 1992)

Thus, while the Institute of Personnel Management in Britain has tens of thousands of members, it has not convinced business managers that it could move centre stage despite the need to implement the ongoing spate of employment and other related legislation that has recently been enacted in this country and internationally. According to Thompson and McHugh (2009), this situation has persisted even since the title 'human resource management' was introduced into the discourse of professionalisation and the growing interest of companies in the change management agenda, which is at the heart of contemporary personnel management. As Leicht (2016b) notes, this has been paralleled in the United States where human relations management was diverted down a different path from the 1970s onwards to that followed by key corporate executives, who were increasingly drawn from financial backgrounds. Human relations personnel instead, in his eyes, were employed mainly as managers to cool out employees in the face of rising union power – having previously focused rather more on the enhancement of worker satisfaction.

This highlights the politics of work in a competitive marketplace in a neo-Weberian sense where human relations experts like industrial psychologists can be seen as the servants of capitalism (Esland, 1980a). In this sense, it is perhaps unfortunate that human resource managers have tended to be sidelined in modern societies by finance professionals. On a more positive note, Swart and Kinnie (2003) have analysed how their policies and processes can contribute to the sharing of important knowledge in organisations. More recently, they have underscored the impact of knowledge sharing through human resources in professional service firms and the development of organisational learning in a study of sixteen professional services firms in Britain and the United States, covering areas from law and management consultancy to the work of software houses and advertising agencies (Swart and Kinnie, 2010). This is reinforced by a further publication by Swart and colleagues (2014) which provides an explicit response to the question of why knowledge sharing is a positive feature of organisational life in knowledge-intensive firms and the importance of engaging commitment to this at all levels, including amongst professional themselves.

Doorewaard and Meihuizen (2000) meanwhile have shown how human resources can support resource strategies based on expertise and efficiency orientations linked to client relations, problem solving and adaptations in such firms. To further accentuate the relatively understated value of the human resources profession in national organisational contexts, Carvalho and Cabral-Cardoso (2008) have demonstrated in Portugal how such professionals achieved functional and numerical flexibility in a combined and interdependent way in management consulting firms. This is not to say, however, that there are no further issues to address. As Hearne, Metcalfe and Piekkari (2012) stress, one of the most notable of these – as in accounting and law – remains that of gender and intersectionality with areas such as ethnicity in global, transnational and national business settings. We shall now turn to look at new and emerging professions in business which have also been beset by similar issues, but have not yet attracted the same kind of critical attention in the literature in modern neo-liberal societies in general and the Anglo-American context in particular (Saks and Brock, 2018).

New and emerging professional groups

A variety of new and emerging professions have recently either joined or are potentially in the process of joining the ranks of established professional groups in business in modern neo-liberal societies. As Kipping, Bühlmann and David (2019) relate, not all – or even most – of the new professions have taken similar pathways to traditional professions or are marked by the classic neo-Weberian notion of exclusionary social closure. Instead, they have sometimes become transformed into the creatures of professional service firms which have come to dominate the professional associations concerned. These associations have in turn gradually abdicated at least part of their jurisdictional controls, including those related to qualifications and enforcement, to the firms involved, which are sometimes national and sometimes more global in scope. Although they have usually been seen as unable or unwilling to compromise on professionalising (Muzio, Hodgson and Faulconbridge, 2011), it can be argued that such occupations do indeed follow a professional strategy of sorts.

Seen through a neo-institutional lens, there are many new knowledge-intensive corporatised groups with professionalisation projects in business, of which some will be illustrated here. These certainly include executive remuneration consultants, who are drawn from a wide range of backgrounds – not least the more established professions of accountancy, law and human resource management (Adamson, Manson and Zacharia, 2015). Here there are different levels of engagement with the professionalising process – at the corporate level and amongst individuals in the field. The majority of executive consultancy firms offering such services to United Kingdom-listed companies are represented by the Remuneration Consultants Group (www.remunerationconsultantsgroup.com), which was founded in 2009. This organisation has developed a voluntary Code of Conduct setting out the role and professional standards of membership bodies. As the name suggests, the work of the consultancies in this example includes advising on executive salaries, and bonus and incentive schemes, based on external market data which are gathered to inform organisational policy at the highest level.

The move towards the professionalisation of executive remuneration consultants has been paralleled by that of executive search consultants. Here the more globalised Association of Executive Search Consultants (www.aesc.org) originally only admitted search firms, but now takes on individuals involved in this activity as members. According to Muzio, Hodgson and Faulconbridge (2011), despite rather different occupational histories, executive search consultants, along with management consultants and project managers, share the following common pattern:

- organisational membership;
- client engagement;

- competence-based closure; and
- internationalisation.

Most importantly in terms of the looser form of social closure that they typically possess in modern neo-liberal countries, such new professions are characterised by a formal knowledge base and control by professional associations, even if these are not standardised or autonomous in nature (Kipping, Bühlmann and David, 2019). However, there is variation. In some countries like Italy, for example, management consultants are even more heterogeneous and lack a strong community of peers that has impeded their professionalisation (Maestripieri, 2019). This differs even from more robust situations where management consultancy has often been seen as less successful than other occupations in developing a regulatory system because its knowledge base is too elusive, fuzzy and perishable to sustain a professional project (Muzio, Kirkpatrick and Kipping, 2011).

The case for project managers as a new corporatised profession, though, is stronger – in Britain at least. Here the Association for Project Management (www.apm.org.uk) was founded in 1972, mirroring the Project Management Institute (www.pmi.org) established three years earlier in the United States, which has a hybrid structure enabling both individual and corporate membership based on various forms of training and certification. As Wang (2019) highlights, the Association for Project Management has recently gained a Royal Charter and has subsequently created the status of Chartered Project Manager – even if there is variable buy-in to the Association in different employment sectors and it has yet to gain statutory regulation. Hodgson, Paton and Muzio (2015) note that this Association has pursued a novel professionalisation strategy by taking advantage of established sources of professional legitimacy and exploring innovative conceptions of professionalism. In this way, from a neo-institutionalist perspective, it has brought together collegial and corporate logics of professionalism (Fincham, 2006).

However, like the other new knowledge-intensive occupational groups covered here, project management can be seen to exhibit 'weak' professionalism as compared to more traditional liberal professions (Fincham, 2006). It is important nonetheless that we have some understanding of the different ways in which the parties involved – such as training bodies, the state, clients, employing organisations, and the occupations themselves – combine to influence these new professional projects (Hodgson, Paton and Muzio, 2015). To these developing professional projects could be added the case of executive coaches in what might be seen as a fledgling, rather than new, corporate profession. As

Salman (2019) observes in her study of this group in France, they are currently more likely to be drawn from self-employed, solo practitioners and freelancers – and, perhaps for this reason, have been largely neglected to date in the literature. But if none of the more localised new and emerging groups so far considered have gained statutory regulation and protection of title, some of them have even less claim to be a profession in terms of neo-Weberian social closure.

These are the aspiring occupations that derive their professional tag more from the claim to be a 'profession' based on discourse analysis than anything more substantive. These occupational groups are not underpinned by the state and may be more difficult to set apart as a profession. Maestripieri (2019) in the previously considered case of Italian management consultants saw them as primarily formed by discourses based on norms, worldviews and values defining what is required for personnel to be considered competent members of the group. Similarly loose boundaries may be found in information technology, where Alvesson (1995) discovered in his early work on a Swedish consulting firm in this area that there is a characteristically flat structure and informal culture amongst those involved. This is also reflected in more specialised fields. For example, Jensen and Kronblad (2020) examined a group of new 'legal tech' start-up personnel in Sweden at the margins of the legal profession responding to digitalisation. They found that those involved crafted and actively enacted a new identity separate to the traditional legal identity – thus undermining the previously strong and relatively homogeneous collegial position of lawyers (Empson, 2007).

This latter example from law underlines that some of the new and emerging, more localised professional fields in business may also be connected to established professions themselves. This can be illustrated further by the field of forensic accounting, which has come into being since the 1980s. As Taminiau, Heusinkveld and Cramer (2019) point out, this is now a recognised service offered not just by accounting firms, but also specialist information technology firms, law firms, research agencies and investigation agencies. Professionals involved in forensic accounting serve clients such as private companies, insurance companies and various governmental agencies. Their role is to engage in fact finding to answer key questions related to actual or potential disputes through settlement or prevention by determining the causes of cases and their financial consequences. Although occupying a small-scale niche as a professional activity at present – with, for instance, only some three hundred specialist forensic accountants in The Netherlands at the time of writing – it is a fast-growing and significant field for the future.

To this group of new and emerging professions in business need to be added the rather longer established group of economists who have become a more widespread and accepted global profession since the last century, with standards of work defined primarily in the United States in their battle to capture particular jurisdictions (Fourcade, 2006). In the recent transnational process of construction and reconstruction of the identity of economists, they seem to have moved some way ahead of engineers, who have a less clear position as a profession in the Anglo-American context. In the United States, engineers were generally replaced in the leadership of private corporations by economists and other experts in commercial knowledge in the early twentieth century (Brante, 2010). The ascendance of the economists as a profession is also reflected in a recent government study in Britain which showed that they were the second highest group of all salary-earning graduates behind medicine, with almost half as much annual income again as engineers (Belfield et al, 2018). As has been seen, while engineers have become very established in Germany, they have remained relatively marginal at the apex of corporate firms in Britain and the United States (Thompson and McHugh, 2009), despite the longstanding nature of many of the composite specialisms of engineering, such as chemical, industrial and mechanical engineering.

Nonetheless, Løwendahl (2005) has outlined the helpful customised services engineers provide, their expertise as employees and their powerful sense of professional ethics. This is accentuated by the study by Breunig, Kvålshaugen and Hydle (2014) of the Norwegian offshore oil, gas and shipping industries. Krause (1996:65), though, remans cynical about engineers in the United States where he perhaps rather harshly notes: "Professions, in theory, are supposed to have codes of ethics. Not so in engineering. One thing that engineers almost never do, given their values, is to complain when they work on projects that maximise profits through cutting back on safety." Even though it is still difficult universally to apply the concept of neo-Weberian closure to engineering in large parts of Europe and North America (Evetts, 1998), this developing area has the potential to become more important within the professionalised business sector. This has recently been highlighted by Adams (2020) in her examination of the relationship of professional engineers and managers in the context of the operation of various institutional logics in Canada. Additional support outside of neo-liberal societies is provided in both China (Kirby, 2011) and Russia (Iarskaia-Smirnova and Abramov, 2016), where – without necessarily existing as an independent professional group – engineering is of higher status and has greater influence than many other expert occupations.

Interprofessional working in business environments

Whatever the setting, as Abbott (1988) has shown, new and emerging professions may face difficulties in developing given the competing interests of established professional groups in protecting and advancing their own jurisdictions in the system of professions. As such, there are parallels in neo-Weberian terms between business and other areas less directly linked to the business field. Feyereisen and Goodrick (2019), for example, have more recently showcased the battle between schools training certified nurse anaesthetists and the medical profession in the more commercialised environment of the United States. Here the timing of a school adopting such graduate programmes was influenced by the extent to which their organisational culture supported physician dominance. This kind of superordinate/subordinate relationship is mirrored in much of the history of health care, as well as that of many other professional fields (Saks, 2015b) – including in business and management where, as has been seen, accountancy and law tend to be the dominant players.

Having discussed the national and international context of various professions and professional service firms in this chapter, there is one area which has not yet been covered in analysing the relational aspect of the power base of professions (Elston, 2004). This is that of potential collaboration between different groups of professionals in the business context. Cromwell and Gardner (2020) discuss aspects of such collaboration in the legal industry. They begin by noting the importance of collaboration in professional–client relationships given the need of professions to deepen their understanding of the business of their corporate clients. They then argue that collaborating in new teams of professionals rather than long-established teams is more likely to generate effective and innovative solutions in areas where the stakes are lower, in terms of potential financial loss. However, it seems that these effects are reversed where higher-stakes issues are concerned as teams with shared perspectives are more likely to take greater risks in providing more innovative solutions.

More challenging perhaps than intra-organisational roles is that of professionals working across the boundaries of both their own organisation and of their own discipline in business settings. This is exemplified by the case of architects working on inter-organisational construction projects in The Netherlands. Bos-de Vos, Liefunk and Lauche (2019) note that, although the professional parties involved had previously interacted in relatively stable role structures, three types of boundary work were seen as occurring:

- *reinstating*: involves emphasis and justification of current roles;
- *bending*: refers to expansion of roles within traditional role definitions; and
- *pioneering*: depicts deliberate transgression of traditional role boundaries.

They argue that each of these responses could be seen as a defensive reaction to the threat of professional marginalisation. Architects also either incrementally or radically changed professional role structures, with greater or lesser effects for ongoing project collaboration. All the responses are seen to be aimed – for better or worse – at creating, shaping and disrupting boundaries that distinguish the work of a professional group from that carried out by others. The categories employed clearly have broader applicability to other settings in examining interprofessional interaction in the business world.

The tensions involved do not mean there are no benefits of collaborations across boundaries. Inter-organisational and interprofessional collaboration has been identified by Noordegraaf (2020) as being valuable moving forward in the modern age. He claims that protective professionalism and the isolationism of professional groups is a thing of the past in business and other contexts in contemporary societies. To overcome the effects of fragmentation, he believes that it is increasingly necessary to interlink professional fields. This may, however, be an optimistic vision in practice in business-related fields. At one remove, in neo-Weberian fashion, the self-interests of particular professions may come into play where there are competing interests involved (Saks, 2016b). These may unhelpfully impede or prevent new or emerging professions from entering the picture, as well as create rivalries between established professions. At another, conflicts are particularly likely to be accentuated between professional groups in a business environment where there is competition between private for-profit firms in the marketplace (Thompson and McHugh, 2009), whether in a local, national or international context (Flood, 2018). Such rivalry is exemplified by the growth of management information services, which has become a professional battleground – not least between accounting firms and consulting services (Abbott, 1988).

Conclusion

In Chapter 5, therefore, in overviewing social, political and economic dynamics at a variety of levels in a more entrepreneurial world, we have now developed an understanding that professions are indeed a key idea in business, as well as the wider society. As noted at the outset of this chapter, we have considered from a mainly neo-institutionalist perspective the role of international professional service firms in the business context. The growth of such professional service firms has been a game changer in scaling up of the analysis of professional activity over the past two or three decades. However, we have also considered their interrelationship with professions in the national and local business environment. In this latter setting we have examined from a largely neo-Weberian framework the position of management as a profession, as well as a number of established and more traditional professions involved in the commercial sector in modern neo-liberal countries. We then discussed the development of an illustrative range of various new and emerging business-related professions, more or less loosely related to the concept of social closure. The interplay between such established and other evolving professional groups was finally explored – including the role that collaboration may play going forward in business settings. This is a good jumping off point into the final chapter, where we shall consider the future of professions in the Anglo-American context in particular and in modern neo-liberal societies in general.

6 Conclusion
The future of professions

Introduction

We have now moved from debating the meaning of professions in Chapter 1 to tracing their history in Chapter 2, discussing the theories related to professional groups in Chapter 3, considering the implications of the recent attacks on them in Chapter 4 to examining their particular relevance to business and management in Chapter 5. The final overarching question addressed in the concluding Chapter 6 is that of whether professions have a future – and, if so, in what form. As we shall see in this chapter, there are many opinions on this by academics and the public alike. At one end of the spectrum, some feel that professions are no longer a fit object of study for social scientists in terms of where the lens of the academic microscope might most beneficially focus in advancing our understanding. Building on the critique of professional groups over the past few decades outlined in Chapter 4, still others believe that professional social closure regimes should be dissolved further in the interests of the wider public. We shall initially explore these radical views which signal the demise of professions and examine their potential implications. However, it is argued in this book that the study of professions is still of vital importance and their role has by no means diminished in neo-liberal societies in late modernity, even if the nature of professionalism is necessarily changing.

In this vein, this chapter focuses on the positive part such groups can play in the future – albeit with adjustment to the shifting circumstances of twenty-first-century neo-liberal societies. Given variations in professional practice, this may involve reforms in the arrangements for particular professions and professional service firms internationally and/or in the specific countries in which they operate. This chapter illustrates possible specific shifts in selected mainstream professions, as well as considering what generic role professions might take in the years ahead in light of technological and other changes – including the increasing application of artificial intelligence. Some have argued in this context that professions should become risk managers or trusted interpreters of information. There is certainly scope too for professions to shed some of their less-desirable characteristics – which includes the neo-Weberian identification of the pursuit of self-interests at the expense of both clients and the common good. In this respect, it is argued that professions should not abandon their most precious asset as embedded in earlier taxonomic approaches of providing a more altruistic orientation in engaging in responsible leadership.

Professions RIP?

We begin with the question as to whether professions are a dying species in terms of the intellectual attention that we give them. Some contributors bemusingly seem to not see the critical issue of the changing role of professions as important in considering the future of work – Simms (2019), for instance, does not include professions at all as a topic in her occupational future casting. It is also extraordinary that this question does not appear anywhere in the agenda of a number of textbooks on business and management, as illustrated by Brooks (2009). Indeed, in the book by Wilson (2004) on *Organizational Behaviour and Work* there is no headline entry on Professions in the Index, but there are six sub-headed entries under the category of Prostitution, one of which relates to professionalism as a form of paid work – where it is controversially argued that the experience of prostitutes parallels that of flight attendants in using their face/body to garner such employment. In the more serious academic examinations of professions, though, it has been suggested by some writers in the United States like Gorman and Sandefur (2011) that the conceptual and theoretical frame of reference in the social sciences should now be concentrated on the use of knowledge and expertise rather than professional groups *per se*. This warrants more focused attention.

This latter view has been especially sharpened by the growing corporatisation of many American professions. Adams (2015), however, does not agree with Gorman and Sandefur (2011), suggesting that it rests on a narrow interpretation of research on professions from a myopic geographical perspective. This is not of course to say that the proposed new academic work stream related to knowledge and expertise should be neglected – as exemplified by the broader analyses by Eyal (2013) of expertise and by Anteby, Chan and DiBenigno (2016) of occupational becoming, doing and relating in organisations. However, while Adams (2015) acknowledges the increasing complexity surrounding professional groups, she also notes their long historical heritage in the literature on both sides of the Atlantic and the ongoing high-impact involvement of self-regulating professions in organisational and societal settings. To be sure, as seen in previous chapters, there has been an increasing shift away from the classic neo-Weberian national statutory self-regulatory professional model of the past in many modern neo-liberal countries towards voluntary self-regulation, independent meta-regulation, and international professional service firms. Nonetheless, this can be encompassed within a neo-Weberian approach and makes the field of professions more rather than less interesting. Hence the expanding, rather than contracting, interest in professional groups in countries from Britain to Canada and beyond is perfectly understandable – especially given the crucial role of professions in global economic development (Brock, Leblebici and Muzio, 2014).

In terms of the academic literature, it should also be stressed that views about the future of the professions will depend very much on the theoretical perspective adopted. As has been seen, for example, some Marxist writers believe that the privileged independent professions of the 1960s and 1970s will become proletarianised with the development of the labour process under capitalism (Braverman, 1998). This process of proletarianisation can be seen to have been carried through in societies with a socialist heritage like Russia and China, where even occupational groups like doctors put on a pedestal elsewhere can generally no longer lay claim to either independence or indeed high socio-economic rewards (Saks, 2015e). As noted in Chapter 4, neo-Weberians like Haug (1973) have also put forward the parallel idea that there may be deprofessionalisation – especially given Weber's own thoughts about progressive disenchantment in industrial societies with the increasing grip of the iron cage of bureaucracy (Parkin, 1982). This neo-Weberian standpoint, alongside the Marxist perspective, as noted in Chapter 3, contrasts with the earlier approach of functionalists like Goode (1960) – to whom we shall return – who see autonomous professionals with high income, status and power as integral to meeting collective needs in modern societies which point to a brighter future for professions.

This poses the question that has occasionally been raised, particularly in the wake of the counter-cultural critique, of what the world would look like without professional groups. Here, as Adams (2017) observes, there has been little in-depth assessment of alternatives to a professionalised world, which, as noted in Chapter 2, has only relatively recently come into existence in the wider sweep of history. She therefore asks whether greater government or corporate regulation would be more efficient, effective and fair. Moreover, if global professional service firms are taking care of their clients, who is protecting the wider public? She then goes on to ask, while self-regulation has been perceived to be flawed in execution, whether it does not have some benefits. The answers to these questions are very material here and were once directly posed to me by a national government I was advising which had become frustrated by the poor performance of a particular elite professional group – and was considering its complete dissolution. The state, after all, as seen in Chapter 3, plays a key role in underwriting professional monopolies from a neo-Weberian perspective and the sanctioning and legitimation of such monopolies need to be justified.

As Saks (2015c) notes, there may be advantages in going back to what may be metaphorically labelled 'the law of the jungle' based on extensive professional de-regulation, including:

- cheapening further the cost of services through more open competition;
- making enrolment and entry to particular occupations easier with the removal of monopolies;
- reducing central state intervention and allowing greater scope for innovation;
- giving more credence to current non-professional staff in the division of labour; and
- providing more direct consumer control of services received.

However, the negative side of de-regulating professions in this way is that it may lead to a dystopian world in which there are no checks and balances in following through the dominant market-based economic logic (Leicht, 2016a). As Saks (2015c) points out, in such a future there may therefore be:

- risks to the consumer without the protection of certified expertise and codes of ethics;
- the widespread prevalence of *caveat emptor* – let the buyer beware;
- financial issues related to the loss of subscriptions to professions as regulatory bodies;
- the lack of a buffer between consumers and the state in representing the public interest; and
- increased bureaucracy in running the system of unregulated occupational groups.

The unruliness of what may result through the formal deconstruction of the professions is clearly highlighted by the vision presented by one of the thought leaders of the counter culture, Ivan Illich (1971). He argues that the new post-professional world that arises from the counterproductive consequences of so-called industrial progress should be based creatively on decentralised 'learning webs', supported by advanced technology. The process of computer-based peer matching would bring together in a de-institutionalised way those who wished to learn about any particular subject – from playing the guitar or speaking languages to conducting different forms of surgery – with others who claimed the skills and expertise to facilitate this. The dynamic that would drive the learning web is the allocation to individuals of a finite number of educational credits which would be surrendered and gained in the process of learning exchange. Illich claims that there would be three main advantages to this novel system:

- Access to available resources whenever individuals desire to learn.
- Empowerment of those who wish to share their knowledge with learners.
- Providing anyone who wants to learn a subject with the opportunity to do so.

However, aside from the contestable and optimistic presumption by Illich (1971) that individuals are self-motivated to learn, there are many difficulties with such a system in attempting to invert industrial growth. For instance, what guarantees are there that there will be sufficient numbers of skilled personnel in particular specialisms in areas like health and finance? Can we assume that the public will be sufficiently knowledgeable to choose appropriate leads for learning? What about considerations of public health and safety in this process? The emergence of the post-professional model in the work of Illich (1973b) is also based on questionable assumptions. It is felt rather naively that it would be brought about by a mass public fervour for change, without clear specification of the precise mechanisms involved. The new society, moreover, would evidently be situated idyllically in small-scale village settings, unfit for modern living – and more suited to rural life in less developed countries. In sum, therefore, while Illich puts forward some stimulating ideas, overturning the professional universe completely as he proposes is not a realistic option. We turn now therefore to examine the prospects for the productive future reform of professionalism in the public interest in modern neo-liberal societies. This analysis of the future begins with a headline analysis of the rationale for the specific reform of three individual professions that have figured prominently in this volume.

The future reform of specific professions

Law

The case for reforming law can be well illustrated in the Anglo-American context. In Britain, as Bargate (2014) has noted, there are ongoing debates about whether the legal profession should continue to be divided into solicitors and barristers in the future or become a fused professional group. In practice, barristers can now conduct litigation, previously the traditional role of solicitors, while solicitors are able to conduct advocacy in the higher courts. Despite the longstanding self-interested protectionism of barristers in defending their historic privileges against solicitors, the two branches are already growing closer together. Bargate therefore believes that there are arguments that a completely conjoined profession may be more in the public interest – not least because:

- It would help in offering a one-stop shop for the public.
- Extra costs for clients are imposed by needless duplication.
- It would facilitate nurturing advocacy talent from a wider pool.

While the legal profession is more seamless in the United States – notwithstanding the split between lawyers serving individual clients from poorer backgrounds and corporate lawyers (Krause, 1996) – this is not to say that a separation of powers in Britain has been without justification historically, including when barristers were specialist advocates and solicitors prepared cases. Further debate about a fused profession in a shifting division of labour would therefore be most helpful.

There are many other key issues with which the legal profession in Britain is grappling, as it looks forward in a period of extremely rapid change. As Sommerlad and colleagues (2015) outline from an explicitly neo-Weberian platform, thinking about these has been prompted by a series of recent regulatory and legislative reforms to the control and ordering of the legal profession in Britain; at a time when it no longer has full powers of self-regulation, it has become subject to an independent legal complaints scheme, and has been opened up to greater competition with non-lawyer providers of legal services. Such issues encompass, as for other mainstream professions in a more global context, how measures to address gender and ethnic diversity can be extended. They also include how lawyers can best:

- meet the needs of poorer constituencies in relation to legal aid;
- devolve legal practice more extensively to unqualified law workers;
- overcome the doctrinal and overly traditional law curriculum;
- include in training more social awareness, commercial and managerial skills; and
- ensure appropriate regulation for international professional service law firms.

What is clearly sought in future – in the face of regulatory, financial and organisational challenges (King, 2015) – is a profession, divided or otherwise, that moderates the dominance of the market and enables lawyers to provide a more open and responsive, high-quality service to all sections of society, educating solicitors and barristers along the way.

Abel (2015) stresses that in so doing, in neo-Weberian terms, the legal profession must be less exploitative of its continuing market shelters and more resistant to wider trends in marketisation. He argues that following the market in the United States in trading off the quality of legal services for lower prices has not helped consumers. In his view, it has led to more poorly paid attorneys in more insecure working conditions. This has rippled through to the fast-rising numbers of graduates who are more likely to be unemployed, have lower starting salaries, law firm layoffs and spiralling educational indebtedness – especially as competition has grown from other professions such as accountancy. All this has disproportionately affected marginalised groups and, as Sommerlad and colleagues (2015) point out, is an easily recognisable picture – albeit in less extreme terms – in Britain too. For the future in the United States, therefore, Abel (2015) calls for, amongst other things:

- a clearer assessment of how many lawyers are needed;
- a more attuned university experience in relation to legal practice;
- more attention to be paid to legal careers for graduates;
- greater equalisation in the distribution of legal services; and
- more ethical behaviour by lawyers in terms of individual misconduct.

The latter will require fuller support from the firms in which legal representatives are employed and the regulators as regards disciplinary action.

Susskind (2017) in his book *Tomorrow's Lawyers* has also given more grounded consideration to the future of the legal profession, beyond wigs, wood-panelled courtrooms and leather-bound tomes. He believes that lawyers will need to work differently in the years ahead, driven by the more-for-less challenge, liberalisation and ever-advancing technology – and facilitated by strategies of efficiency and collaboration, in which clients will increasingly share costs collectively. He claims this would move lawyers towards commoditised, as opposed to bespoke, legal services that will involve working differently. This would include the decomposition and alternative sourcing of tasks, as well as taking on board disruptive legal technologies from document automation to online legal guidance and dispute resolution. Susskind believes this will lead over the next two decades to a new world of change for law firms and in-house legal departments encompassing online courts and global legal businesses based on artificial intelligence. This is in line with more recent analyses, such as that of Armour and Sako (2020) who examine the implications of artificial intelligence for next-generation legal services – even if they highlight that some, but not all, such tasks may still be best carried out through human agency, with the potential for hybridisation of traditional and new business models. As set out in Table 6.1, forward movement for lawyers may well result in a shift in the current legal paradigm.

Table 6.1 Charting the future: The shifting paradigm of the legal profession

Today's legal paradigm	*Tomorrow's legal paradigm*
Legal Service	**Legal Service**
Advisory service	Information service
One-to-one	One-to-many
Reactive service	Proactive service
Time-based billing	Commodity pricing
Restrictive	Empowering
Defensive	Pragmatic
Legal focus	Business focus
Legal Process	**Legal Process**
Legal problem solving	Legal risk management
Dispute resolution	Dispute pre-emption
Publication of law	Promulgation of law
A dedicated legal profession	Legal specialists and information engineers
Print-based	IT-based legal systems

Source: Susskind, R. (2017) *Tomorrow's Lawyers*, 2nd edition, Oxford: Oxford University Press, p. 124.

Such future forecasting may lead to a number of new roles for the next generation of lawyers. As Susskind (2017) argues, the new roles that may emerge are for flexible, open-minded and entrepreneurial lawyers who can adapt to changing market conditions, They are exemplified by, *inter alia*, the expert trusted adviser; the enhanced practitioner; the legal knowledge engineer; the legal technologist; the legal hybrid; the legal process analyst; the legal project manager; the legal data scientist; the research and development worker; the legal management consultant; and the legal risk manager. He argues that such personnel may be employed in an expanding range of businesses from legal tech companies, legal management consultancies and online legal service providers to legal know-how providers, legal process outsourcers and legal leasing agencies making freelance lawyers available to clients. This range will of course also include the now established global law and accounting firms already considered in this volume. In turn, as Susskind points out, law schools will have to adapt their curriculum – to provide education and training through e-learning and other means in twenty-first-century legal skills, rather than simply being 'at the cutting edge of tradition'. This case highlights the multiple dimensions that need to be addressed in any crystal ball gazing over the future of the legal profession in the Anglo-American context and other modern neo-liberal societies.

Accountancy

Similar comments may be made in Britain and beyond about the future of accountancy – an established business profession discussed alongside that of law in the last chapter. In dealing with audit and tax requirements, Susskind and Susskind (2015) believe that accountants will be challenged too by the advent of newer forms of technology – not only with the increasing use of online tax returns, but also with online accounting software. As tax and audit activities become increasingly computerised, rather than paper-based, this may bring closer the day of saturation testing, as opposed to simply sampling a limited array of items in the required documentation. As in law, these changes will have implications for the way jobs are constructed both in smaller companies and Big Four accounting firms. A shrinkage of employment seems very likely at a time when Pitter (2018) estimates that robotics will eliminate some 40 per cent of basic accounting tasks, since these will be conducted more efficiently than by humans. Against this, as Pitter points out, more specialised and higher-level skills in employment roles will be needed on both sides of the Atlantic in areas from data analytics to cybertechnology to support this process.

Conway (2018) more expansively notes that, in terms of reform, accountants will need to be more customer facing in future, with enhanced collaborative, critical thinking and interpersonal skills. As such, crunching numbers will no longer be enough for them going forward – as accountants take on more advisory and consultancy work in contrast to compliance and audit activities. The latter tasks will become relatively low cost, at the same time as repetitive jobs like invoice processing and bank reconciliations are computerised. Faulconbridge, Sarwar and Spring (2020) observe that, from a neo-Weberian viewpoint, this will involve more multi-dimensional, intra-organisational boundary work for accountants, as well as lawyers, if they are to adapt to the novel opportunities and challenges associated with artificial intelligence. Conway (2018) also believes accountants will have to improve their communication skills, promote diversity to a greater extent, exhibit greater transparency, and be more responsive to a broader range of stakeholders in a world of scarce natural resources, rising population and increasing reports of tax avoidance and money laundering on a global scale.

This interpretation of the future is also underlined by Brooks (2018) in the wake of his scathing attack on accountants for their role in the public scandals associated with the bankruptcy of Enron in the United States and the world economic crisis from 2008 onwards, as outlined in Chapter 5. In relation to accountants, Brooks (2018:285) argues that "when they are objective and brave, they protect the world for the better. When they are biased or weak, catastrophe soon follows." He claims that forward movement to avoid further impending worldwide difficulties will require the specific steps below to be implemented to protect the integrity of accountancy in late modernity:

- The separation of accounting and consulting.
- High-standard public auditing of major institutions.
- Greater financial accountability of accountants.
- Regular rotation between auditors and clients.
- More openness about consultancy contracts and other matters.
- Independent regulation of the accountancy profession.

The latter requirement chimes well with the critique by Canning and O'Dwyer (2018) in Chapter 5 of the resistance of the self-regulating accountancy profession in Ireland to positive reform of the regulatory process, in the face of significant malpractice and a weak disciplinary process. They argue from a neo-Weberian and neo-institutionalist perspective in light of the Irish experience that the following generalisable actions should be taken to transition from a delegatory self-regulatory logic to an enhanced public governance logic in accountancy in the context of competing institutional logics:

- Initiating institutional change in governance and disrupting a self-regulatory regime.
- Establishing the structures to realise shifts in governance to a public oversight regime.
- Countering professional efforts at logic assimilation, as a strategy of resistance.
- Coercion in conducting institutional maintenance work to address professional resistance.
- Inserting global shifts in accountancy regulation into the more localised national level.

Canning and O'Dwyer claim that this reform requires engagement with multiple constituencies and not just the more obvious confrontation between the accountancy profession and the state. If such a transformation can be achieved, it is felt that it will lead to brighter future for all concerned.

Medicine

In medicine – on which this volume has also heavily focused in modern neo-liberal societies like Britain and the United States – there are again parallel considerations. Susskind and Susskind (2015) note that this is one of the sectors where the public now has access to most information on the internet, through such sites as NHS Choices and WebMD. In addition, users are now able to sift through databases of doctors, sometimes with review ratings. Offline, there are also computerised diagnostic systems based on scans that not only diagnose, but also recommend treatment plans. Further, physicians – particularly in the United States – now commonly use a digital drug-referencing app that computerises the previously time-consuming task of understanding drug interactions. Medical searches are now available as well to scan tens of thousands of articles in the medical literature for the most appropriate interventions for specific conditions. New technology is very important too in keeping up with developments in medicine such as stem cell science and analysing the human genome. This is in addition to simpler online appointment systems, text messaging to remind people of the time of their visit, and 3-D printing of medical parts, such as artificial limbs and crowns in dentistry. Such innovations in digitalised health care now have swept the globe – certainly in more developed parts of the world, including China (Milcent, 2018).

So, where might the technological revolution take the medical profession in the future? In terms of reform, part of this may involve rolling out the technologies that we already have still further. For one thing, as Susskind and Susskind (2015) point out, there may be an extension of telemedicine whereby health data are fed back electronically to doctors so that remote monitoring and diagnosis may occur around the clock. Alternatively, such data may be used to further assist the process of user self-help, which – aside from possibly forming part of the washback against medical hegemony discussed in Chapter 4 – is likely to become ever more significant in official campaigns based on measures like diet and exercise to combat major health hazards like obesity (Baggott, 2011). Central to this process, as Roberts, Mackenzie and Mort (2019:1) note, is the concept of biosensing, which "uses information technology to understand something about bodies or the environment in which they live, whether the technology is at the cutting edge or not." The applications of biosensing may involve everything from counting the number of steps taken in exercise regimes through Fitbit technology to measuring blood sugar in diabetes through smart meters. Into this equation too comes the mass testing and tracing arrangements that are being implemented worldwide in combatting the Covid-19 pandemic.

Critical in all this is not just future technology *per se*, but – most importantly – the politics of the medical profession and its relationship to clients and other professional groups. As recent history has shown, the balance of interests involved within the neo-Weberian perspective may shape how far physicians are prepared to devolve authority to either users or other health professions such as nurses (Saks, 2015e). In Britain, the regulation of the medical profession, as seen in Chapter 4, has come under much sharper and more independent scrutiny from the state acting on behalf of citizens. There has also been a revolution in medical education in this country arising from the publication by the General Medical Council (2009:14) of *Tomorrow's Doctors*, which aims to ensure that "graduates will make the care of patients their first concern, applying their knowledge and skills in a competent and ethical manner and using their ability to provide leadership and to analyse complex and uncertain situations." These regulatory and educational shifts have generated more optimism about the role that doctors may play in the future, although, as Roche (2018) notes, the challenge is to bring the medical profession more fully on board in the journey to achieve greater openness and accountability – in what, as far as medicine is concerned, may still be a patriarchal society (Witz, 1992) that is also imbued with racial inequalities (Byrne et al, 2020). Otherwise, as in other modern neo-liberal societies like Australia, which has also recently engaged in medical regulatory reform (Short, 2018), there are dangers that elements of the profession will continue to ride the political storms and find other ways of ensuring that their interests continue to prevail, sometimes to the prejudice of the broader public.

However, the context in which the medical profession operates in Britain, as highlighted earlier, is rather different from the United States where there is a much stronger stress on the market in delivering health care. This means that – notwithstanding medical reforms such as Medicare and Medicaid – physicians are working in a relatively uncoordinated, corporatised system with far greater duplication and inequality in health care. The consequence of this is that the United States, with the costliest and most technologically advanced health system in the world, languishes well down the league table of mortality and morbidity in modern societies (Saks, 2015e). Even with such mitigatory effects as Obamacare, this constrains what it is possible for doctors to achieve as a profession in the future in a society with considerable scope for advancing the position of women in medicine (Levin, 2002) and dealing with institutional racism (Gordon-Reed, 2020). As Horowitz (2018) comments, despite state-wide social closure through licensure which allowed the American medical profession to create its own regulatory organisations in hospitals and an ever-wider range of specialisms, the United States is a libertarian and consumerist country which has stymied the kind of medical reform that has occurred in Britain. She is therefore not optimistic about how far there can be a shining future for physicians in the United States given the constraining socio-political context – even if self-interests are overcome and a greater premium is placed on providing better services to clients and the wider public. As Adams (2017) says, any reform will therefore be more gradual, on a region-by-region basis.

The generic reform of the professions

Compelling as these specific examples of reform of individual professional groups may be, though, this book is more focused on narratives about the generic future of professions, rather than speculation about how specific cases of this more powerful and prestigious cluster of occupations are likely to develop in particular socio-political settings. Some indications of what future reforms are necessary in modern neo-liberal societies have already been apparent in the book so far – from enhanced regulatory steps to combat the excesses of international professional service firms and more nationally based professions to the imperative to more forcefully to address gender, ethnic, social-class and other inequalities in the agenda of such groups. These reforms must occur inside and outside professional boundaries to enhance the life chances of both practitioners themselves, their clients and citizens.

What will be central to the general future of professional groups is also the reform of the higher education system that underpins the development of modern professions. Here there will need to be more emphasis on the expansion of online learning courses for professional qualifications – as has been very much in evidence with the global response of universities to the challenge of social distancing associated with the threat of Covid-19 (Saks, 2020a). This will certainly also have to be married to innovative approaches to learning landscapes based on classroom redesign in the more blended forms of learning that evolve (Bell, Stevenson and Neary, 2009). Linked to this, there should be greater opportunities for exploring the role of the student as producer, as opposed to simply a consumer, in the higher education process. This can be traced back to a long-running debate in Britain and the wider European context about how we define the nature and purpose of a university in an era of increased marketisation (Frank, Gowar and Naef, 2019). As Brint (2018) underlines, this is a discussion in which institutions in the United States are also strongly involved in the face of sometimes conflictual intellectual, market and technological logics in a heavily business-driven environment.

A generic view about the future of the professions has most recently been presented by Noordegraaf (2020), who argues, as we have seen in Chapter 5, that the traditional portrayal of professionals as working protectively within well-defined jurisdictional silos has increasing shortcomings. Noordegraaf claims that professions can no longer isolate themselves from outsiders given:

- the heterogeneity and fragmentation of professional fields;
- the increasing interweaving of these fields; and
- dependencies on actors in the external world.

Rather than seeing this as representing a decline or hollowing out of professionalism, he claims that professions are on the positive path to reconfiguration. In this reconstruction, professional and organisational logics within a neo-institutionalist perspective are held to come together and result in professional identities and actions becoming more connected. At the same time, professions are seen as remaining knowledgeable, autonomous and authoritative in a relational universe of clients, managers and others. However, although some of the trends he documents may be occurring in the Anglo-American context, he falls into the trap of abstracting his analysis from any kind of socio-political context – despite countries like China and Russia beyond the neo-liberal context completely casting aside the notion of independent professionalism (Adams et al, 2020). Significantly too Noordegraaf warns against a return to traditional professional values linked to responsible leadership in his idealised future landscape – instead simply arguing for a redefinition of other elements of professionalism as we know it.

In addition to their comments on specific professional groups, Susskind and Susskind (2015) consider the future of professions more generally, with a stress on the impact of technological change. This is especially so in relation to artificial intelligence, which they believe may influence both the way professional work is carried out and the extent to which consumers are empowered *vis-à-vis* the professions. While their analysis examines the already considered professions of law, accountancy and medicine, it also covers other professional groups from architects to teachers in the Anglo-American context. They argue that shifts are already occurring in such areas as how professions store and communicate information, which have clear implications for the sharing of expertise. Lester (2020) suggests that the main impact on the professions of what has been termed as the 'Fourth Industrial Revolution' (Skilton and Hovsepian, 2018) will be occupational transformation rather than the loss of jobs, with more disruptive consequences likely for lower-order occupations. In this respect, Lester (2020) believes that the analysis by Susskind and Susskind (2015) overstates the effects of technological change on professional groups by emphasising too strongly the technical-rational, rather than the creative and interpretative, nature of their work. As such, they underestimate the opportunities for professions in the future – a point underlined by Pettersen (2019) who stresses that artificial intelligence cannot overtake the human element of complex knowledge work without universal rules and solutions.

Moreover, although Susskind and Susskind (2015) acknowledge that one of the classical characteristics of professions is their common set of values including honesty, trustworthiness and a commitment to serving others, this is not strongly followed through in their examination of prospective roles – not least in terms of responsible leadership. Instead, they focus rather one-sidedly on the widespread medium and long-term application of new technologies in the professions, in relation to which their response needs to be nimble. They argue that the application of these ranges from the use of CAD software in design by architects to consultations by video conferencing in appointments for clients with doctors and lawyers. The latter arrangements are already massively increasing in the wake of Covid-19 and are likely to become even more institutionalised in future. They contend that this will be complemented by the employment of intelligent systems performing tasks at or beyond the level of experts. Susskind and Susskind also consider in parallel a variety of other professional templates for the future, from the traditional approach where professionals work alone in silo-based, face-to-face situations to the more stretching networked expert and communities of experience models with greater lateral online connectivity – which are extending nationally and globally with the Covid-19 pandemic.

In a similar way, Flood (2018), while embracing the need for ongoing adaptive changes to Anglo-American professions which appeal to both practitioners and users, underlines the importance of the increased use of technology for the future of professional groups. He argues that this is likely to result in the growing empowerment of, and partnership with, consumers in a new age where greater professional creativity will be needed. Leicht (2018), however, places more emphasis in his neo-Weberian approach on the socio-political context in which professions operate in neo-liberal societies – namely, that of capitalism. While agreeing with the previous authors about the current critical climate that professions are facing and the need for change, he addresses the two major challenges to their authority, as identified in Chapter 4. These are the postmodern war on expertise in opposition to grand scientific narratives, which subverts the quest for collective justice under capitalism through knowledge-based professionalism, and neo-liberal ideologies promoting consumer determination and price competition in the market at the expense of professional judgements as to what is right.

Leicht (2018) believes that professions must counter these twin critiques by adopting at least three main roles in modern neo-liberal societies:

- risk managers in a risk society in which professionals mediate in an impersonal, rational, scientific and technologically infused world;
- trusted interpreters of information where professionals help people sift through the mass of information on social media, and distinguish good from bad; and
- promoters of positive institutional change, particularly in the business contexts in which they are often employed.

In addition, and most pertinently in this context, Leicht sees future professions as playing a fourth key role in bringing values and ideology to clients, policy makers and the public. These values are not well defined by Leicht, but – of all the contributors considered in this chapter – this aspect of his work is closest to the view of the author of this book about the responsible leadership role that professions centrally need to fulfil in the future. It is highly resonant with that of Flood (2018) who rightly identifies reinvigorating client and public trust in relationships with professions as a mainstream aspect of reform going forward.

Responsible leadership and the professions

As Saks (2020b) observes, the role of professions in engaging in responsible leadership is critical for their future at two levels. The first is as a characteristic of the part to be played by professions and a descriptor of a mainstream element of what professional services might look like in the years ahead. The second, and most important in this context, is as a feature of professions that is fundamental to making the transition to an adaptive and functional future world, with professional groups at its heart – supported by clients, citizens, governments and corporate bodies in the private and public sector. We must initially, though, give some greater indication of what is meant by the generic concept of responsible leadership – which it is increasingly fashionable to promote, but not always as easy to define.

The concept of responsible leadership

Kempster and Carroll (2016) note that, while the area of leadership is very well studied, the notion of responsible leadership has been relatively rarely examined. It has largely grown out of the work of writers on corporate social responsibility who felt that the importance of the big challenges facing the world were being subordinated to narrower issues of organisational performance (Hopkins, 2016). Here Brès and his colleagues (2019) have recently identified that there needs to be a generative dialogue between professions and advocates of corporate responsibility given the synergies between their ideas about normative goals and collaborative practice. In terms of responsible leadership in the professions in the private and public sector, this might be seen as moving away from the qualities, abilities and effectiveness of the individual leader towards an emphasis on the purpose, responsibilities and activities of leading figures in realising value for a wide range of stakeholders (Kempster, Maak and Parry, 2020).

However, as Kempster and Carroll (2016) point out, the ensuing concept of responsible leadership is not straightforward; it lies between romanticism and realism – raising further questions such as who is responsible and to what end. They argue that the ten key facets of responsible leadership can be summarised as follows:

- Attention and commitment are given to social responsibility.
- Applicability at all levels, from the individual to the team, organisation and society.
- Goes beyond a shareholder focus in taking a stakeholder perspective.
- Relies on ethical assumptions of a duty to do no harm and do good.
- Sensitive to global intercultural issues, citizens and cosmopolitanism.
- Has a broad outcome orientation including, but going beyond, humanitarianism.
- Engages with sense-making and sense-giving, based on questions of purpose.
- Centred on shared opinions, connecting stakeholders together.
- Focused on the use of resources, identifying where and when disruption is necessary.
- Takes a long-term stakeholder view, rather than a short-term shareholder perspective.

This helpful list stands in a still relatively small, but growing, span of literature on responsible leadership from new rules for global justice (Scholte, Fioramonti and Nhema, 2016) to ethical decision making (Savur and Sandhu, 2017).

Although the particular configuration and the specifics of the constituent elements of responsible leadership can be debated, Kempster and Carroll (2016) provide a useful working framework for considering its future role in the professions. This approach has been further elaborated by Kempster, Maak and Parry (2020) who argue that, in the business world, ambition should stretch beyond seeking to generate financial dividends and aim to produce a broader span of sustainable 'good dividends' enhancing society. These ambitions may not of course be entirely separate, as is clearly indicated by statistical research by Grant Thornton (2019) on the performance of FTSE 350 companies both generally and by sector. Their detailed longitudinal study shows that companies with stronger corporate governance generate more financial value for shareholders and lenders and that the adoption of more responsible leadership should not simply be seen as a ritualistic compliance exercise. This is reinforced by Stangis and Smith (2017) who underline how corporate citizenship in the twenty-first century builds reputation and delivers to the bottom line. The corollary of this is that it makes sense for organisations to make societal purpose part of their business model, based on the wider use of various forms of capital and not just of the financial kind (Kempster, Maak and Parry, 2020) – with all the implications that this has for professions working in institutional and organisational environments in the private and public sector.

The application of the concept of responsible leadership to the professions

In applying the concept of responsible leadership to the professions, the definition set out by Kempster and Carroll (2016) needs to be stiffened and globalised as it is in the work of Kempster, Maak and Parry (2020). In this latter regard, it encompasses the Sustainable Development Goals of the United Nations (2015). These range from combatting poverty and inequality to enhancing the environment and reversing climate change. If anything, such objectives have been accentuated by the Covid-19 pandemic, which involves directly addressing not only the medical issues raised in the global health crisis, but also the no less important question of putting the economy and financial markets on an upward course in the common good. This harmonises with the views of Spence, Voulgaris and Maclean (2017) who stress that professional groups should take politics more seriously, including by showing how their expertise can contribute to the public interest. It also resonates with the ideas of Greenwood, Hinings and Prakash (2017) who argue that the social purpose of professions has been much neglected in the past and needs to be more fully considered in business settings. Within this framework – promoted by the United Nations-endorsed Institute for Responsible Leadership (www.responsible-leadership.org) – professions in the future will need to work in a more interdisciplinary and collaborative manner in sustainably transitioning to the new world.

However, the wider collectivity ethos that they will need to embrace is not new in modern neo-liberal societies such as Britain and the United States. Professional groups have for long had a broader ideological commitment to the public interest, as well as a client orientation, built into their codes of ethics (Saks, 1995). This, indeed, was a major component of the earlier trait conceptions of the professions explored in Chapter 3 of this volume which sought to define the key characteristics of professions (as illustrated by Hickson and Thomas, 1969). As will be recalled, this approach was overtaken by the more sophisticated functionalist theory of professions – based on a trade-off between the ethical and public-interested control by professions of esoteric knowledge of great importance to society and the high income and other rewards reciprocally received by such groups (as exemplified by Barber, 1963). While this sugar-coated view of professional groups, reflecting the ideologies of professions themselves, justly came in for further criticism in terms of its translation into practice (Johnson, 2016), it embodies the notion of responsible leadership in the professions that should be both applied and developed further.

As discussed at the outset of this chapter, those coming from different theoretical perspectives on the professions will doubtless have counterposed opinions about such future possibilities – including whether professional groups can effectively exercise responsible leadership in this way (Saks, 2016b). Historically, as has been seen, Marxist contributors have condemned apparently helpful, client-facing groups like personal service professions for being linked to capitalist interests in neo-liberal societies, as they are held to individualise issues and deflect attention away from the structural source of the problems with which they deal (Esland, 1980a). Such professions as accountancy and law are of course even more directly connected to the sustenance of capitalism by Marxist writers as they help assist in creating surplus value in the process of capital accumulation (Johnson, 1977). Foucauldians too have cast doubt on the progressive role of professions because of their engagement in the state in the process of governmentality (Foucault, 2001). Moreover, as previously discussed, some neo-Weberians, in their focus on competition in the market, remain sceptical about how far the public interest takes precedence over group self-interests in decision making by professions (Perrucci, 1973).

This said, the altruistic ideologies of professions create the potential for more responsible leadership in the future even if they may not always have reflected how they actually operated in the past. But if this highlights a fundamentally desirable future characteristic of professions, they may still need to change in other ways, along the lines of previously discussed contributors in this chapter like Noordegraaf (2020), Susskind and Susskind (2015), Flood (2018) and Leicht (2018), as societal values shift in the Anglo-American context and other neo-liberal settings. Technology may indeed usefully come further to the fore, with greater connectivity of professions to each other, to clients and citizens, and to their wider environment. Equally, the role of professions in the modern world may well further involve such tasks as risk management and reliably interpreting information for clients. The expectation that professions will lead responsibly, though, should be the guiding force shaping the multifaceted direction of professional groups in the years ahead. As such, it needs to be a key driver of the transition to a positive future – the how, and not just the what, of the metamorphosis of professions.

In going back to the professional altruism ideal which traditionally – at an ideological level – lies at the root of the concept of responsible leadership, it is important to recognise in neo-Weberian terms that its specific nature can vary over time, as professions position themselves according to their interests and other factors in the prevailing socio-political context of the day (Berlant, 1975). As such, greater emphasis should be placed on ensuring at every level that there is more professional sensitivity in decision making to a wider range of major stakeholders in business and society in neo-liberal countries in late modernity. At the broadest level, this can be seen as being represented by progressing the Sustainable Development Goals of the United Nations (2015), against which so many organisations and professions themselves now benchmark themselves. Its underpinning values are a vital part of moving the global agenda forward – not least in the midst of the Covid-19 pandemic – and should therefore ideally be crystallised in the ideologies and prospective actions of professional bodies.

Professions, though, do not exist as islands. Moving from a neo-Weberian to a related neo-institutionalist theoretical platform, the professions can be seen as one institution competing with others in a much broader ecological landscape (Suddaby and Muzio 2015). This perspective helpfully takes the study of responsible leadership in the professions further towards the analysis of the wider economic, political and social structure in which they are situated – as exemplified by Kenworthy, MacKenzie and Lee (2016) who highlight the corporate influence on global health governance and Cockerham (2018) who discusses the obstacles and opportunities available in the global governance of public health. Understanding this context is vital as the past performance of professions has not been reassuring in terms of the functionalist trade-off. As a result, the distinctive codes of ethics of professions have all too frequently served as an ideological smokescreen for their activities – leading at best to a more reactive than responsive approach. In consequence, if professions are to be more extensively humanised and act in a more responsible manner as leaders in future (Østergaard, 2018), it is essential that they are encouraged to do so not just through methods of recruitment and socialisation over which they still have some independent control, but also by the state that underwrites their privileges and other key bodies, including the public and private corporate organisations that now typically employ them – alongside clients and citizens themselves (Saks, 2016a).

Conclusion

We should conclude this book by briefly highlighting how professions can best be futureproofed in the Anglo-American context and the wider setting of modern neo-liberal societies, by using the power of metaphor (Liljegren and Saks, 2016). Here it will be recalled from the Arabian Nights tale of Aladdin that the evil sorcerer tricks Aladdin's wife to trade in the lamp containing a powerful genie who can grant the owner's wishes on the pretext of trading 'new lamps for old' (Irwin, 2019). When academics talk of the future of the professions, in exchanging the old lamps of the professions for the glittering new ones of the future, they need to be careful that they are not mistakenly giving up the lamp with the magic genie. This lamp is the one which contains the altruistic ideologies of professions of the past that we continue to need in the modern world if professions are to help us to successfully transition to a new age through responsible leadership, in accord with the public interest (Schuyler et al, 2016). This is the process element without which other pieces in the professional jigsaw will not easily and beneficially fall into place – including through future configurations of technology and complementary but transmuted roles. Moreover, in effecting such a transition, it is vital that a broader range of institutions at the local, organisational, societal and international level provide an enabling framework to support professions acting responsibly within the capitalist economy in which they are situated. If such support can be provided going forward, professions will be able to build on their historic past and become even more of a key idea for business and society in the future.

Bibliography

Abbott, A. (1988) *The System of Professions: An Essay on the Division of Expert Labour*, Chicago, IL: Chicago University Press.

Abbott, A. (2005) 'Linked ecologies: States and universities as environments for professions', *Sociological Theory* 23 (3): 245–274.

Abel, R. L. (1986) 'The transformation of the American legal profession', *Law and Society Review* 20 (1): 7–17.

Abel, R. L. (1989) *American Lawyers*, New York: Oxford University Press.

Abel, R. L. (1998) *The Making of the English Legal Profession*, Frederick, MD: Beard Books.

Abel, R. L. (2003) *English Lawyers between the Market and the State: The Politics of Professionalism*, Oxford: Oxford University Press.

Abel, R. L. (2015) 'An agenda for research on the legal profession and legal education: One American's perspective', in Sommerlad, H., Harris-Short, S., Vaughan, S. and Young, R. (eds) *The Futures of Legal Education and the Legal Profession*, Oxford: Hart Publishing.

Abrams, J. (2013) *Revolutionary Medicine: The Founding Fathers and Mothers in Sickness and in Health*, New York: New York University Press.

Ackroyd, S. (2016) 'Sociological and organisational theories of professions and professionalism', in Dent, M., Bourgeault, I., Dennis, J. and Kuhlmann, E. (eds) *The Routledge Companion to the Professions and Professionalism*, Abingdon: Routledge.

Adams, T. (2015) 'Sociology of professions: International divergencies and research directions', *Work, Employment and Society* 29 (1): 154–165.

Adams, T. (2017) 'Self-regulating professions: Past, present, future', *Journal of Professions and Organization* 4 (1): 70–87.

Adams, T. (2020) 'Professional employees and professional managers: Conflicting logics, hybridity, and restratification', *Journal of Professions and Organization* 7 (1): 101–115.

Adams, T., Clegg, S., Eyal, G., Reed, M. and Saks, M. (2020) 'Connective professionalism: Towards (yet another) ideal type', *Journal of Professions and Organization* 7 (2): 224–233.

Adamson, M., Manson, S. and Zacharia, I. (2015) 'Executive remuneration consultancy in the UK: Exploring a professional project through the lens of institutional work', *Journal of Professions and Organization* 2 (1): 19–37.

Adler, P. S. (2007) 'Marx, socialization and labour process theory: A rejoinder', *Organization Studies* 28 (9): 1387–1394.

Agevall, O. (2016) 'Social closure: On metaphors, professions and a boa constrictor', in Liljegren, A. and Saks, M. (eds) *Professions and Metaphors: Understanding Professions in Society*, Abingdon: Routledge.

Ahmed, H., Brown, A. and Saks, M. (2018) 'Patterns of medical oversight and regulation in Canada', in Chamberlain, J. M., Dent, M. and Saks, M. (eds) *Professional Health Regulation in the Public Interest*, Bristol: Policy Press.

Allsop, J. and Jones, K. (2008) 'Protecting patients: International trends in medical governance', in Kuhlmann, E. and Saks, M. (eds) *Rethinking Professional Governance: International Directions in Health Care*, Bristol: Policy Press.

Allsop, J. and Jones, K. (2018) 'Regulating the regulators: The rise of the United Kingdom Professional Standards Authority', in Chamberlain, J. M., Dent, M. and Saks, M. (eds) *Professional Health Regulation in the Public Interest: International Perspectives*, Bristol: Policy Press.

Allsop, J. and Saks, M. (eds) (2002) *Regulating the Health Professions*, London: Sage.

Alvesson, M. (1995) *Management of Knowledge-Intensive Companies*, Berlin: De Gruyter.

Andersson, T. and Liff, R. (2018) 'Co-optation as a response to competing institutional logics: Professionals and managers in healthcare', *Journal of Professions and Organization* 5 (2): 71–87.

Anteby, M., Chan, C. K. and DiBenigno, J. (2016) 'Three lenses on occupations and professions in organizations: Becoming, doing, and relating', *The Academy of Management Annals* 10 (1): 183–244.

Armour, J. and McCahery, J. A. (eds) (2006) *After Enron: Improving Corporate Law and Modernising Securities Regulation in Europe and the US*, Portland, OR: Hart Publishing.

Armour, J. and Sako, M. (2020) 'AI-enabled business models in legal services: From traditional law firms to next-generation law companies?', *Journal of Professions and Organization* 7 (1): 27–46.

Arney, W. (1982) *Power and the Profession of Obstetrics*, Chicago, IL: University of Chicago Press.

Arnold, B. L. and Kay, F. M. (1995) 'Social capital, violations of trust and the vulnerability of isolates: The social organization of law practice and professional self-regulation', *International Journal of the Sociology of Law* 23 (4): 321–346.

Arnold, P. (2005) 'Disciplining domestic regulation: The World Trade Organization and the market for professional services', *Accounting, Organizations and Society* 30 (4): 299–330.

Ashley, L. and Empson, L. (2017) 'Understanding social exclusion in elite professional service firms: Field level dynamics and the "professional project"', *Work, Employment and Society* 31 (2): 211–229.

Aulakh, S. and Kirkpatrick, I. (2018) 'New governance regulation and lawyers: When substantive compliance erodes legal professionalism', *Journal of Professions and Organization* 5 (3): 167–183.

Baggott, R. (2011) *Public Health: Policy and Politics*, 2nd edition, Basingstoke: Palgrave Macmillan.

Ballakrishnen, S. (2017) '"She gets the job done": Entrenched gender meanings and new returns to essentialism in India's elite professional firms', *Journal of Professions and Organization* 4 (3): 324–342.

Balzer, H. D. (ed) (2016) *Russia's Missing Middle Class: The Professions in Russian History*, Abingdon: Routledge.

Baran, P. (1973) *The Political Economy of Growth*, Harmondsworth: Penguin Books.

Barber, B. (1963) 'Some problems in the sociology of professions', *Daedalus* 92: 669–688.

Bargate, Q. (2014) *Time for a Fused Profession*, London: Bargate Murray.

Barrett, G., Sellman, D. and Thomas, J. (eds) (2005) *Interprofessional Working in Health and Social Care: Professional Perspectives*, Basingstoke: Palgrave Macmillan.

Bartrip, P. (1990) *Mirror of Medicine: A History of the BMJ*, Oxford: Clarendon Press.

Bauman, Z. (1992) *Intimations of Postmodernity*, New York: Routledge.

Baxter, B. (2007) *A Darwinian Worldview: Sociobiology, Environmental Ethics and the Work of Edward O. Wilson*, Farnham: Ashgate.

Beattie, A. (1995) 'War and peace among the health tribes', in Soothill, K., Mackay, L. and Webb, C. (eds) *Interprofessional Relations in Health Care*, London: Edward Arnold.

Becker, H. (1962) 'The nature of a profession', in National Society for the Study of Education (ed) *Education for the Professions*, Chicago, IL: University of Chicago Press.

Belfield, C., Britton, J., Buscha, F., Dearden, L., Dickson, M., van der Erve, L., Sibieta, L., Vignoles, A., Walker, I. and Zhu, Y. (2018) *The Relative Labour Market Returns to Different Degrees Research Report*, London: Institute for Fiscal Studies.

Bell, D. (1962) *The End of Ideology: On the Exhaustion of Political Ideas in the Fifties*, New York: Collier Books.

Bell, D. (1976) *The Coming of Post-industrial Society*, New York: Basic Books.

Bell, L., Stevenson, H. and Neary, M. (eds) (2009) *The Future of Higher Education: Policy, Pedagogy and the Student Experience*, London: Continuum.

Bergman, J. (2020) *Darwinian Eugenics and the Holocaust: American Industrial Involvement*, London: Involgo Press.

Berlant, J. L. (1975) *Profession and Monopoly: A Study of Medicine in the United States and Great Britain*, Berkeley, CA: University of California Press.

Bernanke, B. S., Geitheiner, T. F. and Paulson, H. M. (2019) *Firefighting: The Financial Crisis and Its Lessons*, London: Profile Books.

Bévort, F. and Suddaby, R. (2016) 'Scripting professional identities: How individuals make sense of contradictory logics', *Journal of Professions and Organization* 3 (1): 17–38.

Bierman, L., Brymer, R. A., Dust, S. B. and Hwang, H. (2019) 'Gatekeeping and our moral fabric: Has social capital deterioration vanquished professional oversight?', *Journal of Professions and Organization* 6 (3): 377–386.

Blauner, R. (1964) *Alienation and Freedom: The Factory Worker and His Industry*. Chicago, IL: Chicago University Press.

Blok, A., Lindstrøm, M. D., Meilvang, M. L. and Pedersen, I. K. (2018) 'Trans-local professional projects: Re-scaling the linked ecology of expert jurisdictions', *Journal of Professions and Organization* 5 (2): 106–122.

Blomgren, M. and Waks, C. (2015) 'Coping with contradictions: Hybrid professionals managing institutional complexity', *Journal of Professions and Organization* 2 (1): 78–102.

Bogoch, B. (1997) 'Gendered lawyering: Difference and dominance in lawyer-client interaction', *Law and Society Review* 31 (4): 677–712.

Bolton, S. and Muzio, D. (2008) 'The paradoxical processes of feminization in the professions: The case of established, aspiring and semi-professions', *Work, Employment and Society* 22 (2): 281–299.

Bonner, T. (2000) *Becoming a Physician: Medical Education in Britain, France and the United States 1750–1945*, Baltimore, MD: Johns Hopkins University Press.

Bonnin, D. and Ruggunan, S. (2016) 'Professions and professionalism in emerging economies: The case of South Africa', in Dent, M., Bourgeault, I., Dennis, J. and Kuhlmann, E. (eds) *The Routledge Companion to the Professions and Professionalism*, Abingdon: Routledge.

Borsay, A. and Hunter, B. (eds) (2012) *Nursing and Midwifery in Britain Since 1700*, Basingstoke: Palgrave Macmillan.

Bos-de Vos, M., Liefunk, B. M. and Lauche, K. (2019) 'How to claim what is mine: Negotiating professional roles in inter-organizational projects', *Journal of Professions and Organization* 6 (2): 128–155.

Boston Women's Health Collective (2011) *Our Bodies, Ourselves*, 9th edition, New York: Touchstone.

Bourdieu, P. (1985) 'The social space and the genesis of groups', *Theory and Society* 14 (6): 723–744.

Bourdieu, P. and Wacquant, L. (1992) *An Invitation to a Reflexive Sociology*, Chicago, IL: University of Chicago Press.

Bourdieu, P. and Wacquant, L. (1999) 'On the cunning of imperialist reason', *Theory, Culture and Society* 16 (1): 41–58.

Bourgeault, I., Benoit, C. and Davis-Floyd, R. (eds) (2004) *Reconceiving Midwifery*, Montreal: McGill-Queen's University Press.

Boussard, V. (2018) 'Professional closure regimes in the global age: The boundary work of professional services specializing in mergers and acquisitions', *Journal of Professions and Organization* 5 (3): 279–296.

Boussebaa, M. and Faulconbridge, J. (2018) 'Professional service firms as agents of economic globalization: A political perspective', *Journal of Professions and Organization* 6 (1): 72–90.

Boussebaa, M., Morgan, G. and Sturdy, A. (2012) 'Constructing global firms? National, transnational and neocolonial effects in international management consultancies', *Organization Studies* 33 (4): 465–486.

Bowles, S. and Gintis, H. (1976) *Schooling in Capitalist America*, New York: Basic Books.

Boyle, E. (2013) *Quack Medicine: A History of Combating Health Fraud in Twentieth-century America*, Santa Barbara, CA: Praeger Publishers.

Bradbury, J. (2020) *Constitutional Policy and Territorial Politics in the UK*, Bristol: Bristol University Press.

Bradley, E. H. and Taylor, L. A. (2015) *The American Health Care Paradox: Why Spending More Is Getting Us Less*, New York: Public Affairs.

Brand, P. (1992) *The Origin of the English Legal Profession*, Oxford: Blackwell Publishers.

Brante, T. (2010) 'State formations and the historical take-off of continental professional types: The case of Sweden', in Svensson, L. and Evetts, J. (eds) *Sociology of Professions: Continental and Anglo-Saxon Traditions*, Göteborg: Daidalos.

Braverman, H. (1998) *Labor and Monopoly Capital: The Degradation of Work in the Twentieth Century*, New edition, New York: Monthly Review Press.

Breit, E., Fossestøl, K. and Andreassen, T. (2018) 'From pure to hybrid professionalism in post-NPM activation reform: The institutional work of frontline managers', *Journal of Professions and Organization* 5 (1): 28–44.

Brès, L., Mosonyi, S., Gond, P., Muzio, D. and Rahul, M. (2019) 'Rethinking professionalization: A generative dialogue on CSR practitioners', *Journal of Professions and Organization* 6 (2): 246–264.

Breunig, K. J., Kvålshaugen, R. and Hydle, K. M. (2014) 'Knowing your boundaries: Integration opportunities in international professional service firms', *Journal of World Business* 49: 502–511.

Brint, S. (1994) *In an Age of Experts: The Changing Role of Professionals in Politics and Public Life*, Princeton, NJ: Princeton University Press.

Brint, S. (2018) *Two Cheers for Higher Education: Why American Universities Are Stronger Than Ever – And How to Meet the Challenges They Face*, Princeton, NJ: Princeton University Press.

Brint, S. and Levy, C. S. (2002) 'Professions and civic engagement: Trends in rhetoric and practice, 1875–1995', in Skocpol, T. and Fiorina, M. P. (eds) *Civic Engagement in American Democracy*, Washington, DC: Brookings Institution Press/Russell Sage Foundation.

Brock, D. (2006) 'The changing professional organization: A review of competing archetypes', *International Journal of Management* 8 (3): 157–174.

Brock, D., Leblebici, H. and Muzio, D. (2014) 'Understanding professionals and their workplaces: The mission of the Journal of Professions and Organization', *Journal of Professions and Organization* 1 (1): 1–15.

Brooks, I. (2009) *Organisational Behaviour: Individuals, Groups and Organisations*, 4th edition, Harlow: Prentice Hall.

Brooks, R. (2011) *Cheaper by the Hour: Temporary Lawyers and the Deprofessionalization of the Law*, Philadelphia, PA: Temple University Press.

Brooks, R. (2018) *The Bean Counters: The Triumph of the Accountants and How They Broke Capitalism*, London: Atlantic Books.

Brown, D., Crowcroft, R. and Pentland, G. (eds) (2018) *The Oxford Handbook of Modern British Political History, 1800–2000*, Oxford: Oxford University Press.

Brundage, J. A. (2008) *The Medieval Origins of the Legal Profession*, Chicago, IL: University of Chicago Press.

Bucher, L. and Strauss, A. L. (1961) 'Professions and process', *American Journal of Sociology* 66 (4): 325–334.

Burau, V. (2019) 'Comparative health research', in Saks, M. and Allsop, J. (eds) *Researching Health: Qualitative, Quantitative and Mixed Methods*, 3rd edition, London: Sage.

Burrage, M. (1992) 'Mrs Thatcher against deep structures: Ideology, impact and ironies of her eleven-year confrontation with the professions', Working Paper, Berkeley, CA: Institute of Governmental Studies, University of California.

Burrage, M. (2006) *Revolution and the Making of the Contemporary Legal Profession: England, France and the United States*, New York: Oxford University Press.

Byrne, B., Alexander, C., Khan, O., Nazroo, J. and Shankley, W. (eds) (2020) *Ethnicity, Race and Inequality in the UK: State of the Nation*, Bristol: Policy Press.

Byrne, D. (2018) 'Introduction', in Conway, E. and Byrne, D. (eds) *Contemporary Issues in Accounting: The Current Developments in Accounting Beyond the Numbers*, Basingstoke: Palgrave Macmillan.

Calnan, M. and Gabe, J. (2009) 'The restratification of primary care in England? A sociological analysis', in Gabe, J. and Calnan, M. (eds) *The New Sociology of the Health Service*, Abingdon: Routledge.

Cameran, M., Campa, D. and Clerissi, H. (2020) 'How long is the journey of minorities towards equality in the business world? Evidence from the Australian accounting profession', Crafting the Future(s) of Professional Services, Annual PSF Conference, University of Oxford, July.

Canning, M. and O'Dwyer, B, (2018) 'Regulation and governance of the professions: Institutional work and the demise of "delegated" self-regulation of the accounting profession', in Saks, M. and Muzio, D. (eds) *Professions and Professional Service Firms: Private and Public Sector Enterprises in the Global Economy*, Abingdon: Routledge.

Cant, S. and Sharma, U. (1996) 'Demarcation and transformation within homoeopathic knowledge: A strategy of professionalization', *Social Science and Medicine* 42 (4): 579–588.

Caplow, T. (1954) *The Sociology of Work*, Minneapolis, MN: University of Minnesota Press.

Carchedi, G. (2006) 'On the economic identification of the new middle class', *Economy and Society* 4 (1): 1–86.

Carr, S. (2007) 'Participation, power, conflict and change: Dynamics of service user participation in the social care system of England and Wales', *Critical Social Policy* 27 (2): 266–276.

Carr-Saunders, A. M. and Wilson, P. A. (1933) *The Professions*, Oxford: Clarendon Press.

Cartwight, M. (2018) 'Medieval guilds', *Ancient History Encyclopedia*. Available at: www.ancient.eu/Medieval_Guilds/.

Carvalho, T. (2014) 'Changing connections between professionalism and managerialism: A case study of nursing in Portugal', *Journal of Professions and Organization* 1 (2): 176–190.

Carvalho, T. and Cabral-Cardoso, C. (2008) 'Flexibility through HRM in management consulting firms', *Personnel Review* 37 (3): 332–349.

Chamberlain, J. M. (2015) *Medical Regulation, Fitness to Practise and Revalidation*, Bristol: Policy Press.

Chamberlain, J. M., Dent, M. and Saks, M. (eds) (2018) *Professional Health Regulation in the Public Interest*, Bristol: Policy Press.

Chamberlain, M. (2010) *Old Wives' Tales: A History of Remedies, Charms and Spells*, Reprinted edition, Stroud: The History Press.

Child, J. (2011) *British Management Thought: A Critical Analysis*, Abingdon: Routledge Revivals.

Child, J. (2019) *Hierarchy: A Key Idea for Business and Society*, Abingdon: Routledge.

Childs, B. P., Cypress, M. and Spollett, G. (2017) *Complete Nurse' Guide to Diabetes Care*, Arlington, VA: American Diabetes Association.

Clark, N. and Nixon, C. (2015) *Professional Services Marketing Handbook*, London: Kogan Page.

Clark, T. and Fincham, R. (eds) (2002) *Critical Consulting: New Perspectives on the Management Advice Industry*, Oxford: Blackwell.

Cockerham, G. B. (2018) *Global Governance and Public Health: Obstacles and Opportunities*, London: Rowman & Littlefield.

Coffee, J. C. (2006) *Gatekeepers: The Professions and Corporate Governance*, Oxford: Oxford University Press.

Cohen, L., Wilkinson, A., Arnold, J. and Finn, R. (2005) '"Remember I'm the bloody architect!" Architects, organizations and discourses of profession', *Work, Employment and Society* 19 (4): 775–796.

Collins, D., Dewing, I. and Russell, P. (2009) 'The actuary as a fallen hero: On the reform of a profession', *Work, Employment and Society* 23 (2): 249–266.

Collins, R. (1990) 'Market closure and the conflict theory of the professions', in Burrage, M. and Torstendahl, R. (eds) *Professions in Theory and History: Rethinking the Study of the Professions*, London: Sage.

Conway, E. (2018) 'The future of accountancy – beyond the numbers', in Conway, E. and Byrne, D. (eds) *Contemporary Issues in Accounting: The*

Current Developments in Accounting Beyond the Numbers, Basingstoke: Palgrave Macmillan.

Cook, H. (2013) 'Medicine in Western Europe', in Jackson, M. (ed) *The Oxford Handbook of the History of Medicine*, Oxford: Oxford University Press.

Coombs, J. (2005) *The Rise and Fall of HMOs: An American Health Revolution*, Madison, WI: University of Wisconsin Press.

Cooper, D. L. and Robson, K. (2006) 'Accounting, professions and regulation: Locating the sites of professionalization', *Accounting, Organizations and Society* 31 (4/5): 415–444.

Cornelissen, J. (2005) 'Beyond compare: Metaphors in organizational theory', *Academy of Management Review* 30 (4): 751–764.

Covaleski, M. A., Dirsmith, L. and Rittenburg, L. (2003) 'Jurisdictional disputes at work: The institutionalization of the global knowledge expert', *Accounting, Organizations and Society* 28 (4): 323–355.

Cromwell, J. R. and Gardner, H. K. (2020) 'High-stakes innovation: When collaboration in teams enhances (or undermines) innovation in professional service firms', *Journal of Professions and Organization* 7 (1): 2–26.

Crook, D. (2008) 'Some historical perspectives on professionalism', in Cunningham, B. (ed) *Exploring Professionalism*, London: Institute of Education, University of London.

Cummings, S. L. (ed) (2011) *The Paradox of Professionalism: Lawyers and the Possibility of Justice*, Cambridge: Cambridge University Press.

Cunha, L. G., Gabba, D. M., Ghirardi, J. G., Trubek, D. M. and Wilkins, D. B. (eds) (2018) *The Brazilian Legal Profession in the Age of Globalization: The Rise of the Corporate Legal Sector and Its Impact on Lawyers and Society*, Cambridge: Cambridge University Press.

Denis, J-L., Ferlie, E and van Gestel, N. (2015) 'Understanding hybridity in public organizations', *Public Administration* 93 (2): 273–289.

Denis, J-L., Veronesi, G., Regis, C. and Germain, S. (2019) 'Collegiality as political work: Professions in today's world of organizations', *Journal of Professions and Organization* 6 (3), 323–341.

Dent, M. and Whitehead, S. (eds) (2002) *Managing Professional Identities: Knowledge, Performativity and the 'New' Professional*, London: Routledge.

Dent, M., Bourgeault, I., Denis, J-L. and Kuhlmann, E. (eds) (2016) *The Routledge Companion to the Professions and Professionalism*, Abingdon: Routledge.

Dent, M., Chandler, J. and Barry, J. (eds) (2004) *Questioning the New Public Management*, Aldershot: Ashgate.

Dezalay, Y. and Garth, B. (1996) 'Fussing about the forum: Categories and definitions as stakes in a professional competition', *Law and Social Inquiry* 21 (2): 285–312.

Dezalay, Y. and Garth, B. (2002) *The Internationalization of Palace Wars: Lawyers, Economists, and the Contest to Transform Latin American States*, Chicago, IL: University of Chicago Press.

Dezalay, Y. and Garth, B. (2016) '"Lords of the dance" as double agents: Elite actors in and around the legal field', *Journal of Professions and Organization* 3 (2): 188–206.

Dikötter, F. (2016) *The Cultural Revolution: A People's History, 1962–76*, New York: Bloomsbury Publishing.

Dingwall, R. (2016) 'The ecological metaphor in the sociology of occupations and professions', in Liljegren, A. and Saks, M. (eds) *Professions and Metaphors: Understanding Professions in Society*, Abingdon: Routledge.

Dingwall, R. and Hobson-West, P. (2006) 'Litigation and the threat to medicine', in Gabe, J., Kelleher, D. and Williams, G. (eds) *Challenging Medicine*, 2nd edition, Abingdon: Routledge.

Dingwall, R. and King, M. D. (1995) 'Herbert Spencer and the professions: Occupational ecology reconsidered', *Sociological Theory* 13 (1): 14–24.

Dingwall, R. and Lewis, P. (eds) (1983) *The Sociology of the Professions*, Basingstoke: Macmillan.

Dinovitzer, R., Gunz, H. and Gunz, S. (2014) 'Unpacking client capture: Evidence from corporate law firms', *Journal of Professions and Organization* 1 (2): 99–117.

Dobbin, F. (2009) *Inventing Equal Opportunity*, Princeton, NJ: Princeton University Press.

Donzelot, J. (1979) *The Policing of Families*, New York: Pantheon.

Doorewaard, H. and Meihuizen, H. E. (2000) 'Strategic performance options in professional service organisations', *Human Resource Management Journal* 10 (2): 39–57.

Duffy, J. (1993) *From Humors to Medical Science: A History of American Medicine*, 2nd edition, Champaign, IL: University of Illinois Press.

Durkheim, E. (1964) *The Division of Labor in Society*, New York: Free Press.

Durkheim, E. (1992) *Professional Ethics and Civic Morals*, London: Routledge.

Edgley, C., Sharma, N. and Anderson-Gough, F. (2016) 'Diversity and professionalism in the Big Four firms: Expectation, celebration and weapon in the battle for talent', *Critical Perspectives on Accounting* 35: 13–34.

Ehrenreich, B. and Ehrenreich, J. (1979) 'The professional-managerial class', in Walker, P. (ed) *Between Capital and Labour*, Brighton: Harvester Press.

Elliott, P. (1972) *The Sociology of the Professions*, London: Macmillan.

Elston, M. A. (1991) 'The politics of professional power: Medicine in a changing health service', in Gabe, J., Calnan, M. and Bury, M. (eds) *The Sociology of the Health Service*, London: Routledge.

Elston, M. A. (2004) 'Medical autonomy and medical dominance', in Gabe, J., Bury, M. and Elston, M. A. (eds) *Key Concepts in Medical Sociology*, London: Sage.

Elston, M. A. (2006) 'Attacking the foundations of modern medicine? Antivivisection protest and medical science', in Gabe, J., Kelleher, D. and Williams, G. (eds) *Challenging Medicine*, 2nd edition, Abingdon: Routledge.

Empson, L. (ed) (2007) *Managing the Modern Law Firm: New Challenges, New Perspectives*, Oxford: Oxford University Press.

Empson, L. and Chapman, C. (2006) 'Partnership versus corporation: Implications of alternative forms of governance in professional service firms', *Research in the Sociology of Organizations* 24: 139–170.

Epstein, S. A. (1991) *Wage Labour and Guilds in Medieval Europe*, Chapel Hill, NC: North Carolina University Press.

Eskelinen, T. and Ylönen, M. (2017) 'Panama and the WTO: New constitutionalism of trade policy and global tax governance', *Review of International Political Economy* 24 (4): 629–656.

Esland, G. (1980a) 'Diagnosis and therapy', in Esland, G. and Salaman, G. (eds) *The Politics of Work and Occupations*, Milton Keynes: Open University Press.

Esland, G. (1980b) 'Professions and professionalism', in Esland, G. and Salaman, G. (eds) *The Politics of Work and Occupations*, Milton Keynes: Open University Press.

Etzioni, A. (ed) (1969) *The Semi-professions and Their Organization*, New York: Free Press.

Everett, J. and Green, D. (2006) 'The changing nature of accounting virtues', *Advances in Public Interest Accounting* 12: 119–132.

Evetts, J. (1998) 'Professional identity, diversity and segmentation: The case of engineering', in Olgiati, V., Orzack, L. and Saks, M. (eds) *Professions, Identity and Order in Comparative Perspective*, Onati: Onati International Institute for the Sociology of Law.

Evetts, J. (2000) 'Professions in European and UK markets: The European Professional Federation', *International Journal of Sociology and Social Policy* 18 (11/12): 395–415.

Evetts, J. (2003) 'Reinterpreting professionalism: As discourse of social control and occupational change', in Svensson, L. and Evetts, J. (eds) *Conceptual and Comparative Studies of Continental and Anglo-American Professions*, Göteborg: Göteborg University.

Evetts, J. (2006) 'Organizational and occupational professionalism: The legacies of Weber and Durkheim for knowledge society', in Marcuello, C. and Fados, J. L. (eds) *Sociological Essays for a Global Society: Cultural Change, Social Problems and Knowledge Society*, Zaragoza: Prenas Universitarias de Zaragoza.

Evetts, J. (2010) 'Reconnecting professional occupations with professional organizations: Risks and opportunities', in Svensson, L. and Evetts, J. (eds) *Sociology of Professions: Continental and Anglo-Saxon Traditions*, Göteborg: Daidalos.

Evetts, J. (2011) 'A new professionalism? Challenges and opportunities', *Current Sociology* 59 (4): 406–422.

Evetts, J. (2013) 'Professionalism: Value and ideology', *Current Sociology* 61 (5/6): 778–796.

Eyal, G. (2013) 'For a sociology of expertise: The social origins of the autism epidemic', *American Journal of Sociology* 118 (4): 863–907.

Faulconbridge, J. and Muzio, D. (2008) 'Organizational professionalism in globalizing law firms', *Work, Employment and Society* 22 (7): 7–25.

Faulconbridge, J. and Muzio, D. (2012) 'Professions in a globalizing world: Towards a transnational sociology of the professions', *International Sociology* 27 (1): 136–152.

Faulconbridge, J. and Muzio, D. (2013) 'Global professional service firms and the challenge of institutional complexity: "Field relocation" as a response strategy', *Journal of Management Studies* 53 (1): 89–124.

Faulconbridge, J. and Muzio, D. (2017) 'Global professional service firms and institutionalization', in Seabrooke, L. and Henrikson, L. F. (eds) *Professional Networks in Transnational Governance*, Cambridge: Cambridge University Press.

Faulconbridge, J., Sarwar, A. and Spring, M. (2020) 'Paradoxical boundary work: Creative responses to the impacts of artificial intelligence on accounting and law professional work', Crafting the Future(s) of Professional Services, Annual PSF Conference, University of Oxford, July.

Feyereisen, S. and Goodrick, E. (2019) 'Who is in charge? Jurisdictional contests and organizational outcomes', *Journal of Professions and Organization* 6 (2): 233–245.

Field, M. (1957) *Doctor and Patient in Soviet Russia*, Cambridge, MA: Harvard University Press.

Fincham, R. (2006) 'Knowledge work as occupational strategy: Comparing IT and managing consultancy', *New Technology, Work and Employment* 21 (1): 16–28.

Fine, B., Kinsey, R., Lea, J., Picciotto, S. and Young, J. (eds) (1979) *Capitalism and the Rule of Law*, London: Hutchinson.

Flam, H. (2019) 'Civil society and professions: US civic and politicized lawyering', *Professions and Professionalism* 9 (1): 1–16.

Flood, J. (2011) 'The re-landscaping of the legal profession: Large law firms and professional re-regulation', *Current Sociology* 59 (4): 507–529.

Flood, J. (2018) 'Professions and professional service firms in a global context: Reframing narratives', in Saks, M. and Muzio, D. (eds) *Professions and Professional Service Firms: Private and Public Sector Enterprises in the Global Economy*, Abingdon: Routledge.

Fotaki, M. (2011) 'Towards developing new partnerships in public services: Users as consumers, citizens and/or coproducers in health and social care in England and Sweden', *Public Administration* 89 (3): 933–955.

Foucault, M. (1989) *The Birth of the Clinic*, London: Routledge.

Foucault, M. (1991) *Discipline and Punish: The Birth of the Prison*, London: Penguin Books.

Foucault, M. (2001) *Madness and Civilization: A History of Madness in the Age of Reason*, London: Routledge Classics.

Fourcade, M. (2006) 'The construction of a global profession: The transnationalization of economics', *American Journal of Sociology* 112 (1): 145–195.

Fournier, V. (1999) 'The appeal to "professionalism" as a disciplinary mechanism', *Sociological Review* 47 (2): 656–673.

Fournier, V. (2000) 'Boundary work and the (un)making of the professions', in Malin, N. (ed) *Professionalism, Boundaries and the Workplace*, London: Routledge.

Frank, J., Gowar, N. and Naef, M. (2019) *English Universities in Crisis: Markets without Competition*, Bristol: Policy Press.

Freidson, E. (1970) *Profession of Medicine: A Study in the Sociology of Applied Knowledge*, New York: Dodd, Mead & Co.

Freidson, E. (1986) *Professional Powers: A Study of the Institutionalization of Formal Knowledge*, Chicago, IL: University of Chicago Press.

Freidson, E. (1994) *Professionalism Reborn: Theory, Prophecy and Policy*, Chicago, IL: University of Chicago Press.

Freidson, E. (2001) *Professionalism: The Third Logic*, Cambridge: Polity Press.

Friedman, A. L. (2019) 'Juxtapositioning populism and professionalism', *Professions and Professionalism* 9 (2), 1–16.

Friedman, M. (1962) *Capitalism and Freedom*, Chicago, IL: University of Chicago Press.

Gabbioneta, C, Garnett, P. and Muzio, D. (2020) 'When it is hard to say "no" to a client: The impact of the client and the professional's characteristics on client capture', Crafting the Future(s) of Professional Services, Annual PSF Conference, University of Oxford, July.

Gadd, I. A. and Wallis, P. (eds) (2002) *Guilds, Society and Economy in London 1450–1800*, London: Centre for Metropolitan History, Institute of Historical Research/Guildhall Library.

Ganesh, S. and McAllum, K. (2012) 'Volunteering and professionalization: Trends in tension?', *Management Communication Quarterly* 26 (1): 152–158.

Gans, H. J. (1972) *People and Plans: Essays on Urban Problems and Solutions*, London: Pelican Books.

General Medical Council (2009) *Tomorrow's Doctors: Outcomes and Standards for Undergraduate Medical Education*, London: GMC.

Giddens, A. (1981) *The Class Structure of the Advanced Societies*, 2nd edition, London: Hutchinson.

Goldblatt, D. (2018) *The Games: A Global History of the Olympics*, London: Pan Macmillan.

Goldthorpe, J. (1982) 'On the service class, its formation and future', in Giddens, A. and Mackenzie, G. (eds) *Social Class and the Division of Labour*, Cambridge: Cambridge University Press.

Goode, W. (1960) 'Encroachment, charlatanism and the emerging profession: Psychology, sociology and medicine', *American Sociological Review* 25: 902–914.

Goodrick, E. and Reay, T. (2011) 'Constellations of institutional logics: Changes in the professional work of pharmacists', *Work and Occupations* 38 (3): 372–416.

Gordon-Reed, A. (ed) (2020) *Racism in America: A Reader*, Cambridge, MA: Harvard University Press.

Gorman, E. and Sandefur, R. (2011) '"Golden age", quiescence, and revival: How the sociology of professions became the study of knowledge-based work', *Work and Occupations* 38 (3): 275–302.

Graf, E., Sator, M. and Spranz-Fogasy, T. (2014) *Discourses of Helping Professions*, Amsterdam: John Benjamins Publishing.

Granfield, R. and Mather, L. (eds) (2009) *Private Lawyers and the Public Interest: The Evolving Role of Pro Bono in the Legal Profession*, New York: Oxford University Press.

Grant Thornton (2019) *Corporate Governance and Company Performance*, London: Grant Thornton.

Greenspan, A. and Wooldridge, A. (2018) *Capitalism in America: A History*, London: Penguin Books.

Greenwood, E. (1957) 'The attributes of a profession', *Social Work* 2 (3): 45–55.

Greenwood, R. and Suddaby, R. (2006) 'Institutional entrepreneurship in mature fields: The Big Five accounting firms', *Academy of Management Journal* 49 (1): 27–48.

Greenwood, R., Hinings, C. R. and Prakash, R. (2017) '25 years of the Professional Partnership (P2) form: Time to foreground its social purpose and herald the P3?', *Journal of Professions and Organization* 4 (2): 112–122.

Gubrium, J. and Holstein, J. (2003) 'Analyzing interpretive practice', in Denzin, N. and Lincoln, Y. (eds) *Strategies of Qualitative Inquiry*, Thousand Oaks, CA: Sage.

Hall, R. H. (1968) 'Professionalization and bureaucratization', *American Sociological Review* 33: 92–104.

Haller, J. (2009) *The History of American Homeopathy: From Rational Medicine to Holistic Health Care*, New Brunswick, NJ: Rutgers University Press.

Halliday, T. C. (1987) *Beyond Monopoly: Lawyers, State Crises, and Professional Empowerment*, Chicago, IL: University of Chicago Press.

Harrington, B. (2015) 'Going global: Professionals and the micro-foundations of institutional change', *Journal of Professions and Organization* 2 (2): 103–121.

Harrington, B. (2017) 'Habitus and the labor of representation among elite professionals', *Journal of Professions and Organization* 4 (3): 282–301.

Hartmann, M. (1995) 'Bank lawyers: A professional group holding the reins of power', in Dezalay, Y. and Sugarman, D. (eds) *Professional Competition and Professional Power: Lawyers, Accountants and the Social Construction of Markets*, London: Routledge.

Harvey, D. (1990) *The Condition of Postmodernity: An Enquiry into the Origins of Cultural Change*, Oxford: Blackwell Publishers.

Hasselbalch, J. and Seabrooke, L. (2018) 'Professional strategies and enterprise in transnational projects', in Saks, M. and Muzio, D. (eds) *Professions and Professional Service Firms: Private and Public Sector Enterprises in the Global Economy*, Abingdon: Routledge.

Haug, M. (1973) 'Deprofessionalization: An alternative hypothesis for the future', in Halmos, P. (ed) *Professionalization and Social Change*, Sociological Review Monograph No. 20, Keele: University of Keele.

Haug, M. (1988) 'A re-examination of the hypothesis of physician depro-fessionalization', *Milbank Quarterly* 66 (S2): 48–56.

Hayes, C. and Jacobs, K. (2017) 'The processes of inclusion and exclusion: The role of ethnicity and class in women's relation with the accounting profession', *Accounting, Auditing and Accountability Journal* 30 (3): 565–592.

Hearne, J., Metcalfe, B. D. and Piekkari, R. (2012) 'Gender, intersectionality and international human resource management', in Stahl, G. K., Björkman, I. and Morris, S. (eds) *Handbook of Research in International Human Research Management*, 2nd edition, Cheltenham: Edward Elgar.

Hellberg, I. (1990) 'The Swedish veterinary profession and the Swedish state', in Torstendahl, R. and Burrage, M. (eds) *The Formation of Professions: Knowledge, State and Strategy*, London: Sage.

Hellberg, I., Saks, M. and Benoit, C. (eds) (1999) *Professional Identities in Transition: Cross-cultural Dimensions*, Södertälje: Almqvist & Wiksell International.

Hendrikx, P. (2018) 'Priced not praised: Professional identity of GPs within market-oriented healthcare reform', *Journal of Professions and Organization*, 5 (1): 12–27.

Henriksson, L., Wrede, S. and Burau, V. (2006) 'Understanding professional projects in welfare service work: Revival of old professionalism?', *Gender, Work and Organization* 13 (2): 174–192.

Heusinkveld, S., Gabbioneta, C., Werr, A. and Sturdy, A. (2018) 'Professions and (new) management occupations as a contested terrain: Redefining jurisdictional claims', *Journal of Professions and Organization* 5 (3): 248–261.

Hickson, D. J. and Thomas, M. W. (1969) 'Professionalization in Britain: A preliminary measure', *Sociology* 3 (1): 37–53.

Hitt, M. A., Bierman, L., Uhlenbruck, K. and Shimizu, K. (2006) 'The importance of resources in the internationalization of professional service firms: The good, the bad and the ugly', *Academy of Management Journal* 49 (6): 1137–1157.

Hobson-West, P. and Timmons, S. (2015) 'Animals and anomalies: An analysis of the UK veterinary profession and the relative lack of state reform', *Sociological Review* 64: 47–63.

Hodgson, D., Paton, S. and Muzio, D. (2015) 'Something old, something new? Competing logics and the hybrid nature of new corporate professions', *British Journal of Management* 26 (4): 745–759.

Hoffman, T. (2011) *Guilds and Related Organisations in Great Britain and Northern Ireland: A Bibliography*, London: Birkbeck College, University of London.

Hopkins, M. (ed) (2016) *CSR and Sustainability: From the Margins to the Mainstream*, Sheffield: Greenleaf Publishing.

Horne, J. (1971) *Away with All Pests: An English Surgeon in People's China 1954–69*, New York: Monthly Review Press.

Horowitz, R. (2013) *In the Public Interest, Medical Licensing and the Disciplinary Process*, New Brunswick, NJ: Rutgers University Press.

Horowitz, R. (2018) 'Let the consumer beware: Maintenance of licensure and certification in the United States', in Chamberlain, J. M., Dent, M. and Saks, M. (eds) *Professional Health Regulation in the Public Interest*, Bristol: Policy Press.

Horrobin, D. (1977) *Medical Hubris: A Reply to Ivan Illich*, London: Eden Press.

Hsiao, W. C. and Hu, L. (2013) 'The state of medical professionalism in China: Past, present and future', in Alford, W. P., Winston, K. and Kirby, W. C. (eds) *Prospects for the Professions in China*, Abingdon: Routledge.

Hughes, E. (1963) 'Professions', *Daedalus* 92: 655–668.

Humphrey, C., Loft, A. and Woods. M. (2009) 'The global audit profession and the international financial architecture: Understanding regulatory relationships at the time of financial crisis', *Accounting, Organizations and Society* 34 (6/7): 810–825.

Iarskaia-Smirnova, E. and Abramov, R. (2016) 'Professions and professionalization in Russia', in Dent, M., Bourgeault, I., Denis, J-L. and Kuhlmann, E. (eds) *The Routledge Companion to the Professions and Professionalism*, Abingdon: Routledge.

Ilcan, S. and Basok, T. (2004) 'Community government: Voluntary agencies, social justice and the responsibilisation of citizens', *Citizenship Studies* 8 (2): 129–144.

Illich, I. (1971) *Deschooling Society*, London: Marion Boyars.

Illich, I. (1973a) 'The professions as a form of imperialism', *New Society*, 13 September.

Illich, I. (1973b) *Tools for Conviviality*, New York: Harper & Row.

Illich, I. (1976) *Limits to Medicine: Medical Nemesis – The Expropriation of Health*, London: Marion Boyars.

Irwin, R. (2019) *Tales from 1,001 Nights: Aladdin, Ali Baba and Other Favourites*, Harmondsworth: Penguin Books.

Jenkins, P. (2012) *A History of the United States*, Basingstoke: Palgrave Macmillan.

Jensen, S. H. and Kronblad, C. (2020) 'From suits to geeks: How lawyers in legal tech create and enact a new professional identity in opposition to traditional lawyers', Crafting the Future(s) of Professional Services, Annual PSF Conference, University of Oxford, July.

Johnson, D. and Chaudhry, H. (2012) *Medical Licensing and Discipline in America: A History of the Federation of State Medical Boards*, Lanham, MD: Lexington Books.

Johnson, M. (ed) (2015) *Precariat, Labour, Work and Politics*, Abingdon: Routledge.

Johnson, T. (1973) 'Professions', in Hurd, G. (ed) *Human Societies: An Introduction to Sociology*, London: Routledge and Kegan Paul.

Johnson, T. (1977) 'The professions in the class structure', in Scase, R. (ed) *Industrial Society: Class Cleavage and Control*, London: Allen & Unwin.

Johnson, T. (1995) 'Governmentality and the institutionalization of expertise', in Johnson, T., Larkin, G. and Saks, M. (eds) *Health Professions and the State in Europe*, London: Routledge.

Johnson, T. (2016) *Professions and Power*, Abingdon: Routledge Revivals.

Johnson, T., Larkin, G. and Saks, M. (eds) (1995) *Health Professions and the State in Europe*, London: Routledge.

Jones, C. and Porter, R. (1994) 'Introduction', in Jones, C. and Porter, R. (eds) *Reassessing Foucault: Power, Medicine and the Body*, London: Routledge.

Jonnergård, K. and Erlingsdóttir, C. (2012) 'Variations in professions' adoption of quality reforms: The cases of doctors and auditors in Sweden', *Current Sociology* 60 (5): 672–689.

Kaplan, A. (2018) 'European management and European business schools: Insights from the history of business schools', in Siebert, S., (ed) *Management Research: European Perspectives*, Abingdon: Routledge.

Kaye, B. (1960) *The Development of the Architectural Profession in Britain: A Sociological Study*, London: Allen & Unwin.

Keenan, M. (2012) *Child Sexual Abuse and the Catholic Church: Gender, Power and Organizational Culture*, Oxford: Oxford University Press.

Kelleher, D. (2006) 'Self-help groups and their relationship to medicine', in Gabe, J., Kelleher, D. and Williams, G. (eds) *Challenging Medicine*, 2nd edition, Abingdon: Routledge.

Kelner, M., Wellman, B., Pescosolido, B. and Saks, M. (eds) (2003) *Complementary and Alternative Medicine: Challenge and Change*, London: Routledge.

Kempster, S. and Carroll, B. (2016) *Responsible Leadership: Realism and Romanticism*, Abingdon: Routledge.

Kempster, S., Maak, T. and Parry, K. (eds) (2020) *Good Dividends: Responsible Leadership of Business Purpose*, Abingdon: Routledge.

Kenez, P. (2017) *A History of the Soviet Union from the Beginning to Its Legacy*, 3rd edition, New York: Cambridge University Press.

Kenworthy, N., MacKenzie, R. and Lee, K. (eds) (2016) *Case Studies on Corporations and Global Health Governance: Impacts, Influence and Accountability*, London: Rowman & Littlefield.

Kerr, C., Dunlop, J., Harbison, F. and Myers, C. (1960) *Industrialism and Industrial Man*, Cambridge, MA: Harvard University Press.

Kessell, R. (1958) 'Price discrimination in medicine', *Journal of Law and Economics* 1 (1): 20–53.

King, T. (2015) 'The future of legal education from the profession's viewpoint: A brave new world?', in Sommerlad, H., Harris-Short, S., Vaughan, S. and Young, R. (eds) *The Futures of Legal Education and the Legal Profession*, Oxford: Hart Publishing.

Kipping, M., Bühlmann, F. and David, T. (2019) 'Professionalization through symbolic and social capital: Evidence from the careers of elite consultants', *Journal of Professions and Organization* 6 (3): 265–285.

Kirby, W.C. (2011) 'Engineers and the state in modern China', in Alford, W. P., Winston, K. and Kirby, W. C. (eds) *Prospects for the Professions in China*, Abingdon: Routledge.

Kirkpatrick, I. (2016) 'Hybrid managers and professional leadership', in Dent, M., Bourgeault, I., Denis, J-L. and Kuhlmann, E. (eds) *The Routledge Companion to the Professions and Professionalism*, Abingdon: Routledge.

Kirkpatrick, I. and Veronesi, G. (2019) 'Researching health care management using secondary data', in Saks, M. and Allsop, J. (eds) *Researching Health: Qualitative, Quantitative and Mixed Methods*, London: Sage.

Klegon, D. (1978) 'The sociology of the professions: An emerging perspective', *Sociology of Work and Occupations* 5 (3): 259–283.

Klein, R. (2013) *The New Politics of the NHS: From Creation to Reinvention*, 7th edition, London: Radcliffe Publishing.

Koesel, K. J., Bunce, V. J. and Weiss, J. C. (eds) (2020) *Citizens and the State in Authoritarian Regimes: Comparing Russia and China*, New York: Oxford University Press.

Krause, E. (1996) *The Death of the Guilds: Professions, States and the Advance of Capitalism, 1930 to the Present*, New Haven, CO: Yale University Press.

Kuhlmann, E. and Annandale, E. (eds) (2012) *The Palgrave Handbook of Gender and Healthcare*, 2nd edition, Basingstoke: Palgrave Macmillan.

Kuhlmann. E. and Saks, M. (eds) (2008) *Rethinking Professional Governance: International Directions in Healthcare*, Bristol: Policy Press.

Kuhlmann, E., Allsop, J. and Saks, M. (2009) 'Professional governance and public control: A comparison of medicine in the United Kingdom and Germany', *Current Sociology* 57 (4): 511–528.

Kumar, K. (1991) *Prophecy and Progress: The Sociology of Industrial and Post-industrial Society*, New edition, Harmondsworth: Penguin Books.

Kvålshaugen, R., Hydle, K. M., and Brehmer, P-O. (2015) 'Innovative capabilities in international professional service firms: Enabling trade-offs between past, present, and future service provision', *Journal of Professions and Organization* 2 (2): 148–167.

Laing, R. D. and Esterson, E. (1973) *Sanity, Madness and the Family*, New edition, Harmondsworth: Penguin Books.

Lander, M. W., Heugens, P. and van Oosterhout, H. (2017) 'Drift or alignment? A configurational analysis of law firms' ability to combine profitability with professionalism', *Journal of Professions and Organization* 4 (2): 123–148.

Lander, M. W., Koene, B. A. S. and Linssen, S. N. (2013) 'Committed to professionalism: Organizational responses of mid-tier accounting to conflicting institutional logics', *Accounting, Organizations and Society* 38 (2): 130–148.

Larkin, G. (1995) 'State control and the health professions in the United Kingdom: Historical perspectives', in Johnson, T., Larkin, G. and Saks, M. (eds) *Health Professions and the State in Europe*, London: Routledge.

Larson, M. S. (1977) *The Rise of Professionalism: A Sociological Analysis*, Berkeley, CA: University of California Press.

Larson, M. S. (1990) 'On the matter of experts and professionals, or how it is impossible to leave nothing unsaid', in Torstendahl, R. and Burrage, M. (eds) *The Formation of Professions: Knowledge, State and Strategy*, London: Sage.

Le Bianic, T. and Svensson, L. (2008) 'European regulation of professional regulation: A study of documents focusing on architects and psychologists in the EU', *European Societies* 10 (4): 567–595.

Le Fanu, J. (2011) *The Rise and Fall of Modern Medicine*, 2nd edition, London: Abacus.

Leathard, A. (ed) (2003) *Interprofessional Collaboration: From Policy to Practice in Health and Social Care*, London: Brunner/Routledge.

Lee, T. A. (1995) 'The professionalization of accountancy: A history of protecting the public interest in a self-interested way', *Accounting, Auditing and Accountability Journal* 8 (4): 48–69.

Lees, D. S. (1966) *The Economic Consequences of the Professions*, London: Institute of Economic Affairs.

Leicht, K. T. (2016a) 'Market fundamentalism, cultural fragmentation, postmodern skepticism, and the future of professional work', *Journal of Professions and Organization* 3 (1): 103–117.

Leicht, K. T. (2016b) 'The professionalization of management', in Dent, M., Bourgeault, I., Denis, J-L. and Kuhlmann, E. (eds) *The Routledge Companion to the Professions and Professionalism*, Abingdon: Routledge.

Leicht, K. T. (2018) 'Professions and entrepreneurship in international perspective', in Saks, M. and Muzio, D. (eds) *Professions and Professional Service Firms: Private and Public Sector Enterprises in the Global Economy*, Abingdon: Routledge.

Lemmings, D. (2004) 'Ritual, majesty and mystery: Collective life and culture among English barristers, serjeants and judges, c.1500-c.1830', in Pue, W. W. and Sugarman, D. (eds) *Lawyers and Vampires: Cultural Histories of the Legal Profession*, Portland, OR: Hart Publishing.

Lester, S. (2014) *Association and Self-regulation in Smaller UK Professions*, Taunton: Avista Press.

Lester, S. (2016) 'The development of self-regulation in four UK professional communities', *Professions and Professionalism* 6 (1): 1–14.

Lester, S (2020) 'New technology and professional work', *Professions and Professionalism* 10 (1): 1–15.

Levin, B. (2002) *Women and Medicine*, 3rd edition, Lanham, MD: Scarecrow Press.

Li, J. (2019) 'All roads lead to Rome: Internationalization strategies of Chinese law firms', *Journal of Professions and Organization* 6 (2): 156–178.

Light, D. (1995) 'Countervailing powers: A framework for professions in transition', in Johnson, T., Larkin, G. and Saks, M. (eds) *Health Professions and the State in Europe*, London: Routledge.

Liljegren, A. and Saks, M. (eds) (2016) *Professions and Metaphors: Understanding Professions in Society*, Abingdon: Routledge.

Liljegren, A., Höjer, S. and Forkby, T. (2014) 'Laypersons, professions, and governance in the welfare state: The Swedish child protection system', *Journal of Professions and Organization* 1 (2): 161–175.

Littler, C. (1982) *The Development of the Labour Process in Capitalist Societies: A Comparative Study of the Transformation of Work Organization in Britain, Japan, and the USA*, London: Heinemann Educational.

Liu, S. (2018) 'Boundaries and professions: Towards a processual theory of action', *Journal of Professions and Organization* 5 (1): 45–57.

Løwendahl, B. R. (2005) *Strategic Management of Professional Service Firms*, Copenhagen: Copenhagen Business School Press.

Lymbery, M. (2000) 'The retreat from professionalism: From social worker to care manager', in Malin, N. (ed) *Professionalism, Boundaries and the Workplace*, London: Routledge.

Lyotard, J. (1984) *The Postmodern Condition: A Report on Knowledge*, Minneapolis, MN: University of Minnesota Press.

Macdonald, K. (1995) *The Sociology of the Professions*, London: Sage.

Maestripieri, L. (2019) 'Fragmented fields: Professionalisms and work settings in Italian management consultancy', *Journal of Professions and Organization* 6 (3): 357–376.

Malhotra, N. and Morris, T. (2009) 'Heterogeneity in professional service firms', *Journal of Management Studies* 46 (6): 895–922.

Malin, N. (ed) (2000) *Professionalism, Boundaries and the Workplace*, London: Routledge.

Malin, N. (2020) *De-professionalism and Austerity: Challenges for the Public Sector*, Bristol: Policy Press.

Marks, F., Leswing, K. and Fortinsky, B. (1972) *The Lawyers, the Public and Professional Responsibility*, Chicago, IL: American Bar Foundation.

Mars, G. (1982) *Cheats at Work: Anthropology of Workplace Crime*, London: George Allen & Unwin.

McCaig, C. (2018) *The Marketisation of Higher Education*, Bingley: Emerald Publishing.

McCann, L. and Granter, E (2019) 'Beyond "blue-collar professionalism": Continuity and change in the professionalization of uniformed emergency services work', *Journal of Professions and Organization* 6 (2): 213–232.

McClelland, C. (1991) *The German Experience of Professionalization: Modern Learned Professions and Their Organization from the Early Nineteenth Century to the Hitler Era*, Cambridge: Cambridge University Press.

McGillivray, A. (2004) 'He would have made a wonderful solicitor: Law, modernity and professionalism in Bram Stoker's Dracula', in Pue, W. W. and Sugarman, D. (eds) *Lawyers and Vampires: Cultural Histories of Legal Professions*, Portland, OR: Hart Publishing.

McKinlay, J. (1977) 'The business of good doctoring or doctoring as good business: Reflections on Freidson's view of the medical game', *International Journal of Health Services* 7 (3): 459–483.

McKinlay, J. and Arches, J. (1985) 'Towards the proletarianization of physicians', *International Journal of Health Services* 15 (2): 161–195.

Medvetz, T. and Sallaz, J. J. (eds) (2018) *The Oxford Handbook of Pierre Bourdieu*, Oxford: Oxford University Press.

Merino, B. D., Mayper, A. G. and Tolleson, T. D. (2010) 'Neoliberalism, deregulation and Sarbanes-Oxley: The legitimation of a failed corporate governance model', *Accounting, Auditing and Accountability Journal* 23 (6): 774–792.

Milcent, C. (2018) *Healthcare Reform in China: From Violence to Digital Healthcare*, Basingstoke: Palgrave Macmillan.

Miles, S. H. (2005) *The Hippocratic Oath and the Ethics of Medicine*, Oxford: Oxford University Press.

Milewa, T. (2004) 'Local participatory democracy in Britain's health service: Innovation or fragmentation of a universal citizenship?', *Social Policy and Administration* 38 (3): 240–252.

Miller, P., Kurunmäki, L. and O'Leary, T. (2008) 'Accounting, hybrids and the management of risk', *Accounting, Organizations and Society* 33 (7/8): 942–967.

Millerson, G. (1964) *The Qualifying Associations*, London: Routledge & Kegan Paul.

Moore, S. and Newbury, A. (2017) *Legal Aid in Crisis: Assessing the Impact of Reform*, Bristol: Policy Press.

Mors, M. L., Rogan, M. and Lynch, S. (2018) 'Boundary spanning and knowledge exploration in a professional services firm', *Journal of Professions and Organization* 5 (3): 184–205.

Murphy, R. (1990) 'Proletarianization or bureaucratization: The fall of the professional', in Torstendahl, R. and Burrage, M. (eds) *The Formation of Professions: Knowledge, State and Strategy*, London: Sage.

Muzio, D. and Ackroyd, D. (2005) 'On the consequences of defensive professionalism: Recent changes in the legal labour process', *Journal of Law and Society* 32 (4): 615–642.

Muzio, D. and Flood, J. (2012) 'Entrepreneurship, managerialism and professionalism in action: The case of the legal profession in England and Wales', in Reihlen, M. and Werr, A. (eds) *Handbook of Research on Entrepreneurship in Professional Service Firms*, Cheltenham: Edward Elgar.

Muzio, D., Ackroyd, S. and Chanlat, J-F. (2008) 'Introduction: Lawyers, doctors and business consultants', in Muzio, D., Ackroyd, S. and Chanlat, J-F. (eds) *Redirections in the Study of Expert Labour: Established Professions and New Expert Occupations*, Basingstoke: Palgrave Macmillan.

Muzio, D., Brock, D. and Suddaby, R. (2013) 'Professions and institutional change: Towards an institutionalist sociology of the professions', *Journal of Management Studies* 50 (5): 699–721.

Muzio, D., Hodgson, D. and Faulconbridge, J. (2011) 'Towards corporate professionalization: The case of project management, management consultancy and executive search', *Current Sociology* 59 (4): 443–464.

Muzio, D., Falconbridge, J., Gabbioneta, C. and Greenwood, R. (2016) 'Bad applies, bad barrels and bad cellars: A boundaries perspective on professional misconduct', in Palmer, D., Smith-Crowe, K. and Greenwood, R. (eds) *Organizational Wrongdoing: Key Perspectives and New Directions*, Cambridge: Cambridge University Press.

Muzio, D., Kirkpatrick, I. and Kipping, M. (2011) 'Professions, organizations and the state: Applying the sociology of the professions to the case of management consultancy', *Current Sociology* 59 (6): 805–824.

Muzzin, L. and Martimianakis, M. A. (2016) 'The professoriate and professionalism in the academy', in Dent, M., Bourgeault, I., Denis, J-L. and Kuhlmann, E. (eds) *The Routledge Companion to the Professions and Professionalism*, Abingdon: Routledge.

Nancarrow, S. and Borthwick, A. (2021) *The Allied Health Professions: A Sociological Perspective*, Bristol: Policy Press.

Navarro, V. (1976) *Medicine under Capitalism*, New York: Prodist.

Navarro, V. (1978) *Class Struggle, the State and Medicine: An Historical and Contemporary Analysis of the Medical Sector in Great Britain*, London: Martin Robertson.

Navarro, V. (1986) *Crisis, Health and Medicine: A Social Critique*, London: Tavistock.

Neal, M. and Morgan, J. (2000) 'The professionalisation of everyone? A comparative study of the development of professions in the United Kingdom and Germany', *European Sociological Review* 16 (1): 9–26.

Nettleton, S. (1992) *Power, Pain and Dentistry*, Buckingham: Open University Press.

Newton, K. and van Deth, J. (2010) *Foundations of Comparative Politics*, Cambridge: Cambridge University Press.

Nichols, T. (2017) *The Death of Expertise: The Campaign against Established Knowledge and Why It Matters*, Oxford: Oxford University Press.

Noordegraaf, M. (2015) 'Hybrid professions and beyond: (New) forms of public professionalism in changing organizational and societal contexts', *Journal of Professions and Organization* 2 (2): 187–206.

Noordegraaf, M. (2018) 'Enterprise, hybrid professionalism and the public sector', in Saks, M. and Muzio, D. (eds) *Professions and Professional Service Firms: Private and Public Sector Enterprises in the Global Economy*, Abingdon: Routledge.

Noordegraaf, M. (2020) 'Protective or connective professionalism? How connected professionals can (still) act as autonomous and authoritative experts', *Journal of Professions and Organization* 7 (2): 205–223.

Noordegraaf, M. and Schinkel, W. (2011) 'Professional capital contested: A Bourdieusian analysis of conflicts between professionals and managers', *Comparative Sociology* 10 (1): 97–125.

O'Rourke, K. (2019) *A Short History of Brexit: From Brentry to Backstop*, London: Pelican Books.

Ogilvie, S. (2019) *The European Guilds: An Economic Analysis*, Princeton, NJ: Princeton University Press.

Olakivi, A. and Niska, M. (2017) 'Rethinking managerialism in professional work: From competing logics to overlapping discourses', *Journal of Professions and Organization* 4 (1): 20–35.

Olgiati, V. (1995) 'Process and policy of legal professionalization in Europe: The deconstruction of a normative order', in Dezalay, Y. and Sugarman, D. (eds) *Professional Competition and Professional Power: Lawyers, Accountants and the Social Construction of Markets*, London: Routledge.

Olgiati, V. (2003) 'Geo-political constructionism: The challenge of Europe to the comparative sociology of the professions', in Svensson, L. and Evetts, J. (eds) *Conceptual and Comparative Studies of Continental and Anglo-American Professions*, Göteborg: Göteborg University.

Olgiati, V. (2010) 'The concept of profession today: A disquieting misnomer?', *Comparative Sociology* 9 (6): 804–842.

Olgiati, V., Orzack, L. and Saks, M. (eds) (1998) *Professions, Identity and Order in Comparative Perspective*, Onati: Onati International Institute for the Sociology of Law.

Olsen, K. M., Sverdrup, T. E. and Kalleberg, A. L. (2019) 'Turnover and transferable skills in a professional service firm', *Journal of Professions and Organization* 6 (1): 2–16.

Østergaard, E. K. (2018) *The Responsive Leader*, London: LID Publishing.

Parkin, F. (1979) *Marxism and Class Theory: A Bourgeois Critique*, London: Tavistock.

Parkin, F. (1982) *Max Weber*, London: Routledge.

Parry, N. and Parry, J. (2019) *The Rise of the Medical Profession*, Abingdon: Routledge Revivals.

Parsons, T. (1952) *The Social System*, London: Tavistock.

Pascale, R. (1990) *Managing on the Edge*, Harmondsworth: Penguin.

Pattison, I. (1984) *The British Veterinary Profession 1791–1948*, London: J.A. Allen.

Peeters, R. (2013) 'Responsibilisation on government's terms: New welfare and the governance of responsibility and solidarity', *Social Policy and Society* 12 (4): 583–595.

Perkin, H. (1989) *The Rise of Professional Society: England Since 1880*, London: Routledge.

Perreault, T., Bridge, G. and McCarthy, J. (eds) (2015) *The Routledge Handbook of Political Ecology*, Abingdon: Routledge.

Perrucci, R. (1973) 'In the service of man: Radical movements in the professions', in Halmos, P. (ed) *Professionalization and Social Change*, Sociological Review Monograph No. 20, Keele: University of Keele.

Pettersen, L. (2019) 'Why artificial intelligence will not outsmart complex knowledge work', *Work, Employment and Society* 33 (6): 1058–1067.

Pickard, S. (2009) 'The professionalization of general practitioners with a special interest: Rationalization, restratification and governmentality', *Sociology* 43 (2): 250–267.

Pickard, S. (2010) 'The role of governmentality in the establishment, maintenance and demise of professional jurisdictions: The case of geriatric medicine', *Sociology of Health and Illness* 32 (7): 1072–1086.

Pitter, A. (2018) 'Job disruption is quickly coming to accounting, too', *Accounting Today*, 19 March.

Pomeranz, W. E. (2019) *Law and the Russian State; Russia's Legal Evolution from Peter the Great to Vladimir Putin*, London: Bloomsbury Academic.

Porter, R. (1992) 'Introduction', in Porter, R. (ed) *The Popularization of Medicine 1650–1850*, London: Routledge.

Porter, R. (1995) *Disease, Medicine and Society, 1550–1860*, 2nd edition, Cambridge: Cambridge University Press.

Porter, R. (2001) *Quacks: Fakers and Charlatans in English Medicine*, Stroud: Tempus Publishing.

Porter, R. (2002) *Blood and Guts: A Short History of Medicine*, London: Allen Lane.

Portwood, D. and Fielding, A. (1981) 'Privilege and the professions', *Sociological Review* 29 (4): 749–773.

Poulantzas, N. (1975) *Political Power and Social Classes*, London: New Left Books.

Pound, R. (1977) *The Lawyer from Antiquity to Modern Times with Particular Reference to the Development of Bar Associations in the United States*, St Paul, MI: West Publishing Company.

Power, M. (2003) 'Evaluating the audit explosion', *Law and Policy* 25 (3): 185–202.

Quack, S. and Schüßler, E. (2015) 'Dynamics of regulation of professional service firms: National and transnational developments in law and accounting', in Empson, L., Muzio, D., Broschak, J. and Hinings, B. (eds) *The Oxford Handbook of Professional Service Firms*, Oxford: Oxford University Press.

Ramnath, A. (2017) *The Birth of an Indian Profession: Engineers, Industry and the State, 1900–47*, New Delhi: Oxford University Press.

Ramsden, E. (2013) 'Science and medicine in the United States of America', in Jackson, M. (ed) *The Oxford Handbook of the History of Medicine*, Oxford: Oxford University Press.

Raphael, D. (1990) *Problems of Political Philosophy*, 2nd edition, London: Macmillan.

Reay, T. and Hinings, C. R. (2009) 'Managing the rivalry of competing institutional logics', *Organization Studies* 30 (6): 629–652.

Redbird (2017) 'The new closed shop? The economic and structural effects of occupational licensure', *American Sociological Review* 82 (3): 600–624.

Reed, M. I. (2012) 'Masters of the universe: Power and elites in organization studies', *Organization Studies* 33 (2): 203–221.

Reed, M. I. (2018) 'Elites, professions, and the neoliberal state: Critical points of intersection and contention', *Journal of Professions and Organization* 5 (3): 297–312.

Reihlen, M., Werr, A. and Seckler, C. (2018) 'Entrepreneurship and professional service firms: The team, the firm, the ecosystem and the field', in Saks, M. and Muzio, D. (eds) *Professions and Professional Service Firms: Private and Public Sector Enterprises in the Global Economy*, Abingdon: Routledge.

Ritzer, G. and Jeffrey, N. S. (2018) *Sociological Theory*, 10th edition, Thousand Oaks, CA: Sage.

Roberts, C., Mackenzie, A. and Mort, M. (2019) *Living Data: Making Sense of Health Biosensing*, Bristol: Bristol University Press.

Roche, W. (2018) 'Medical regulation for the public interest in the United Kingdom', in Chamberlain, J. M., Dent, M. and Saks, M. (eds) *Professional Health Regulation in the Public Interest*, Bristol: Policy Press.

Rogowski, R. (1995) 'German corporate lawyers: Social closure in autopoietic perspective', in Dezalay, Y. and Sugarman, D. (eds) *Professional Competition and Professional Power: Lawyers, Accountants and the Social Construction of Markets*, London: Routledge.

Roszak, T. (1995) *The Making of a Counter Culture*, Berkeley, CA: University of California Press.

Roth, J. (1974) 'Professionalism: The sociologists' decoy', *Work and Occupations* 1: 6–23.

Rothgang, H., Cacace, M., Frisin, L., Grimmeisen, S., Schmid, A. and Went, C. (eds) (2010) *The State and Healthcare: Comparing OECD Countries*, Basingstoke: Palgrave Macmillan.

Rowe, P. G. and Wang, B. (2013) 'Formation and re-formation of the architecture profession in China: Episodes, underlying aspects and present needs', in Alford, W. P., Winston, K. and Kirby, W. C. (eds) *Prospects for the Professions in China*, Abingdon: Routledge.

Rueschmeyer, D. (1988) 'Comparing legal professions: A state-centred approach', in Abel, R. L. and Lewis, P. (eds) *Lawyers in Society*, Berkeley, CA: University of California Press.

Rutkow, I. (2010) *Seeking the Cure: A History of Medicine in America*, New York: Scribner.

Saks, M. (1983) 'Removing the blinkers? A critique of recent contributions to the sociology of professions', *Sociological Review* 31 (1): 1–21.

Saks, M. (1987) 'The politics of health care', in Robins, L. (ed) *Politics and Policy-making in Britain*, London: Longman.

Saks, M. (ed) (1992) *Alternative Medicine in Britain*, Oxford: Clarendon Press.

Saks, M. (1995) *Professions and the Public Interest: Medical Power, Altruism and Alternative Medicine*, London: Routledge.

Saks, M. (1996) 'From quackery to complementary medicine: The shifting boundaries between orthodox and unorthodox medical knowledge', in Cant, S. and Sharma, U. (eds) *Complementary and Alternative Medicines: Knowledge in Practice*, London: Free Association Books.

Saks, M. (1997) 'East meets West' in Porter, R. (ed) *Medicine: A History of Healing*, London: Ivy Press.

Saks, M. (1998) 'Deconstructing or reconstructing professions? Interpreting the role of professional groups in society', in Olgiati, V., Orzack, L. and Saks, M. (eds) *Professions, Identity and Order in Comparative Perspective*, Onati: Onati International Institute for the Sociology of Law.

Saks, M. (2000) 'Medicine and the counter culture', in Cooter, R. and Pickstone, J. (eds) *Medicine in the 20th Century*, Amsterdam: Harwood Academic Publishers.

Saks, M. (2002a) 'Empowerment, participation and the rise of orthodox bio-medicine', in Byrt, R. and Dooher, J. (eds) *Empowerment, and Participation: Power, Influence and Control in Contemporary Health Care*, Dinton: Quay Books.

Saks, M. (2002b) 'Professionalization, regulation and alternative medicine', in Allsop, J. and Saks, M. (eds) *Regulating the Health Professions*, London: Sage.

Saks, M. (2003a) *Orthodox and Alternative Medicine: Politics, Professionalization and Health Care*, London: Sage.

Saks, M. (2003b) 'The limitations of the Anglo-Anglo-American sociology of the professions: A critique of the current neo-Weberian orthodoxy', *Knowledge, Work and Society* 1 (1): 11–31.

Saks, M. (2006) 'The alternatives to medicine', in Gabe, J., Kelleher, D. and Williams, G. (eds) *Challenging Medicine*, 2nd edition, Abingdon: Routledge.

Saks, M. (2008) 'Policy dynamics: Marginal groups in the healthcare division of labour in the UK', in Kuhlmann, E. and Saks, M. (eds) *Rethinking Professional Governance: International Directions in Healthcare*, Bristol: Policy Press.

Saks, M. (2010) 'Analyzing the professions: The case for a neo-Weberian approach', *Comparative Sociology* 9 (6): 887–915.

Saks, M. (2012) 'Defining a profession: The role of knowledge and expertise', *Professions and Professionalism* 2: 1–10.

Saks, M. (2014) 'The regulation of the English health professions: Zoos, circuses or safari parks?', *Journal of Professions and Organization* 1 (1): 84–98.

Saks (2015a) 'Health policy and complementary and alternative medicine', in Kuhlmann, E., Blank, R., Bourgeault, I. and Wendt, C. (eds) *The Palgrave International Handbook of Healthcare Policy and Governance*, Basingstoke: Palgrave Macmillan.

Saks, M. (2015b) 'Inequalities, marginality and the professions', *Current Sociology Review* 63 (6): 850–868.

Saks, M. (2015c) 'Professions RIP? Reflections on the future of professionalism', Conference on professions, professionalism and professional learning, University of Huddersfield, July.

Saks, M. (2015d) 'The academic menagerie: Reflections on higher education in England', Presentation at Ontario Institute for Studies in Education, University of Toronto, March.

Saks, M. (2015e) *The Professions, State and the Market: Medicine in Britain, the United States and Russia.* Abingdon: Routledge.

Saks, M. (2016a) 'Professions and power: A review of theories of professions and power', in Dent, M., Bourgeault, I., Denis, J-L. and Kuhlmann, E. (eds) *The Routledge Companion to the Professions and Professionalism*, Abingdon: Routledge.

Saks, M. (2016b) 'Review of theories of professions, organizations and society: Neo-Weberianism, neo-institutionalism and eclecticism', *Journal of Professions and Organization* 3 (2): 170–187.

Saks, M. (2018a) 'Regulation and Russian medicine: Whither medical professionalisation?', in Chamberlain, J. M., Dent, M. and Saks, M. (eds) *Professional Health Regulation in the Public Interest*, Bristol: Policy Press.

Saks, M. (2018b) 'The medical profession, enterprise and the public interest', in Saks, M. and Muzio, D. (eds) *Professions and Professional Service Firms: Private and Public Sector Enterprises in the Global Economy*, Abingdon: Routledge.

Saks, M. (2020a) 'Higher education and coronavirus in the UK', Presentation on coronavirus and its impact on the higher education sector, United Nations Institute for Training and Research webinar, June.

Saks, M. (2020b) 'Responsible leadership and futureproofing the professions: New lamps for old?', Crafting the Future(s) of Professional Services, Annual PSF Conference, University of Oxford, July.

Saks, M. (ed) (2020c) *Support Workers and Health Professions in International Perspective: The Invisible Providers of Health Care*, Bristol: Policy Press.

Saks, M. and Adams, T. (2019) 'Neo-Weberianism, professional formation and the state: Inside the black box', *Professions and Professionalism* 9 (2): 1–14.

Saks, M. and Allsop, J. (eds) (2019) *Researching Health: Qualitative, Quantitative and Mixed Methods*, 3rd edition, London: Sage.

Saks, M. and Brock, D. (2018) 'Professions and organizations: A European perspective', in Siebert, S. (ed) *Management Research: European Perspectives*, Abingdon: Routledge.

Saks, M. and Muzio, D. (eds) (2018) *Professions and Professional Service Firms: Private and Public Sector Enterprises in the Global Economy*, Abingdon: Routledge.

Salaman, G. (1979) *Work Organisations: Resistance and Control*, London: Longman.

Salman, S. (2019) 'Towards a 'client professionalization' process? The case of the institutionalization of executive coaching in France', *Journal of Professions and Organization* 6 (3): 286–303.

Sandefur, R. (2007) 'Lawyers' pro bono service and American-style civil legal assistance', *Law and Society Review* 41 (1): 79–112.

Saunders, P. (1986) *Social Theory and the Urban Question*, 2nd edition, London: Hutchinson.

Saunders, P. (2007) *Urban Politics: A Sociological Interpretation*, Abingdon: Routledge.

Savoldi, R. and Brock, D. (2019) 'Opening the black box of PSF network internationalization: An exploration of law firm networks', *Journal of Professions and Organization* 6 (3): 304–322.

Savur, S. and Sandhu, S. (eds) (2017) *Responsible Leadership and Ethical Decision-making*, Bingley: Emerald Publishing.

Scambler, G. and Higgs, P. (eds) (1998) *Modernity, Medicine and Health*, London: Routledge.

Scholte, J. A., Fioramonti, L. and Nhema, A. G (eds) (2016) *New Rules for Global Justice: Structural Distribution in the Global Economy*, London: Rowan & Littlefield.

Schuyler, K. G., Baugher, J. E. and Jironet, K. (eds) (2016) *Creative Social Change: Leadership for a Healthy World*, Bingley: Emerald Publishing.

Sciulli, D. (2005) 'Continental sociology of professions today: Conceptual contributions', *Current Sociology* 53 (6): 915–942.

Sciulli, D. (2009) *Professions in Civil Society and the State: Invariant Foundations and Consequences*, Leiden: Brill.

Scott, W. R. (1966) 'Professionals in bureaucracies: Areas of conflict', in Vollmer, H. M. and Mills, D. L. (eds) *Professionalization*, Englewood Cliffs, NJ: Prentice-Hall.

Scott, W. R. (2008) 'Lords of the dance: Professionals as institutional agents', *Organization Studies* 29 (2): 219–238.

Seabrooke, L. (2014) 'Epistemic arbitrage: Transnational professional knowledge in action', *Journal of Professions and Organization* 1 (1): 49–64.

Seabrooke, L. and Tsingou, E. (2015) 'Professional emergence on transnational issues: Linked ecologies on demographic change', *Journal of Professions and Organization* 2 (1): 1–18.

Sennett, R. (2003) *Respect: The Formation of Character in an Age of Inequality*, New York: Norton.

Sharples, J., Webster, R. and Blatchford (2016) *Making Best Use of Teaching Assistants: Guidance Report*, London: Education Endowment Foundation.

Shaw, G. B. (1946) *The Doctor's Dilemma*, Harmondsworth: Penguin Books.

Short, S. (2018) 'Birth of the hydra-headed monster: A unique antipodean model of health workforce governance', in Chamberlain, J. M., Dent, M. and Saks, M. (eds) *Professional Health Regulation in the Public Interest*, Bristol: Policy Press.

Simms, M. (2019) *The Future of Work*, London: Sage.

Skelcher, C. and Smith, S. R. (2015) 'Theorizing hybridity: Institutional logics, complex organizations, and actor identities: The case of nonprofits', *Public Administration* 93 (2): 433–448.

Skilton, M. and Hovsepian, F. (2018) *The 4th Industrial Revolution: Responding to the Impact of Artificial Intelligence on Business*, Basingstoke: Palgrave Macmillan,

Slaughter, M. J. (2007) 'Globalization and declining unionization in the United States', *Industrial Relations* 46 (2): 329–346.

Smigel, E. O. (1964) *The Wall Street Lawyer: Professional Organization Man?*, Glencoe, IL: Free Press.

Sommerlad, H. (2017) 'The new "professionalism" in England and Wales: Talent, diversity, and a legal precariat', in Headworth, S., Nelson, R. L., Dinovitzer, R. and Wilkins, D. B. (eds) *Diversity in Practice: Race, Gender and Class in Legal and Professional Careers*, Cambridge: Cambridge University Press.

Sommerlad, H. and Ashley, L. (2018) 'The implications for gender of work in professional service firms: The case of law and accountancy', in Saks, M. and Muzio, D. (eds) *Professions and Professional Service Firms: Private and Public Sector Enterprises in the Global Economy*, Abingdon: Routledge.

Sommerlad, H. and Sanderson, P. (2018) *Gender, Choice and Commitment: Women Solicitors in England and Wales and the Struggle for Equal Status*, Abingdon: Routledge Revivals.

Sommerlad, H., Harris-Short, S., Vaughan, S. and Young, R. (2015) 'The futures of legal education and the legal profession', in Sommerlad, H., Harris-Short, S., Vaughan, S. and Young, R. (eds) *The Futures of Legal Education and the Legal Profession*, Oxford: Hart Publishing.

Sox, H. C. (2007) 'The ethical foundations of professionalism: A sociologic history', *CHEST Journal* 131 (5): 1532–1540.

Spangler, E. (1986) *Lawyers for Hire*, New Haven, CO: Yale University Press.

Spary, E. (2013) 'Health and medicine in the Enlightenment', in Jackson, M. (ed) *The Oxford Handbook of the History of Medicine*, Oxford: Oxford University Press.

Spence, C., Voulgaris, G. and Maclean, M. (2017) 'Politics and the professions in a time of crisis', *Journal of Professions and Organization* 4 (3): 261–281.

Spencer, H. (1896) *The Principles of Sociology*, Volume 3, London: Williams and Norgate.

Stacey, M. (1980) 'Charisma, power and altruism', *Sociology of Health and Illness* 2 (1): 64–90.

Standing, G. (2011) *The Precariat: The New Dangerous Class*, London: Bloomsbury Academic.

Stangis, D. and Smith, K. V. (2017) *The Executive's Guide to 21st Century Corporate Citizenship*, Bingley: Emerald Publishing.

Starr, P. (1982) *The Social Transformation of American Medicine*, New York: Basic Books.

Stevens, R. (1998) *American Medicine and the Public Interest*, Berkeley, CA: University of California Press.

Stevens, R. (2003) *Medical Practice in Modern England: The Impact of Specialization and State Medicine*, Piscataway, NJ: Transaction Publishers.

Strawbridge, D. and Strawbridge, J. (2020) *Practical Self-sufficiency: The Complete Guide to Sustainable Living Today*, London: Penguin Books/Random House.

Stringfellow, L. and Thompson, A. (2014) 'Crab antics? Contesting and perpetuating status hierarchies in professional service firms', *Journal of Professions and Organization* 1 (2): 118–136.

Suddaby, R. and Muzio, D. (2015) 'Theoretical perspectives of the professions', in Empson, L., Muzio, D., Broschak, J. and Hinings, B. (eds) *The Oxford Handbook of Professional Service Firms*, Oxford: Oxford University Press.

Suddaby, R. and Viale, T. (2011) 'Professionals and field-level change: Institutional work and the professional project', *Current Sociology* 59 (4): 423–441.

Suddaby, R., Cooper, D. J. and Greenwood, R. (2007) 'Transnational regulation of professional services: Governance dynamics of field level organizational change', *Accounting, Organizations and Society* 32 (4/5): 333–362.

Sugarman, D. (1995) 'Who colonized whom? Historical reflections on the intersection between law, lawyers and accountants in England', in Dezalay, Y. and Sugarman, D. (eds) *Professional Competition and Professional Power: Lawyers, Accountants and the Social Construction of Markets*, London: Routledge.

Susskind, R. (2017) *Tomorrow's Lawyers*, 2nd edition, Oxford: Oxford University Press.

Susskind, R. and Susskind, D. (2015) *The Future of the Professions: How Technology Will Transform the Work of Human Experts*, Oxford: Oxford University Press.

Svennson, L. (1999) 'Professionals as a new middle class: The Swedish case', in Hellberg, I., Saks, M. and Benoit, C. (eds) *Professional Identities in Transition: Cross-cultural Dimensions*, Södertälje: Almqvist & Wiksell International.

Svensson, L. and Evetts, J. (eds) (2010) *Sociology of Professions: Continental and Anglo-Saxon Traditions*, Göteborg: Daidalos.

Swart, J. and Kinnie, N. (2003) 'Sharing knowledge in knowledge-intensive firms', *Human Resource Management Journal* 13 (2): 60–75.

Swart, J. and Kinnie, N. (2010) 'Organisational learning, knowledge assets and HR practices in professional service firm', *Human Resource Management Journal* 20 (1): 64–79.

Swart, J., Kinnie, N., van Rosenberg, Y. and Yalabik, Z. Y. (2014) 'Why should I share my knowledge? A multiple foci of commitment perspective', *Human Resource Management Journal* 24 (3): 269–289.

Swedberg, R. and Agevall, O. (2016) *The Max Weber Dictionary: Key Words and Central Concepts*, 2nd edition, Stanford, CA: Stanford University Press.

Synnot, A. and Hill, S. (2019) 'Public involvement in health research', in Saks, M. and Allsop, J. (eds) *Researching Health: Qualitative, Quantitative and Mixed Methods*, 3rd edition, London: Sage.

Taminiau, Y., Heusinkveld, S. and Cramer, L. (2019) 'Colonization contests: How both accounting and law firms gain legitimacy in the market for forensic accounting', *Journal of Professions and Organization* 6 (1): 49–71.

Tang, J. and Smith, E. (eds) (1996) *Women and Minorities in American Professions*, New York: SUNY Press.

Tawney, R. H. (1921) *The Acquisitive Society*, London: Bell & Sons.

Taylor, B. (1995) 'Amateurs, professionals and the knowledge of archaeology', *British Journal of Sociology* 46 (3): 499–508.

Tazzyman, A., Ferguson, J., Boyd, A., Bryce, M., Tredinnick-Rowe, J., Price, T. and Walshe, K. (2020) 'Reforming medical regulation: A qualitative study of the implementation of medical revalidation in England, using Normalization Process Theory', *Journal of Health Services Research and Policy* 25 (1).

Thistlethwaite, J. and Paterson, M. (2016) 'Private governance and accounting for sustainability networks', *Environment and Planning C: Government and Policy* 34 (7): 1197–1221.

Thomas, P. and Mungham, G. (1983) 'Solicitors and clients: Altruism or self-interest', in Dingwall, R. and Lewis, P. (eds) *The Sociology of the Professions*, Basingstoke: Macmillan.

Thompson, P. (2007) 'Adler's theory of the capitalist labour process: A pale(o) imitation', *Work, Employment and Organization* 28 (9): 1359–1368.

Thompson, P. and McHugh, D. (2009) *Work Organisations: A Critical Approach*, 4th edition, Basingstoke: Palgrave Macmillan.

Tonkens, E. (2016) 'Professions, service users and citizenship: Deliberation, choice and responsibility', in Dent, M., Bourgeault, I., Denis, J-L. and Kuhlmann, E. (eds) *The Routledge Companion to the Professions and Professionalism*, Abingdon: Routledge.

Turner, B. (1995) *Medical Power and Social Knowledge*, 2nd edition, London: Sage.

United Nations (2015) *Transforming Our World: The 2030 Agenda for Sustainable Development*, Geneva: UN.

Venkataraman, S. (1997) 'The distinctive domain of entrepreneurship research: An editor's perspective', in Katz, J. A. and Brockhaus, R. (ed) *Advances in Entrepreneurship, Firm Emergence and Growth*, Volume 3, Greenwich, CT: JAI Press.

Volti, R. (2008) *An Introduction to the Sociology of Work and Occupations*, Thousand Oaks, CA: Pine Forge Press.

von Nordenflycht, A. (2010) 'What is a professional service firm? Toward a theory and taxonomy of knowledge-intensive firms', *Academy of Management Review* 35 (1): 155–174.

Waddington, I. (1984) *The Medical Profession in the Industrial Revolution*, London: Gill & Macmillan.

Wallis, R. and Morley, P. (1976) 'Introduction', in Wallis, R. and Morley, P. (eds) *Marginal Medicine*, London: Peter Owen.

Wang, K. (2019) *Professionalising Project Management in Company-Oriented Contexts: Cross-Case Study in Construction, Defence and IT Companies in the UK*, PhD thesis, School of Engineering, University of Manchester.

Ward, V. C. (2017) *Legal Profession: Is It for You?*, London: Bruce & Holly.

Waring, J. (2014) 'Restratification, hybridity and professional elites: Questions of power, identity and relational contingency at the points of professional-organisational intersection', *Sociology Compass* 8: 688–704.

Watson, T. (2017) *Sociology, Work and Organisation*, 7th edition, Abingdon: Routledge.

Webb, J., Schirato, T. and Danaher, G. (2002) *Understanding Bourdieu*, London: Sage.

Webber, A. (2019) 'Diversity in HR: Is it really a "white female" profession?', *Personnel Today*, 26 February.

Weber, M. (1968) *Economy and Society: An Outline of Interpretive Sociology*, New York: Bedminster Press.

Weber, M. (2011) *Methodology of the Social Sciences*, Piscataway, NJ: Transaction Publishers.

Weininger, E. B. and Lareau, A. (2018) 'Pierre Bourdieu's sociology of education: Institutional form and social inequality', in Medvetz, T. and Sallaz, J. J. (eds) *The Oxford Handbook of Pierre Bourdieu*, Oxford: Oxford University Press.

White, S. (2000) *Russia's New Politics: The Management of a Postcommunist Society*, Cambridge: Cambridge University Press.

Whiting, M., May, S. and Saks, M. (2020) 'Exclusionary social closure and the professionalization of veterinary medicine in the UK: A self-interested or public interested endeavour?', *Professions and Professionalism* 10 (1): 1–19.

Whittle, A., Mueller, F. and Carter, C. (2016) 'The "Big Four" in the spotlight: Accountability and professional legitimacy in the UK audit market', *Journal of Professions and Organization* 3 (2): 119–141.

Wilensky, H. (1964) 'The professionalization of everyone?', *American Journal of Sociology* 70 (2): 137–158.

Wilson, F. M. (2004) *Organizational Behaviour and Work: A Critical Introduction*, 4th edition, Oxford: Oxford University Press.

Witz, A. (1992) *Professions and Patriarchy*, London: Routledge.

Further reading

Adams, T. (2017) 'Self-regulating professions: Past, present, future', *Journal of Professions and Organization* 4 (1): 70–87.

Brooks, R. (2018) *The Bean Counters: The Triumph of the Accountants and How They Broke Capitalism*, London: Atlantic Books.

Chamberlain, J. M., Dent, M. and Saks, M. (eds) (2018) *Professional Health Regulation in the Public Interest*, Bristol: Policy Press.

Dent, M., Bourgeault, I., Denis, J-L. and Kuhlmann, E. (eds) (2016) *The Routledge Companion to the Professions and Professionalism*, Abingdon: Routledge.

Johnson, T. (2016) *Professions and Power*, Abingdon: Routledge Revivals.

Kempster, S., Maak, T. and Parry, K. (eds) (2020) *Good Dividends: Responsible Leadership of Business Purpose*, Abingdon: Routledge.

Liljegren, A. and Saks, M. (eds) (2016) *Professions and Metaphors: Understanding Professions in Society*, Abingdon: Routledge.

Ogilvie, S. (2019) *The European Guilds: An Economic Analysis*, Princeton, NJ: Princeton University Press.

Saks, M. (2015) *The Professions, State and the Market: Medicine in Britain, the United States and Russia*. Abingdon: Routledge.

Saks, M. (2016) 'Review of theories of professions, organizations and society: Neo-Weberianism, neo-institutionalism and eclecticism', *Journal of Professions and Organization* 3 (2): 170–187.

Saks, M. and Muzio, D. (eds) (2018) *Professions and Professional Service Firms: Private and Public Sector Enterprises in the Global Economy*, Abingdon: Routledge.

Sommerlad, H., Harris-Short, S., Vaughan, S. and Young, R. (eds) (2015) *The Futures of Legal Education and the Legal Profession*, Oxford: Hart Publishing.

Susskind, R. and Susskind, D. (2015) *The Future of the Professions: How Technology Will Transform the Work of Human Experts*, Oxford: Oxford University Press.

Index

Abbott, A. 15, 22–3, 78, 116, 142
Abel, R. L. 35, 38, 96, 100, 103, 151
Abramov, R. 46
academic profession 21, 25, 43, 44, 46, 79, 96, 99, 100
accountancy 1, 13, 37, 4, 42, 44, 56, 71–2, 100, 103, 106, 117, 118, 121, 123, 125, 130–3, 134, 135, 136, 138, 140, 142, 151, 153–5, 159, 164
Ackroyd, D. 110
Ackroyd, S. 6, 10–11
action-based processual theories of professions 55
actuaries 74, 130, 133
acupuncture 68, 93–4
Adams, T. 14, 68, 102, 110, 124, 125, 141, 146–8, 157
Adler, P. S. 108
Agevall, O. 44, 60–1
Alder Hey hospital 98
allied health professions 14, 64
Allitt, Beverley 98
Allsop, J. 24, 29, 30, 98
alternative therapies 30, 68, 70, 74, 81, 89, 93, 94
altruism 9, 11, 12, 51, 52, 71, 146, 164, 165, 166
Alvesson, M. 140
amateurism 8, 9, 59
American Association of University Professors 43
American Bar Association 38, 39, 40, 82
American Institute of Certified Public Accountants 42

American Medical Association 32–3, 38, 70
American Sociological Association 43
anaesthesiology 33
Anderson-Gough, F. 135
Anglo-American context 2, 5, 6, 10, 14–16, 20, 25, 26, 41, 43, 45, 49–80, 87, 94, 95, 101, 108, 110, 118, 123, 130, 134, 137, 141, 144, 150, 153, 159, 160, 164, 166; *see also* Britain and United States
animal experimentation 94
Annandale, E. 72
Anteby, M. 11, 146
anti-tax haven measures 117
Apartheid 47
apothecaries 28, 31, 63, 67
archaeologists 59
Arches, J. 108
architects 8, 24, 42–3, 44, 46, 71, 82, 87, 92, 142, 143, 159
Argentina 117
Armour, J. 152
Arthur Andersen 125
articles 36
artificial intelligence 146, 152, 154, 159
Ashley, L. 123, 134, 135–6
Asian solicitors 135
Association for Project Management 139
Association of Certified Chartered Accountants 130
Association of Executive Search Consultants 138

Printed in the United States
By Bookmasters